People of North East India:
Bio-Cultural Dimensions

People of North East India: Bio-Cultural Dimensions

Edited by
R. Khongsdier
Sarthak Sengupta

KALPAZ

ISBN: 978-93-5128-238-9

Price: ₹ 990

First Published, 2017

Published by

Kalpaz Publications
C-30, Satyawati Nagar,
Delhi – 110052
E-mail: kalpaz@hotmail.com
Ph.: 9212142040

Printed at: G. Print Process, Delhi

Cataloging in Publication Data—DK
Courtesy: D.K. Agencies (P) Ltd. <docinfo@dkagencies.com>

People of North East India : bio-cultural dimensions / edited by Romendra Khongsdier, Sarthak Sengupta.
pages cm
Contributed articles.
Includes bibliographical references.
ISBN 9789351282389

1. Ethnology—India—Assam. 2. Ethnology—India—Meghalaya. 3. Physical anthropology—India—Assam. 4. Physical anthropology—India—Meghalaya. I. Khongsdier, R., 1963- editor. II. Sengupta, Sarthak, 1955- editor.

GN635.I4P46 2016 DDC 305.8009541 23

Contents

Preface

It is indeed a great pleasure to give our readers this volume on "People of North East India: Bio-cultural Dimensions" as a snapshot. North East India is a small India in terms of diversity in ecology, ethnicity, language and culture. It is, therefore, a fertile area for anthropologists and other scientists interested in the study of human evolution and variation. In this volume, we brought out fifteen articles contributed by anthropologists of the region concerning language of material culture in terms of utensils and receptacles, gender issues in matrilineal and patrilineal societies, proselytisation of local populations, traditional political institutions, agricultural rituals, social and biological consequences of intermixture, growth and development of children, food habits, gynecological and obstetric problems faced by them, health and nutritional conditions as indicated by demographic and anthropometric traits.

Almost all the papers presented in this volume are directly or indirectly concerned with the ongoing process of change at different levels and forms of biological and cultural aspects of human populations due to different factors. Some changes may be temporary or permanent and irreversible. Other changes are the reflection of the accommodation and plasticity of human society and the limits to that plasticity and some other changes may be indicative of evolutionary processes and the interaction of biology and culture in relation to the environment. Indeed the subject matter of change is very complex and it remains the major issue of many disciplines including anthropology and sociology. We hope that the articles in this volume are helpful to general readers and different scholars interested in populations of North East India. Last but not least, we are indebted to all the authors who have made their valuable contributions without which this volume would not have been in its present form.

R. Khongsdier
Sarthak Sengupta

List of Tables

Contributors

A. KAPESA

Department of Anthropology, North-Eastern Hill University, Umshing-Mawkynroh, Shillong-793022, India.

ABIGAIL LALNUNENG

Department of Anthropology, North-Eastern Hill University, Umshing-Mawkynroh, Shillong-793022, India.

A.N.M. IRSHAD ALI

Department of Anthropology, Guwahati University, Guwahati-781014, India.

BARNALI DAS

Department of Anthropology, Guwahati University, Guwahati-781014, India.

BIRINCHI K. MEDHI

Department of Anthropology, Guwahati University, Guwahati-781014.

CHANDANA SARMAH

Department of Anthropology, Guwahati University, Guwahati-781014, India.

DALI DUTTA

Department of Anthropology, Dibrugarh University, Assam, 786 004, India.

DHRUBA KUMAR LIMBU

Department of Anthropology, North-Eastern Hill University Umshing-Mawkynroh, Shillong-793022, India.

GEETIKA RANJAN

Department of Anthropology, North-Eastern Hill University, Umshing-Mawkynroh, Shillong-793022, India.

HAPPYSTONE SYNGKON

Department of Anthropology, North-Eastern Hill University Umshing-Mawkynroh, Shillong-793022, India.

JURI BORAH

Department of Anthropology, Dibrugarh University, Dibrugarh, Assam, 786004

LUCY ZEHOL

Department of Anthropology, North-Eastern Hill University, Umshing-Mawkynroh, Shillong-793022, India.

MINI BHATTACHARYYA

Department of Anthropology, Guwahati University, Guwahati-781014, India.

QUEENBALA MARAK

Department of Anthropology, North-Eastern Hill University, Umshing-Mawkynroh, Shillong-793022, India.

R. KHONGSDIER

Department of Anthropology, North-Eastern Hill University, Umshing-Mawkynroh, Shillong-793022, India.

R.K. ATHPARIA

North Eastern Social Research Centre (NESRC), Jagriti, GMCH Road, Christian Basti, Guwahati, Assam, 781005.

RITU GEU GOSWAMI

National Institute of Public Co-operation and Child Development, Khanapara, Guwahati-781022, India.

SARTHAK SENGUPTA

Department of Anthropology, Dibrugarh University, Assam, 786004, India.

SUDIPTA GHOSH

Department of Anthropology, North-Eastern Hill University, Umshing-Mawkynroh, Shillong-793022, India.

THEPUVEKHO DAWHUO

Department of Anthropology, North-Eastern Hill University, Umshing-Mawkynroh, Shillong-793022.

VALENTINA PAKYNTEIN

Department of Anthropology, North-Eastern Hill University, Umshing-Mawkynroh, Shillong-793022, India.

1

Role of Acculturation and Assimilation in the Growth of Assamese Muslim People, their Society and Culture

—*A.N.M. Irshad Ali*

Introduction

Anthropological and sociological studies on the spread of Islam have concerned themselves mainly with the problems of 'culture contact' or 'acculturation' because the introduction of Islamic beliefs into different local societies involved radical socio-political changes, apart from the more personal aspects of conversion (Rigby, 1966: 268). As Islam spread to various parts of the world, it gradually took over many elements and features of indigenous folk traditions. The presence of indigenous folk elements in the social life of various local Muslim communities is to some extent explainable in terms of proselytisation of local populations into Islam. While examining the interrelationships between the Islamic doctrines and the local cultures that have become Islamized, G. Von Grunebaum (1955) states that there are different ways in which conflict, co-existence and interaction of the Islamic high culture and local cultures can be described.

Several anthropological and sociological studies in culture contact between Islam and various local communities and cultural traditions, in parts of the world, have demonstrated the extent of Muslim influence on various spheres of social life of the traditional cultures and the patterns of adoption and assimilation of Islamic elements by the traditional cultures. Some of these studies have also referred to a 'syncretism' between Islamic and traditional customs and rituals (Geertz, 1965; Greenberg, 1941; 1946; Lewis, 1966; Rigby, 1966; Weekes, 1984). Such syncretism is also discernible in North-east India and Assam (Ali, 2006:141-149).

The empirical observations of the socio-cultural life of the Muslims of India, made by anthropologists and sociologists, have suggested that the religious and social life of the Muslims of India exhibit a peculiar synthesis of Islam and local folk traditions. It has been demonstrated that Muslim familial life exhibits a peculiar synthesis of Islam and Hindu traditions (Hashim, 1970), that the kinship terminology of the Muslims is comparable to that of the Hindus (Vreede-de-Steurs, 1968) and the marriage customs of the Muslims are often characterised by a curious mixture of Hindu and Muslim rituals (Uddin, 1972). Divorce and remarriage among the Muslims in India have studied by a number of scholars (Ahmad, 2003). A study of a group of convert Muslims shows that Islam, which is essentially patrilineal in orientation, co-exists along with a matrilineal kinship system (Dube, 1969; Kutty, 1972). Several studies have revealed that while the Muslims claim adherence to the principles and practices ordained by Islam, there is considerable divergence between the formal and the actual religious beliefs and practices of the Muslims in different parts of India (Ahmad, 1984). Mandelbaum (1972) has discussed the social aspects of Islam as one of the 'introduced religions' to India and also the socio-cultural variations among different local Muslim communities in India. Another field of interest to anthropologists and sociologists in India has been castes among the Indian Muslims. Elements of Hindu caste system have percolated into the social organisation of many other non-Hindu communities including Muslims of India. This is partly due to the influence of the majority community on the social life of other communities and partly due to the mass conversion of the Hindus into other religions at different times. As a result of the latter process, a considerable section of the Hindu population, especially from among the lower castes, accepted Islam and other faiths. But they could not wean themselves away from the organisational framework of the Hindu society (Aggarwal, 1966; Ahmad, 1962;

Ahmad, 1973; Ansari, 1960; Guha, 1965; Gupta, 1956; Khan, 1968; Misra, 1964; Mondal, 1991).

The above mentioned studies clearly indicate that the socio-cultural life of the Muslims of India, in many respects, exhibits similarities to those of the Hindus and that there is a synthesis of Islam and Hindu traditions. In this context, a few examples may be cited with a view to indicating the influence of local Hindu traditions on the Indian Muslims. The Meos of Mewat in Rajasthan were converted into Islam long back. These Muslim Meos claim themselves as the descendants of Rama, Laxmana and Arjuna. These Meos employ Brahmin priests in their marriage and other ceremonies. The stories of the Ramayana and the Mahabharata are still prevalent among these Meos. The Meos have several exogamous clans (Aggarwal, 1966; 1969). In addition, in Bengal a large number of Patuas (scroll painters) were converted into Islam during the time of Muslim reign in the sixteenth century. At present, these convert Muslim Patuas live as a separate community both from the Hindus and other Muslims. The Muslim Patuas make idols of the Goddesses of *Durga, Kali, Saraswati, Laxmi, Sitala* and *Manasa* and sell these idols at the time of festivals in the market. Some of these Patuas perform *mukhagni* (the ceremony of putting fire on the face of the corpse) before burying a dead. A majority of the female Patuas put on vermilion. With a view to averting evil eyes, to getting rid of sickness and crises and for prosperity, these Patuas offer puja in the Hindu shrines (Bandopadhya, 1974).

The concept of Islamisation has been used by several scholars to analyse the process of social change among the Muslim communities in India and elsewhere. Geertz (1965) was probably the first scholar to express the conceptualisation of 'Islamisation'. Islamisation is viewed as a 'cultural process whereby groups and individuals distinguish themselves from non-Muslims by purifying themselves of the so-called un-Islamic customs and practices'. Broadly speaking, Islamisation has been followed by different Muslim communities in India to either legitimise or to reconcile themselves with the law of Islam (*Shariat*) and yet continue to remain as an integral part of the wider societal context within which they are embedded (Ahmad, 1976). This is evident in the writings of Mishra (1964) on the Muslim communities of Gujarat. Both Mandelbaum (1972) and Singh (1986) have analysed the process of social change among the Indian Muslims by using the concept of Islamisation.

Islam in Assam and the Growth of Assamese Muslim People

Kamrupa, the ancient Assam, came into contact with the Muslims in 1206 A.D. for the first time when the Turkish army led by Muhammad bin Bakhtiyar made an expedition to Tibet through this region. However, Islam had won very little over the indigenous people during this early period of Assam-Muslim contact. Nevertheless, the sign of Islam is said to have appeared in Assam during this period after the invasion made by Ikhtiyaruddin Mali Yuzbak, the ruler of Gauda, in 1257 A.D. The ruler erected a mosque to celebrate his victory and also initiated Friday congregational services. In fact, Islamisation took place during the next stage following the invasions of Assam made by a number of Muslim invaders.

The history of Assam during the period from the fifteenth to seventeenth centuries was mainly concerned with the Assam-Muslim conflicts. These conflicts arose out of the ambitions of the Muslims to extend their territories further to the east; the intervention of the Ahoms in the affairs of the rival prince of Cooch Bihar; and the violation by the Ahoms of the terms of the treaties entered by them with the Muslims. The first Muslim invasion during the Ahom's rule occurred in 1527 A.D. when Turbak invaded Assam and the Muslims suffered defeat. The Muslims who were captured and taken prisoners by the Ahoms were settled in different parts of Assam. These prisoners are supposed to be the earliest Muslims in the Assam Valley.

Mir Jhumla invaded Assam in 1662 A.D. and as per a treaty, which was enacted in 1663 A.D., part of Assam was transferred to the possession of the Muslims. Finally, in 1682 A.D., the Ahoms expelled the Muslims and then re-established their rule over the territory till 1886 A.D. when the British came to occupy Assam (Bhuyan, 1949; Gait, 1963).

History suggests that the Muslims never really gained enough of a foothold in the Assam Valley. But the Assam-Muslim contact has cultural significance. Every Muslim invasion contributed a little towards the strengthening and propagation of Islamic faith in Assam. Infiltration and migration of the Muslim population into different parts of Assam at various dates and conversion of local people to Islam are the primary factors responsible for the growth of Muslim population in Assam. As a result of the Assam-Muslim contact, some traits of the Islamic culture were assimilated by the indigenous people.

Like Muslim communities in other parts of India, the Assamese Muslims are the product of prolonged interaction between Islam and local cultures. As pointed out earlier, Assam came into contact with the Muslims for the first time in 1206 A.D. when a Turkish army led by Muhammad bin Bakhtiyar Khiliji made an expedition to Tibet through this region. He was followed by some other Muslim invaders. In 1352 A.D., a Muslim army under Turbak invaded Assam. The forces of the Ahom king defeated the Muslims and those who were taken prisoners were settled in different parts of the state. They married Assamese women and, after a few generations, their descendants immersed themselves so deeply into the indigenous culture that they lost whatever Islamic mornings their ancestors ever had. Descendants of these soldiers today are called Marias. The traditional occupation of the Maria is brass-working which is practiced by many Marias even to this day.

The Assamese Muslims

The present day Assamese Muslims would thus appear to be composed of the descendents of (a) Muslim soldiers captured by the Ahom rulers in the battle of 1532 A.D.; (b) the Muslim clergies who propagated Islam; (c) the Muslim artisans brought to Assam by the rulers of Assam from time to time and appointed to various departments of the state Government (Bhuyan, 1949:4) and (d) the converts to Islam at different historical times.

The common name for the indigenous Muslims of Assam is *Goria*. There are various views of the origin of this word. It could denote the introduction of the faith by invaders from the ancient Muslim Bengal capital of Gaura. According to another view, the term could refer to people who bury their dead (*gor*) in a graveyard. A third view is that the term refers to the traditional occupation of the Muslim settlers.

The Assamese Muslims identify themselves with Assam, their homeland and Assamese as their language. These Muslims identify with the common culture they have share with the Assamese people. The Assamese Muslims, who are referred to as Asamiya Musalman, are the descendants of the early migrants to Assam between the thirteenth and seventieth centuries who married locally as well as the converts who belonged to various indigenous populations. Besides language, the Assamese Muslims shares many other elements of culture with the Assamese. There are many points of socio-cultural identity between the Assamese Muslims and the Assamese people. A majority of Assamese Muslims are rural inhabitants and peasants.

As in the case of many other local Muslim communities in other parts of the India, the Assamese Muslims have also not been able to keep themselves away from the influence of indigenous folk traditions. These Muslims have been observing folk, unwritten customs, convention and habits handed down from generations. Thus, indigenous cultural traditions have been playing a significant role in the socio-cultural life of the contemporary Assamese Muslims.

From the cultural point of view the whole population of North-east India and Assam could be divided into three categories : (i) those tribal communities living in the hills and those who are more or less isolated and free from the impact of 'Sanskritic' or other organised cultures (except in the case of tribes with Buddhistic connections); (ii) those tribal groups living in the hills and plains, who have retained their tribal identity but who have been acculturated in various degrees as a result of their living in close proximity of and contact with non-tribal Sanskritised majority or through the impact of Buddhism or Christianity or Islam ; and (iii) those societies which are more or less Sanskritised, where the population is almost wholly (like the Meities) or partly as in the case of the Assamese society made up of earlier Mongoloid stocks. The indigenous (Assamese) Muslims of this region, although not Sanskritised from the religious point of view, are culturally part of this milieu (Datta, 1985: 18).

Society and Culture

The overwhelming majority of the Assamese Muslims are rural inhabitants and peasants. Their main crop is paddy rice of several local varieties. Other crops include maize and wheat, pulses such as black grams, oil seeds such as mustard, jute, sugarcane and seasonal vegetables. Many farmers supplement their income with wage labour and various types of petty trade and commerce. Some Muslims in eastern Assam produce agar wood oil (aquilaria agalocha), from which the choicest of perfumes are made. The trees are infected by a disease which creates the scent, especially appreciated by Arabs who purchase the oil in Bombay. Urban Muslims pursue a more diversified occupational pattern including the professions.

Rural Assamese Muslims live in clustered hamlets and villages surrounded by their fields. While Muslims and Hindus generally live in villages of their own, there are many villages and towns where both groups reside as their neighbours. In such cases, each community maintains a separate identify largely through its exclusive religious and social groups. At the same time, spatial proximity and sharing of a number of institutions have provided opportunities for social contact. Intermarriage, however, is not common. Towns are inhabited by both groups everywhere.

The basic unit of the kinship system among Assamese Muslims is the nuclear family household, unlike the extended family system so common in other parts of India and the non-industrial world. Although this household is a discrete socio-economic unit, it often forms part of a wider kin group. The effective kin group would include a number of family households among whom mutual assistance is a recognised ideal and practice.

Assamese Muslim families are patriarchal and descent is traced through the father. The rules of succession and inheritance are patrilineal, but these principles are sometimes modified by the wishes of the original owner. Women are entitled on inherit one-eight of the father's property.

The family life of the Assamese Muslims exhibits a peculiar synthesis of Islam and the traditions of the local Hindus. The kinship terminology of the Muslims is comparable to that of the Hindus. Like the Hindus, certain types of coactive behaviour patterns between certain categories of kin are also present among the Muslims. Avoidance in relations between father-in-law and daughter-in-law and between husband's elder brother and younger brother's wife is found among both Muslims and Hindus.

The formalities of an Assamese Muslim marriage cover two separate ceremonies: the ring ceremony (*magni* or *angathi pindhua*), which is followed by the actual marriage ceremony (*nikah*). After finalisation of the negotiations, a party consisting of close kin and the parents of the groom-to-be visits the future brides' home. The party carries a gold ring, silk clothes and sweets as presents. The negotiations are sealed with the presentation of the engagement ring to the future bride. In performing *nikah*, the proposal and acceptance are made in the presence of three elderly and respectable males, one of whom acts as *ukil* (chief negotiator) and two as witnesses - the *ukil* the consent of the bride and groom to the marriage. The *imam* then recites verses from the Quran. By and large, Assamese Muslims are Sunnis and follow the norms of Sunni marriages. However, the practice of cross-cousin marriage is not encouraged.

The marriage customs of Muslims are characterised by a mixture of Hindu and Muslim rituals. Muslims fix the date of marriage in consultation with both Hindu and Muslim almanacs. Among the Assamese Muslims, the bride and groom take ceremonial bath on the day of marriage and exchange betel nuts with their respective family and friends. *Bianam* (songs sung by Hindu females during marriage) is prevalent among the Muslims. A local custom known as *athmongola* is also observed by Muslims, whereby the bride and groom attend a feast given by the bride's parents on the eighth day following the wedding. Both Muslims and Hindus arrange marriages in all months except *Puh* (December/January), *Chot* (March/April), *Bhado* (August-September) and *Kati* (October/November). Muslims usually do not plan marriages during the lunar month of Ramadan. During the days of February and March, rural people are not engaged in agriculture and have enough leisure time to celebrate marriage.

Generally, a rural Assamese Hindu wife gives birth to her first child in her parents' home. Muslim wives also follow this custom. Like Hindus, Muslim mothers protect the newborn baby from evil spirits by keeping a fire burning and iron implements in the room. Among traditional rural Assamese, the mother cuts the umbilical cord immediately after birth with a bamboo split. The cord is buried to protect the baby from society. The part of the umbilical cord remaining attached to the baby dries out and detaches automatically. In many cases, this dried cord is used to quiet a crying baby by allowing the baby to drink a drop of water from a pot into which the umbilical cord has been dipped. Muslims bring a newborn baby out ceremonially to the courtyard in the presence of a gathering of women on a day following detachment of the umbilical cord.

Aqiqa is a naming ceremony of close kin and is performed on the seventh, fourteenth, or twenty-first day after the birth of a baby. The head of the newborn in shaved. A cow or a goat is sacrificed. The circumcision (*sunnat, khatna or Mussalmani*) ceremony calls for another gathering of close kin. A boy is usually circumcised between the ages of five and ten years. The person who performs the surgery is called a *badia* or *hajam*.

A Hindu girl is kept in seclusion during the time of her first menstrual period; so, too, is a Muslim girl. Muslims, like Hindus, perform post-mortuary rites on the third and between the seventh and tenth days after death (according to Islamic custom, post-mortuary rite is preferably performed on the fourtieth day after death).

Elements of the Hindu caste system have also influenced the social structure of the Assamese Muslims. They are broadly divided into three 'caste-like' groups: Syeds, Sheikhs and Marias. The Syeds, who have the highest social status, claim to be descendants of Prophet Muhammad. A majority of the Sheikhs are presumably descendants of local peoples, including some who have been converted to Islam. The Marias, third in social status, are descendants of the Muslim soldiers captured during the Muslim invasion of 1532 A.D. Their traditional calling is brass working. Sheikhs are most common, followed by Marias and Syeds. Each of them maintains some degree of autonomy on a social plane and social relations, including marriage, are confined within the group. However, the spread of religious knowledge, the expansion of education and the levelling influence of contemporary economic forces are gradually breaking down the social barriers among these groups. The rural Assamese Muslim women, compared to men, are more backward and sub-servient because of a number of factors, one of which is the influence of purdah, which keeps women in seclusion (although not to the degree that women must wear the *burqa*, a cloth shroud from head to feet excepting the eyes, as is required in other parts of the Indo-Pakistan sub-continent). The Muslims community is apathetic about providing formal education to women, preferring instead that they get married. Large numbers of girls from rural Muslim families have no opportunity to continue schooling beyond secondary levels.

In recent decades, especially since Independence, many urban Muslim women have seen their opportunities increase measurably. Some have entered the professions and there are now-a-days a number of stages, screen and radio artists with popular followings. Social change is paving the way for many women to come out of the confines of the four walls of their homes.

As for language, there are slight regional variations in the culture of Assamese Muslims between rural and urban areas and also between eastern and western Assam. In parts of western Assam, there are strong feelings not only against kin marriage, but also against marriages between members of the same lineage. In eastern Assam, endogamous marriage is accepted by the Syeds. Among the western rural Assameses, wedding ceremonies continue through the night; in eastern Assam, the ceremonies are short and are performed in the afternoon. In parts of eastern Assam, women participate in both planting and harvesting crops; in the west, they take part only in the planting (Ali, 2013: 39-58).

Conclusion

There are a number of ways in which elements of Islamic tradition and indigenous cultural values and beliefs co-exist and interact in the regional socio-cultural context and more particularly in the case of the Assamese Muslim social life. It is a kind of socio-cultural context, which is a meeting point of two sets of factors: the religious ideology of Islam and the indigenous socio-cultural norms. The former prevails in the obligatory ritualistic spheres and the latter prevails in the social, cultural and economic spheres. The two sets of divergent factors influence each other, exist in mutual association and interact in such a way that each makes adaptive to the other. Thus, the Assamese Muslim social life shows a combination of influences from two different sources: a part of Assamese Muslim social life is derived from the Islamic socio-cultural tradition and another part of it is derived from the indigenous folk cultural tradition.

The assimilation between Islamic tradition and Assamese culture can be viewed as a product of prolonged interaction between two traditions: the Islamic Great Tradition and the Indo-Islamic Little Tradition which have been conceptualised by Momin (1975: 580). The Islamic Great Tradition is based on the Koran, Hadith (opinions and decisions of Prophet Muhammad) and Shariat (the religious law of Islam). On the other hand, the Indo-Islamic tradition is based on the folk, unwritten customs, conventions and habits handed down from generations.

The situation of acculturation and assimilation of Islamic tradition and Assamese culture obtaining in Assam region is to a considerable extent similar to those obtained in various parts of the world where Islam has come into contact with various traditional societies through the spreading process of the religion. Studies of many such situations have clearly indicated that socio-cultural life of the people who have embraced Islam is not a replica of the Islamic society envisioned and given shape by Prophet Muhammad (Greenberg, 1941; Lewis, 1966; Mujeeb, 1967; Weekes, 1984). In this context, reference may be made to Geertz (1957) who has stated that the Javanese town of Modjokuto in many respects has still preserved the peasant cultural traditions of rural Java, including a religious system that combines Islam, Hinduism and older animistic beliefs.

References

Aggarwal, P.C. (1969). Changing religious practices: their relationship to secular power in a Rajasthan Village. *Economic and Political Weekly*, 4(12): 547-51.

Aggarwal, P.C. (1966). A Muslim sub-caste in Northern India: Problem of cultural integration. *Economic and Political Weekly*, I (4):159-161.

Ahmad, Imtiaz (Ed.)(1973). *Caste and Social Stratification among Muslims in India*. Delhi: Monohar Book Service.

Ahmad, Imtiaz (Ed.)(1976). *Family Kinship and Marriage among Muslims in India*. New Delhi: Monohar Book Service.

Ahmad, Imtiaz (Ed.)(1984). *Ritual and Religion among Muslims in India.* New Delhi: Monohar Publications.

Ahmad, Imtiaz (Ed.)(2003). *Divorce and Remarriage among Muslims in India.* New Delhi: Monohar Publishers and Distributors.

Ahmad, Zarina (1962). The Muslim caste in Uttar Pradesh. *Economic and Political Weekly*, 14(7):325-35.

Ansari, Ghaus (1960). Muslim caste in India. *The Eastern Anthropologist*, 19(2): 104-111.

Bandopadhaya, O. K. (1974). *Dekha Hoi Nai.* Calcutta: Ananda Publishers.

Bhuyan, S.K. (1949). *Anglo-Assamese Relations.* Guwahati: Department of Historical and Antiquarian Studies.

Datta, Birendranath (1985). The study of folklore material of North-East India: The case for taking an integrated and multidimensional approach. *The Assam Academy Review*, I:15-31.

Dube, L. (1969). *Matriliny and Islam: Religion and Society in Laccadives.* University of Saugar Monographs in Anthropology and Sociology. No. 1, Delhi: National Publishing House.

Gait, Edward (1963). *A History of Assam*, 3rd edition. Calcutta: Thacker Spink and Co. Pvt. Ltd.

Greenberg, J. (1941). Some aspects of Negro Muhammedan culture contact among the Hausa. *American Anthropologist*, 43:51-61.

Greenberg, J. (1946). *The Influence of Islam on a Sudanese Religion.* Monographs of the American Ethnological Society, Vol. 10. New York: J. J. Augustin.

Geertz, Clifford (1957). Ritual and social change: A Javanese example. *American Anthropologist*, 59:32-54.

Geertz, Clifford (1965). Modernisation in a Muslim society: The Indonesian Case. In: R.N. Bellah (Ed.), *Religion and Progress in Modern Asia*, pp. 201-11. New York: The Free Press.

Grunebaum, G. Von (1955). The problem: Unity and diversity. In: G. Von. Grunebaum (Ed.), *Unity and Diversity in Muslim Civilisation*, pp.17-37. Chicago: University of Chicago Press.

Guha, Uma (1965). Caste among rural Bengali Muslims. *Man in India*, 45(2): 167-69.

Gupta, R. (1956). Caste ranking and intercaste relations among the Muslims of a village in North-Western Uttar Pradesh. *The Eastern Anthropologist*, 10(1): 30-42.

Hashim, Amir Ali (1970). *The Meos of Mewat.* New Delhi: Oxford and IBH Publishing Company.

Herskovits, M.J. (1938). *Acculturation, the Study of Culture Contact.* New York: J.J. Augustin.

Irshad Ali, A.N.M. (1986). Reflection of Islamic Tradition in Assamese Folklore. *Bulletin of the Assam State Museum.* Vol. VIII.

Irshad Ali, A.N.M. (2006). Cultural syncretism in North-East India: The case of the Assamese Muslim. *Humankind*, 2:141-49.

Irshad Ali, A.N.M. (2013). Ethno history, society and culture of the Assamese Muslims. In: Manoj Kr. Talukdar and Jagadish Dutta (Eds.), *Looking East Probing Deep*, pp. 39-58. Guwahati: APPOCUS.

Khan, Zillur (1968). Caste and Muslim peasantry in India and Pakistan. *Man in India*, 48(2):133-48.

Kutty, A.R. (1972). *Marriage and Kinship in an Island Society*. University of Saugar Monographs in Anthropology and Sociology, No. 2. Delhi: National Publishing House.

Lewis, I.M. (Ed.)(1966). *Islam in Tropical Africa*. London: Oxford University Press.

Mandelbaum, David G. (1972). *Society in India*. Bombay: Popular Prakashan.

Misra, S.C. (1964). *Muslim Communities in Gujarat*. Bombay: Asia Publishing House.

Momin, A.R. (1975). Muslim Caste: Theory and Practice. *Economic and Political Weekly*, 10(14):580-82.

Mondal, S.R. (1991). *Stratification, Hierarchy and Ethnicity in East and North-East India*. New Delhi: Daya Publications.

Mujeeb, M. (1967). *The Indian Muslims*. London: George Allen and Unwin Ltd.

Rigby, P.J.A. (1966). Sociological factors in the contact of the Gogo of Central Tanzania with Islam. In: I.M. Lewis (Ed.), *Islam in Tropical Africa*, pp. 248-96. London: Oxford University Press.

Singh, Yogendra (1986). *Modernisation of Indian Tradition*. Jaipur: Rawat Publications.

Smith, C.S. (1986). *Macmillan Dictionary of Anthropology*. London: The Macmillan Press Ltd.

Uddin, Qama. (1972). Marriage customs among Muslims of Western U.P. *Indian Journal of Social Work*, 33:215-16.

Vreede-de-Steurs, C. (1968). *Pardah: A Study of Muslim Women's Life in Northern India*. Essen: Van Gorkum and Co.

Weekes, R.V. (Ed.) (1984). *Muslim Peoples: A World Ethnographic Survey*, 2nd edition. West Port, Connecticut: Greenwood Press.

2

The Construction of Gender in the North-east: An Anthropological Critique

—Lucy Zehol

The Notion of Gender

In its most recent usage, 'gender' seems to have first appeared among the American feminists who wanted to insist on the fundamentally social quality of distinctions based on sex. The word denoted a rejection of the biological determinism implicit in the use of such terms as 'sex' or 'sexual difference.' While emphasising on the multiplicity of possibility of ways of conceptualising as well as experiencing, 'performing' or 'doing gender,' Connell (2002) offers the following working definition of 'gender' as "the structure of social relations that centres on the reproductive arena and the set of practices (governed by this structure) that brings reproductive distinction between bodies into social processes." In this definition, 'gender' is intimately linked with meanings and interpretations of not only reproductions and sexual bodies but also expands beyond that realm to structure and other social processes as in Mauss's terminology in which gender could be given the status of a 'total social fact'.

In everyday conversation, however, the term 'gender' may more often be used interchangeably with 'sex' as a categorical reference, i.e., 'male' and 'female' which are two examples of 'gender'. The distinction between 'sex and gender,' as analytical categories, can be traced back to developments in sociological, medical sciences and cultural anthropology during the twentieth century. Whereas de Beauvoir's (1949) political criticism of the subordination of women, titled 'the second sex,' linked the cultural devaluation of women in western society to biological differences between men and women. Rubin (1975) explored the notion of a sex or gender system, whereby the 'raw resources' of male and female bodies become 'gendered' products through processes of socialisation, normative behaviours, hegemonic representation, etc.

The 'raw resources' referred to by Rubin were defined by a conception of bio-medical differences between 'male' and 'female.' Research on chromosomes, gonads, differences between the genitals, hormones, brain size and psychology (men have more grey matter, women more white matter) and secondary characteristics, such as body fats distributions (including breasts) and bodily hair. Bio-medical research has consistently sought to link such differences to innate 'personalities' or psychological explanations for perceived differences in behaviour and effective experiences, whereas sociologists and social-cultural anthropologists as well as many psychologists have tended rather to focus on the ways in which symbolic meaning and practices are associated with biological features of 'sex' to 'cultural construct of gender.'

Since the nineties, theorists have drawn attention to the fact that the medical assignment of 'sex' at birth is also a culturally constructed practice. Hubbard (1990) cites Anne Fausto-Sterling estimation that one-two per cent of babies are actually born with ambiguous sexual characteristics (chromosomal, gonad, genital sex do not always corroborate with one another) and proposes the existence of at least five sexes. Like Judith Butler (1990), Hubbard sees the surgical procedures to 'correct' the genitals of intersexes infants as an example of science being used to force upon 'natural' bodies to conform to cultural perceptions.

In response to the increasing abstraction of gender theory, with everything being reduced to cultural constructions, Moi's (2001) essay on 'what is a woman' argues the need to abandon the 'gender' concept altogether and return to a theory embedded within a material world. Her 'lived body' concept proposes that a person's identity interaction with experience of their world is directly related to the materiality of his/her body, its physical attributes and capacities, the reactions it evokes from others and its 'situation' within a historically specific cultural environment. Moreover, the body's inhabitant has projects and goals which determined the way a person interacts with this 'situation.' Thus, the limits of the 'gender concept' which tends to imply that people are subject to the roles imposed upon them by 'culture' and transcended by the 'lived body' theory. However, as Young (2002) points out in the essay on "lived body versus gender" such a conceptualisation is more useful to describe individual experience than macro-logical social structure and their organisation. Young concludes that 'gender' continues to be necessary in political and sociological approaches to gender relations.

Anthropology and Gender

Anthropological studies have highlighted cross-cultural variation in human behaviour, social structure and belief/meaning of systems, which in the early twentieth century helped to draw attention to the social and historical specificity of the Western notion of gender and denied their having an ontological or biological basis. However, as have been argued by Moore (1998) and other feminist anthropologists, male bias and gender blindness or ethnocentrism has been a marked feature of the formational stages of anthropology as a discipline. Moore (1998) remarked that women were observed, photographed and documented by anthropologists, but their opinions were generally not represented or even listened to. She attributes this to the fact that a majority of anthropologists up to the sixties or seventies and beyond were male and therefore not only found it difficult to approach women, (social context) but also tended to assume that men made better informants as they were likely to have political/ritual power and knowledge, an assumption resulting from their knowledge of their own (i.e. Western) societies. Moore (1998) notes that even female ethnographers were likely to hold this view, since they had been educated within the male-dominated Western academic system. The impression that male informants were more 'articulate' is understood as indication that their statements/models of society were simply more intelligible (familiar) to social scientists.

The fundamental paradigm which emerged and continues to be very significant within the anthropological approach to the study of gender relations is the study of kinship. This situates gender within social structure which has significant implications for power and economic relations. But the relegation of women to mere symbols or commodities within structural systems reiterates a male world-view in which women and their activities are considered to merely serve the purposes of men or social reproduction.

Margaret Mead (1935) drew attention to the process of socialisation and its influence upon culturally different patterns of gendered behaviour and experience, including sexuality in the first half of the twentieth century. But the social changes within Europe and America led women anthropologists in the sixties and seventies to investigate gender relations across cultures with a political imperative, especially in asking whether women's sub-ordination was universal or a feature unique to capitalist society. Ortners' (1974) complex reasoning that women are seen as 'closer to nature' than men as a result of their association with children and the 'domestic sphere' because of their reduced mobility enforced by lactation and pregnancy led her to conclude that this could explain their 'devaluation' in most or all societies.

Rosaldo (1980), however, in the use and abuse of anthropology proposed, as Moore (1998) did in feminist anthropology, that women and feminist anthropology should look to develop new lines of questioning rather than follow male paradigms of seeking to explain perceived 'universals' or simply cataloguing women's experiences as examples of their sub-ordinations.

Such questions include the social, cultural and historical specificities of gender relations and the ways they are symbolically represented or articulated in practices. Visweswaran (1994), in defining feminist anthropology, notes the danger of focusing on gender relations leading to a 'decentred' approach in which women once again slip into margins can be avoided by paying particular attention to women-women relations and the power differentials between them. We must learn to ask more often how things happened in order to find out why they happened. We must pursue not universal, general causality but meaningful explanation: "It now appears to me that woman's place in human social life is not in any direct sense a product of the things she does, but of the meaning her activities acquire through concrete social interaction" (Rosaldo, 1980). Further, as Scott (1986) proposed, we need to replace the notion that social power is unified, coherent and centralised with something like Foucault's concept of power as dispersed constellations of unequal relationships, discursively constituted in social fields of force. Therefore, the notion of gender is open to challenges and is being contested.

Construction of Gender among the Khasis and Naga

Generally, in academic and non-academic works women particularly of the tribes of the north-eastern region of India, better known as the North-east, are assumed to enjoy higher social status and privileges *vis-à-vis* their counterparts in the rest of the country. Often statements and arguments are largely based on the tribal societies having 'no *purdah* system,' 'no restriction on their movement' or 'no restriction on food habits,' 'attires'. Various reports on pre-marital sex and widow re-marriage or the fact that when a woman is in trouble or when she is ill-treated by her husband she is supported by her parents, brothers and clan members. For instance, Furer-Haimendorf (1939) writes that "many women in more civilised parts of India may well envy the women of the Naga Hills, their high status and their free and happy life and if you measure the cultural level of the people by the social position and personal freedom of its women you will think twice before looking down on the Nagas as savages." The above perspective arises because tribal women were either compared to Hindu or Muslim or Western women by the colonial writers.

This chapter seeks to construct a picture of how gender is constituted in the Khasi (matrilineal) and Naga (patrilineal) societies as case studies from the North-east India as constructed by local scholars. The Khasi are one of the few remaining matrilineal tribes in India, while the Naga were once feared as head-hunters and yet admired for their material culture are taken as an example of patrilineal-patrilocal complex consisting of patrilineality, patrilocality, warfare and male supremacy situated in the political faultline of North-east India.

The various ideologies and assumptions that have influenced anthropological theories of matriliny are lucidly analysed in Nongbris' (2000) essay on *Khasi Women and Matriliny: A Tansformation in Gender Relation*. She notes two theories: the disintegration model, which asserts that matrilineal systems of inheritance are essentially unstable and cannot survive in market based economies and the 'resilience' model, which focuses on the strength of matriliny, in particular, the support it provides to women in matrilineal societies. Nongbri argues that the theories are not mutually exclusive and that, while matriliny as a system has certain advantages, it may prove susceptible to change within a global context of capitalist patriarchy.

In describing the Khasi matrilineal society Nongbri (2000) explicitly draws explicit attention to dominating power structures in politics, as well as cultural conceptions of men and women, which assert male superiority. For example, the term *u rangbah,* which means 'adult man,' also means 'bearer or carrier, while a common simile *ka kynthei ka-khynnah* translatable as 'the woman, the child' analogically suggests that women are like children. A man is said to have twelve units of strength while a woman has one. This belief underlay the conception of men as 'protectors and guardians of the weaker sex.' By using the agency of language to undermine the position of women, according to Nongbri, men ensure themselves of a firm ideological base to maintain their dominance in society.

Authority in a household is shared (which may cause conflict) between a mother's elder brother and her husband. But the sole inheritance of ancestral property is the youngest daughter who is thus less dependent economically on her male relatives than a woman in patrilineal societies. It must be noted that the youngest daughter *(ka khadduh)* also inherits significant responsibilities including cremation of her mother and provision of welfare to any family members in need. She is actually only the custodian of the ancestral property since she is not permitted to sell without consulting her mother's brother and father. Further, Nongbri notes that the institution of the *khadduh* is blamed by some for the lack of responsibility taken by divorced husband for the welfare of their children; they assume the youngest sisters will take care of them.

Nongbri (2000) also notes that *khadduh* is expected to display a high standard of morality and uphold tradition; any inappropriate behaviour may lead to her disinheritance. The divided loyalties of men between their natal households (MB) and affinal households can result in unfortunate women being neglected from both sides. However, Nongbri argues that this has also led to Khasi women being innovative and resilient, active in the productive process to ensure their economic security.

In the matrilineal system of the Khasi, gender asymmetry is visible in different aspects of their lives. The system is closely tied with indigenous belief system which is premised on the ritual unity of the sibling group. In this system where the descent is traced from the women's line, gender revolves around authority and residential pattern. In their inheritance pattern, the youngest daughter though inherits the ancestral property is not free to deal with it as she pleases. While women uphold the tradition of the family, authority is concentrated in the hands of men as shared between a mother's brother and father. This reduces her only as the custodian of the property as the control of power is vested in the hands of her male matri-kin (Nongbri, 2000; Mukhim, 2009).

In their clan organisation, the *Iing* (the smallest unit of Khasi kinship) is not a residential unit. It is comprised of many households. Thus, while a man shares a common ritual with his clan members, he shares a common residence with his wife and children. As the Khasi household is matrilocal in nature, a man keeps one foot in the mother's house and another foot at his wife's. A man here occupies two roles; that of a father and of a maternal uncle or mother's brother. However, the conflicting role of a father and the mother's brother only consolidate the position of a man. Women, on the other hand, are under the control of the brother and protection and support of the husband. As such, women have no independence identity (Nongbri, 2000). In the matrilineal set up of the Khasis, gender asymmetry is thus based on the principle of male dominance. As the writings of Nongbri (2000) shows, even the language of the Khasis too gives picture of their asymmetrical gender relations. For instance, terms like *rangbah* is denotative of male dominance where *rang* comes from *shynrang* meaning men and *bah* means to carry on the back.

The sayings of the Khasis also categorise women and children under the same category.

With the onset of modernity and the advent of Christianity, many factors made inroads into this indigenous traditional set up. Though the system still functions as a unique system of descent with women as the upholder of family's tradition, there have been many problems facing this system. Education and Christianity are considered agents posing threat to their matrilineal system by taking away the people from their belief system and change in occupational structure leading to disintegration of village endogamy. The conflicting role of the father and that of the mother's brother have further consolidated the position of men (Nongbri, 2000).

Women in the Khasi Hills are excluded from the *Dorbar Shnong* which is the traditional local governance. It is a male-centric organisation (Mukhim, 2009). There is a common saying in Khasi, *haba la kynih ka ïar kynthei la wai ka pyrthei*, meaning, when the hen crows, it will be the end of the world or the world will be ruined (See also, Pakyntein in this volume). Women have no part at all in the administration, only men occupy the position of the *Laskar* and *Sordar* (who administer justice like magistrates) in rural areas and women can never be the village headmen.

The *Dorbar Shnong* practices male suffrage because all males who have reached around eighteen years of age are admitted to the *Dorbar Shnong* as voting members. Young males function as *Ki Nongpyrta Shnong* to announce meetings of the *Dorbar* and other community matters. Women would come to the *Dorbar* only when cases or matters concerning them were discussed. As politics is considered a male prerogative, very few women came forward to contest in electoral politics, as a result of which decision-making and administration is concentrated in the hands of men. In spite of the social and economic system, yet when it comes to politics the long held tradition still prevails.

Perusal of the statistics of the women representation in the Parliament, State Legislature and District Councils indicates their participation is negligible. While women play an active role in the social and economic field, yet very few come forward to contest in the electoral politics. Women turn out in large numbers to exercise their franchise and in some polling booths women voters exceed those of men. But so far the representation of women in the Parliament, Legislative Assembly and District Councils is dismal.

Most women are not aware of politics; in fact, they have little knowledge of politics and outside world other than their household works. It appears that a majority of the women themselves are not sensitised in contesting the election as traditional conditioning is still strong (Khatso, 2004).

What is more sharp of the gender imbalances of Khasi matriliny is the findings on their reproductive health and reproductive rights which figures the lowest status of reproductive health in the country and that many couples still use the traditional methods of family planning (Khongsdier, 1992). Moreover, Pakyntein's (2000) study conducted in urban Shillong shows a perceptible sex preference for girl child among female respondents than the male in the Khasi society, as one would expect from a matrilineal society.

Coming to the patrilineal society, descent is traced from men. Men are considered the upholder of the family's tradition while women are only temporary members of her natal family and establish her permanent status only after her marriage. In the patrilineal system of the Northeast, men are considered as the head of the family, clan and village. They are the representatives of their respective units and as such, they represent the decision-making body. As Zehol (2006) noted the husband takes all major decisions inside and outside the family. The wife may be consulted and may even indirectly influence her husband. Yet, the issue is that thought patriarchies depends on their wives or mothers, they contrive to make the importance of motherhood invisible. Thus, gender asymmetry is visible in the light of men as the head in the family and society at large who wields authority in their hands and women who follow the headship of their men.

The concept of what is feminine and what is considered as masculine seems to manifest itself in every aspect of their life. For instance, the structure of the society itself sanctions to men and women different status. Men are always given the title of a householder while women are only acknowledged in the society as daughter of the father or wife of her husband. A woman's dependent status itself shows asymmetrical relations based on gender which is structured in different institutions of the society.

As descent is traced from the male line, women are not entitled to inherit any ancestral property. If a person does not have sons, then the right to inherit goes to the next kin. In this light, son preference becomes very apparent in the patrilineal society in order to uphold the tradition of the family. We can take instance from the Zeliangrong Nagas where husbands could even divorce their wives if they fail to give them sons (Newmai, 1998). However, this does not mean that girls are not welcome in the family. As compared to the mainland Hindu society, there is no sex discrimination yet a matter of preference for a boy child in the region. The birth of a girl is always welcome in the family to help the parents, but not as upholder of the family's tradition. Thus, patriarchy seems to favour boys over a girl child for the said reason and it is a matter of family's pride and for security reasons to have someone of their own to inherit the name, line and ancestral property in terms of land, field and woodland.

Further, gender based practices appears to be deeply rooted in the culture of the Naga patrilineal societies as it is apparent in the taboos, folklores and sayings of the people which are passed down through oral tradition. As Aier (2008) writes about the Naga society that the construction of gender identity within the strictly patriarchal system draws its inspiration from such tradition and narratives which immortalises and reveres male ancestors as progenitors, whereas the female ancestors are pushed to the background and are simply forgotten.

In the same way, Zehol (2006) also noted that sayings which are passed down in the form of oral text gives a picture of masculine principle as the dominant label and femininity as subordinate to such dominant principle. Even taboo imposed on men not to sleep with his wife or touch women's things before going to war or hunting are indicative of such patriarchal principles

Moreover, Zehol's (1998) account of gender relation in Naga patrilineal society draws attention to women in patrilineal society's economic dependence on men. Although women especially in the rural villages are often active in the production process and their activities are essential for the maintenance of economic continuity of their societies, they do not have the opportunity to accumulate wealth.

In addition, the customary laws of the various Naga tribes are clearly in favour of the men, who continue to subscribe to them in order to retain their superiority *vis-à-vis* the women in their own societies. The factors like education, occupation and religion do not seem to have had any success towards overcoming such gender bias among the men though the women are not without such bias either (Vitso, 2003).

It is generally believed that in Naga society, girls are to marry whomsoever they like and parents simply agree to their will. But the facts reveal that among some Naga tribes, the opposite is the reality. Parents among the Angami and Konyak tribes arrange marriages (Kelhou, 1998; Zehol, 1998). A woman, as daughter, is not entitled to own any of the ancestral property. If a woman is the only child, the ancestral property will be given to her fathers' immediate male relatives.

It is the women who usually perform the sacred rituals in religious ceremonies. Yet, in one of the most popular Angami Naga festivals *Sekrenyi* (feast of purification), women are not allowed to fetch water from the spring or other sources due to fear of defilement. Men do not take even the food cooked by them and they are prohibited even to go near the men or to walk past them. All this prohibition takes place on the day of the secret ritual called *Pri.*

As agents in the maintenance of tribe/community boundaries, however, Zehol and Zehol (2009) argued that women's knowledge in the domestic realm regarding food practices and rituals (granary) or their preparation gives women a certain sense of power and prestige in their families. It is important to note that since women are economically dependent on their families, it is understandable that maintaining ritual purity and observing prescriptions of boundary maintenance becomes a prerogative for them.

In terms of political empowerment, Khasi or Naga women whether belonging to matrilineal or patrilineal society were still not allowed to take part in the deliberations of the traditional village durbar/council. Such observations on women not playing leadership roles in political or socio-religious matters are, however, not peculiar of the tribal societies. Today, Khasi and Naga women indeed have experienced significant improvement in lifestyle and opportunities but they have a long way to go before they achieve equity within their respective society.

We can, therefore, observe that the gender ideology of the Khasi and Naga tribes of North-east shows that the structure and customary laws of the society are clearly in favour of men. This is despite the changes that are taking place in the region with the introduction of Christianity and Modernisation. Values of what constitute masculinity and femininity seem to be under the control of the traditional system which is grounded with men as the dominant figure. However, gender gap is wider in the Naga society as compared to that of the Khasi society as matriliny is advantageous for women (Mukhim, 2009).

The need for a critique of patriarchy and a redefinition of the term matriarchy has been argued by Goettner-Abendroth (2009) in her book *Societies of Peace: Matriarchies Past, Present and Future*. According to her, even if matriarchal studies started more than 140 years ago with the works of Bachofen and Morgan, their works did not have a true scientific foundation because patriarchal-biased presuppositions distorted their findings. Moreover, modern matriarchal studies put an end to the common prejudice that, matriarchy means 'women's rule'. It is true that in patriarchal societies women are ruled by men. Matriarchal societies are in no way the simple reversal of this scenario. In matriarchies, mothers are at the centre of culture without ruling over other members of the society. The aim is not to have power over others and over nature, but to follow maternal values, i.e., to nurture the natural, social and cultural life based on mutual respect. In other word, the governing principle of matriarchal societies is balance, rather than domination (Goettner-Abendroth, 2009). If we treat the opposition between male and female as problematic rather than known, as something contextually defined, repeatedly constructed, then we must constantly ask not only what is at stake in proclamations or debates that invoke gender to explain or justify their positions but also how implicit understandings of gender are being invoked and re-inscribed.

Challenges

Hence, issues that present serious challenges for Anthropology of gender are: (a) the multiplicity of conceptualising as well as experiencing gender, (b) in the context of anthropology of gender studies, it must be critical. The Anthropology of Gender must be in a continual state of critical dialogue with itself, the world around and with the differences between its definitions of reality (contextually specific ways) that stem from longstanding gender asymmetries deeply rooted in cultures. Gender, provides a way to decode meaning and experience and to understand the complex relationship among various forms of human interaction.

References

Aier, Anungla (2008). Folklore, Folk Ideas and Gender among the Naga. *Eastern Quarterly: Gender Studies in the North-east*, 5:87-93.

Butler, Judith (1990). *Gender Trouble: Feminism and the Subversion of Identity.* New York: Rutledge.

Connell, R. W. (2002). *Gender.* Cambridge: Polity Press.

de Beauvoir, Simone (1949). *The Second Sex*. Canada: Penguin Books Ltd.

Furer-Haimendorf, C. von (1939). *The Naked Naga.* London: Methuen and Co. Ltd.

Goettner-Abendroth, Heide (2009). *Societies of Peace: Matriarchies Past, Present and Future*. Toronto: Inanna Publications and Education Inc.

Hubbard, Ruth (1990). *The Politics of Women's Biology.* New Brunswick: Rutgers University Press.

Kelhou (1998). Women in Angami Society. In: Lucy Zehol (Ed.), *Women in Naga Society,* pp. 55-61. New Delhi: Regency Publication.

Khatso, Kezhaleno (2004). *Khasi Women and Electoral Politics: A Study of the Greater Shillong Area*. Unpublished Ph.D. Thesis. Shillong: NEHU.

Khongsdier, R. (1992). Some demographic traits among the Pnar of Sutnga and Moopala in Jaintia Hills District of Meghalaya. *Man in India,* 72 (4): 491- 495.

Mead, Margaret (1935). *Sex and Temperament in Three Primitive Societies.* New York: Morrow.

Moi, Toril (2001). *What is a Woman?* New York: Oxford University Press.

Moore, Henrietta L. (1998). *Feminism and Anthropology*. Cambridge: Polity Press.

Mukhim, Patricia (2009). Khasi Matrilineal Society: Challenges in the Twenty-first Century. In: Heide Goettner-Abendroth (Ed.), *Societies of Peace: Matriarchies Past, Present and Future*, pp. 193-204. Toronto: Inanna Publications and Education Inc.

Newmai, Hunibou (1998). *Women in Naga Society*. New Delhi: Regency Publications.

Nongbri, Tiplut (2000). Khasi women and matriliny: Transformations in gender relations. *Gender, Technology and Development*, 4(3): 359-95.

Ortner, Sherry (1974). Is Female to Male as Nature is to Culture? In: *M*. Rosaldo and M. Lamphere *(Eds.), Woman, Culture and Society*, pp. 68-87. Stanford: Stanford University Press.

Pakyntein, Valentina (2000). Gender preference in Khasi Society: An evaluation of Tradition, Change and Continuity. *Indian Anthropologist*, 30:27-35.

Rosaldo, M.Z. (1980). The use and Abuse of Anthropology: Reflections on feminism and cross-cultural understanding. *Signs: Journal of Women in Culture and Society*, 5(3): 389-417.

Rubin, Gayle (1975). The traffic in Women: Notes on the political economy of Sex. In: R.R. Reiter (Ed.), *Towards an Anthropology of Women*, 157-210. New York: Monthly Review Press.

Scott, Joan (1986). Gender: A useful category of historical analysis. *The American Historical Review*, 91(5):1053-75.

Viswewaran, Kamala (1994). *Fictions of Feminist Ethnography*. Minneapolis: University of Minnesota Press.

Vitso, Adino (2003). *Customary Law and Women: The Chakhesang Naga*. New Delhi: Regency Publications.

Young, Iris Marion (2002). Lived body versus gender: Reflections on social structure and subjectivity. *Ratio*, 15: 410–28.

Zehol, Lucy (2006). Gender issues in the tribal society of North-East India: Some observations. *Bulletin of the Department of Anthropology Dibrugarh University*, 34: 99-10.

Zehol, Lucy (Ed.) (1998). *Women in Naga Society*. New Delhi: Regency Publications.

Zehol, Lucy and Kevekha Kevin Zehol (2009). *The Legendary Naga Village: A Reader (Khezhakeno)*. Nagaland: Heritage Publishing House.

3

Dynamics of Gender Roles in Khasi-Pnar Matrilineality

— Valentina Pakyntein

Introduction

The Khasi-Pnar is the indigenous people inhabiting Meghalaya in North-east India. The matrilineal principle of descent, inheritance and succession is an age-old practice of the people in matrilineal societies as hypothetically inferred, which confer more autonomy on women as compared to patriarchal ones. This chapter is an attempt to discuss gender roles, keeping in view the dynamic nature of human society in general and the Khasi-Pnar society in particular during the last century. The chapter is compressed into the following sections:

1. Traditional Gender Roles in Khasi society and the underlying and values.
2. Changing Society and impingement of the Gender Roles.
3. Concluding Remarks: Issues and Queries.

In the Khasi-Pnar society, descent is traced through the female and each clan traced their descent to the apical ancestress. Women have the right over their children by dint of the matronymic principle and children take the clan's name of the mother. Incessancy of the clan devolves on women. A mother is a pivotal in the family; she is responsible for the upbringing and socialisation of children. The father is regarded as the provider among the Khasi, but not among the Pnar following the original beliefs. The position of a husband and father in the War Khasi family is much higher compared with that of the Khynriam Khasi owing to the fact that among them both sons and daughters inherit the parental property (Das Gupta, 1981).

Traditional Gender Roles in Khasi Society and the Underlying Values

Reproductive role of women is acclaimed and there are many rituals for the expecting mother and a safe delivery of the child (Mawrie, 1981). In Khasi society, an issueless woman is ridiculed as *Iap-Duh* (extinct-line). Even if perpetuation of the clan depends on women, Khasi society has frowned upon an issueless man alike. A special ceremony is performed for members of the clan who died without an issue (Gordon, 1907). This ceremony is a symbolic obviation of childlessness. The role of both the sexes in procreation is considered significant for the continuity of the group.

A Khasi man had two major roles to play, viz., *U Kni* (maternal uncle) and *U Kpa* (father) in his family of orientation and procreation, respectively. A man's obligation and duties was ambivalent, particularly if he is the eldest maternal uncle. As the maternal uncle he has to take care of his niece family and property. The maternal uncle also plays an important role in the upbringing and welfare of the sister's children, besides his socio-economic and socio-religious duties to his other lineage members. As a husband and father, his obligation is that of provider and protector to his wife and children. The conflicting roles between maternal uncle and husband are minimised among the Pnar following the traditional religion, because they adapt to the 'visiting husband system' even in today's context.

In the agrarian society, land is an important asset. Land as an important asset is within the control of the clan council. The clan or lineage with landed property serves as an important economic unit. In the past society when clan-land was abundant and people depended on it for their livelihood, the role of the maternal uncle in the clan council was no doubt important. The council could distribute or allocate land whether for agricultural purpose, housing, or otherwise. The inheritress of the clan-landed-property is the youngest daughter among the majority of the Khasi-Pnar. The eldest daughter in certain section of the War Khasi inherits the clan property. It has always been portrayed that though women enjoy property rights, but in this society as in most matrilineal societies, men exert control over their sister's or niece's property. The inheritress acts as a custodian of the clan landed property, while the manager is the eldest maternal uncle among the Khasi-Pnar. However, neither the inheritress nor the manager has the power and authority over the use and disposal of clan property, because other members of the lineage have a say. The manager can, however, influence any decision as the adviser of the lineage in general. But a mother or senior women of the clan will have a say in the clan property.

The ancestral property passes from mother to daughter. Among the War Khasi there is an exception to this rule, both male and female children inherit the ancestral and acquired property in equal share, with the exception that the youngest daughter is given something in addition to her share (Gurdon, 1907).When it comes to self-acquired property of the family, at parental discretion, other children can inherit irrespective of male or female. The inheritress of the lineage-property by dint of her privileges have more responsibilities and obligation to her family members. The house of the youngest daughter among the Khasi is looked up by a member of the matri-kin as a refuge in the midst of any contingency (Nongbri, 1996). Thus, the obligation of looking after the parents, house the orphans of her sisters and shelter her divorced/separated brother and sister rest on her. The right to property is equally complement by her social duties.

Women also directly or indirectly participate in the socio-religious and socio-political activities. Performance of family socio-religious rites and ceremonies are in the hands of males, but conventionally arranged in the household of the youngest daughter of the family. The youngest daughter is also regarded as the holder and keeper of religion (*Ka bat ia ka Niam*). Her house is known as the foundation house (*ka iing-seng*). It is here that members of the family assembled for family rituals and propitiation of ancestors and ancestress, or other rituals relating to the family and its members. She prepares the articles for the rituals (Gordon, 1907; Mawrie, 1981). The actual rites may be conducted by the maternal uncle, or by the diviner (*Nongknia*), or by the priest (*Lyngdoh*) ordained from a particular lineage or clan. In the past Khasi society, death rituals are very elaborate and take place in many stages and it is usually in the house of the youngest daughter that these important rites take place. The rights and privileges of the youngest daughter and maternal uncle in Khasi society extend to socio-religious activities. In the socio-economic and socio-religious institutions, the youngest daughter and maternal-uncle hold significant rights, privileges and duties among the Khasi-Pnar. Their role is being replaced by that of *Syiem* (chief) and *Syiem Sad* in the socio-political domain.

The political and administrative affairs are considered men's domain in the traditional set-up both in Khasi and Pnar societies. Unlike the Ashanti women in Ghana (Rattray, 1969), women in the Khasi matrilineal society of Meghalaya have no active roles in the public domain. Khasi women were barred from attending any of the councils (*durbar*) be it at the village or at the state level. The simile-*ynda kynih ka iar kynthei, ka pyrthei ruh lawai* (meaning when the hen crows the world is nearing its end) and *ksan rympei rem dorbar*, meaning a winner in the family a loser in the council) - repudiates women's participation in politics. These sayings insinuated that though women are pivotal in the affair of the family and clan, men are decision-makers in the public sphere. Thus, women have no direct role in politics, except that successions to political offices pass through the female line, i.e., from the current *Syiem* to his sister's son. The office of the State-priesthood (*Syiem-sad*), which is accorded to the *Syiem's* mother or eldest sister, is a token of the religio-political nature of the Khasi-Pnar *Syiemship*. Through this, the official political status women symbolic role in politics is ensured. It is also through this office that the *Syiem-sad* performs her role in state rituals and advises the appointment of the next chief. She is entrusted with the custody of rites and ceremonies of the states in order that her moral force may serve as a restraining hand, a power behind the throne (Lyngdoh, 1989). This political office of *Ka Syiem Sad* is observable till date in the annual Nongkrem festival. Although the public-domain is directly under men's control, men succeed to traditional political offices via the female line, i.e., brother to sister's son or sister daughter's son and in some Khasi states women figured as symbolic head more associated with rituals of political nature.

The above paragraphs highlight the rights and duties of the key-figures in Khasi-Pnar societies. Nakane (1967) terms the youngest daughter and the eldest maternal uncle as the 'Pair-status' who perform the socio-economic and socio-religious roles within the family and lineage in accordance with the norms laid down by the society. This term can be extended to the *Syiem* and *Syiem-sad* who perform the traditional socio-political and religio-political roles.

Nakane (1967) has pointed out the conflicting gender roles in Khasi matriliny. She elaborates the problems faced by the eldest maternal uncle and the youngest daughter. She refers to the subordinate position of the man who marries an heiress and also to the problems encountered by a woman who marries the maternal uncle, who is the man of authority in his respective lineage and clan. According to her, this is one of the reasons for the high rate of divorce and separation in the Khasi society. The position of man as a husband is stable and better-off if he marries a non-heiress. A woman who marries a non-authority man gets the full support of her husband economically. The role of the maternal uncle in such a family also declines. Nongbri (1996) reiterates the above view when she states that the Khasi kinship imposes a dual loyalty upon men.

In Khasi-Pnar societal set-up, men and women have certain rights, privileges and functions, accorded by traditional practices, thereby contributing to the continuity of the social structure. In this context, one can argue the complementary gender roles and the valuing of both sexes in the traditional social norms and institutions. Thus, gender roles are firmly embedded in the matriarchal social-structures and institutions. Examining the gender roles in the Khasi-Pnar society, one cannot ignore the complementary nature of the structured-roles. The traditional gender roles have been construed in a way that men and women could not function in isolation. The foci of roles on the youngest daughter and the eldest maternal uncle indicated the complementary nature of the position of men and women in the family and lineage - the basic units of the Khasi social-structure. If the younger brothers have no authority the other elder sisters have no property. The functions of one depend on the reciprocal roles and duties of the other, but as clan members, every individual has rights and duties. The cementing bond in the social structure of both

Khasi-Pnar largely depends on the 'key-roles' assigned to the 'key-figures' in the society and these function at the family level or lineage. The structural-gender roles at present continue, but need to be redefined and reformulated with the changing times.

Changing Society and Gender Role at Present

The Khasi society has undergone through a sea of changes in the discernible past. The British colonial rule directly impacted the polity of self-governance as well as effectuated many aspects of the society. Facilitated by the foreign rule, missionaries penetrated into the region successfully, where earlier attempts had failed. The conversion to Christianity forwarded many changes in their beliefs and practices. The introduction of formal education and healthcare by the missionaries, modernise many aspects of their culture. The colonial rule and changes in the polity after independence, along-with progressing formal education, precipitated changes in the society's polity, economy, etc. With the changing society and economy, the concept of property acquires a new meaning, although its ownership and management was uncontested in the past. The setting up of political headquarters brought about an aggregation of people from varied ethnic groups at the centres. Gradually, urbanisation begins and urbanism as a new way of life takes-shape. The accumulative changes open up new vista of job opportunities, white and blue collar, which are of no significance in the past slash and burn economy. The patterns of relationship shift from kinship and village ties to other dimension of private-public relationship/partnership, whether in the social, economic, political or religious spheres. These accruing changes metamorphose individual's roles and statuses, snowballing into curtailment of certain roles and addendum others.

The matrilineal principle of descent and inheritance is being questioned at the initial stage of Christianisation. However, judicial support of the British government with more people converted to Christianity there followed a lulling period where matrilineal principle is observed and traditional norms being followed. The juxtaposition with people of patriarchal culture and values have contravened with the traditional Khasi worldviews and the underlying values. Amidst the mix-cultural groups the local norms, customs and traditions are questioned, or look-at negatively both by the insiders and the outsiders. In the second half of the twentieth century, certain Khasi individuals and groups summoned to contest the matrilineal system and vindicated the patrilineal principle of descent and inheritance. These groups actively advocated the patriarchal values, through meetings, seminars, discussions etc. at the public or private platform.

The natives of Meghalaya have had a long contact with the outside world, thereby affecting many aspects of their traditional institutions, besides weakening the matrilineal-structure. The Khasi came into contact with the people in the plains of Bengal for trade and commerce since the early part of the nineteenth century. On the other hand, the contact of the Pnar with the Hindu culture dates back to the fifteenth century (Mathur, 1979). The British occupation in this part of the country during the early ninteenth century has brought about a profound impact on many aspects of their cultures and traditions. The contact of the Khasi and Pnar with the Hindus also influences certain sections of the people notably the War Khasi and the War Jaintia on the present Bangladesh border and the Pnar in Jaintia Hills. Their beliefs and customs, to a certain extent, have been Hinduised. The major changes, however, occurred with the organised effort of the Western missionaries in proselytising and introducing formal education. The British occupancy of this area has brought about a chain of changes from administrative to cash economy, changing religion, development in communication and so on. After the post-independence period, more changes occurred in the society political and economic aspects. These combined factors affect the normative roles of the traditional matrilineal structure. Thus, the rights, privileges and duties of both men and women need to be redefined in the present context.

The traditionally etched statuses and rights, obligations and duties, needs to be redefined and reorganise at tandem with the ever transforming society. The motley causes of undergoing changes in the society play havoc with people's beliefs, ideologies and values. Many issues stem from the perplexity and ambiguity of individual expedient role, fulfillment and status expectations. Notwithstanding, matrilineal principle of descent, residence, inheritance and succession is still binding on a majority of the Khasi at present. At best one can argue about the resiliency of Khasi matriarchy even if not in its pristine form.

Motherhood continues to be an ideal image for women. Perpetuation of the clan is the vested role of women and changes in the society have not impinged on this sacred duty. However, inter-community marriages in a multi-cultural urban setting brought about men's bestowal to the continuity of their clans. A majority of the children of Khasi males, who married non-Khasi women, take their father's clan name; a few of them undergo through the traditional (and revived) ceremony of *Tang-Jait* meaning incorporation of the new clan into the Khasi society. Besides, few Khasi families (Khasi to Khasi marriage) take the father's clan instead of the mother's (Pakyntein, 1996). Thus, a handful of males also contribute to the reproduction of clan-members, which is impossible in the past.

There has been a major reorganisation and redefinition of men's role as a result of the changes in the society's belief-system, economy, modernisation, contact with other cultures, etc. The role of man as a husband and father is fortified with the Christian doctrine that a woman should subdue to her husband and that of the father as the bread-earner of the family. Modernisation opens the gate to various means of livelihood, such as white-collar salaried jobs and a range of other occupations. Trade and commerce flourishes with the introduction of cash economy. These in a way bolster the men's position in the family set-up as compared to the substantive economy in the past. In the past, a man who married an heiress lived in the shadow of the maternal uncle, whereas a man who married a non-heiress had a comparatively stable position in his family of procreation. At present, whether a man marries an heiress or not, his position is reinforced, especially when the family depends on his income for the needs of the family. In addition, a man overall socio-economic status influences his position whether in his mother's house or his wife.

The role and position of the maternal uncle also needs to be redefined. The emphasised role of a man as a husband and father has weakened the position of the maternal uncle in his sister's family, though he continues to be respected. His position needs to be appraises *vis-à-vis* the sister's husband with respect to economic status, educational status, morality, etc. Among the Christians, the duty of maternal uncle as family priest is relinquished, thereby enhancing the role of the father in the family. The increasing population diminishes the size of clan property and pushes the clan members to migrate elsewhere in search of better economic opportunities. This in turn vanquished the role of maternal uncle in controlling the clan property resources. The pull between the avuncular and paternal authority has led to the emergence of the mother figure as a dominant personality in the family (Nongbri, 1996).

The rights and duties of the youngest daughter in Khasi society have been affected by various factors of change. She continues to inherit the family property and has more control and authority over it, because the position of the maternal uncle is weakened. Many legal-battles have been fought over the mismanagement (sale) of ancestral property by the youngest daughter or/and her husband. The religious duty of the youngest daughter, like that of the maternal uncle, is relegated among the Christians. Her house is no longer the pivot where lineage members revolve for family rituals. It became a centre for social bonding instead of a centre for socio-economic and socio-religious activities. In the past, the socio-economic and socio-religious roles of the youngest daughter were complementary to those of the maternal uncle. Her position is enhanced with the weakened position of the maternal uncle. The socio-economic status of the youngest daughter's husband may influence their position in the family relationship and the society as a whole. In addition, educational status, economic opportunities and general urban way of life may strengthen her position or undermine it.

In the agricultural society, the concept of non-working does not exist; men, women and even children are allocated with specific economic duties. Modern economic life and changing life style, especially in the urban areas, introduces the concept of 'house-wife.' The women, who are labelled as house-wives, do not consider themselves better-off in status as compared to the working-women. Thus, such women shy away from the community life unless they are well-educated, or have substantive economic asset and status to back them up. Non-working women generally have less power of decision-making in the family and a man as a bread-earner in such a family has more power and authority.

Women actively participate in all Christian churches. Each church, irrespective of the sect, has women's wings where women have praise and worship sessions and through such wings women extend their socio-religious and other activities. Women in Meghalaya could give a sermon in such gathering but not in the general worship session. Many women teach in 'Sunday-school,' which consists mostly of children and adolescents. Women in the Presbytarian Churches are not elected as church-elders (*Tymmen Basan*). There have been cases where women are proposed, but the Church Organising Committee negates such proposals. Because of such instances, there is a clear instruction from the church authority not to vote for women as church-elders. Though we have women pastors, none has been given a pastorate to preside officially. There are also women missionaries who work for the churches. However, women basically perform supplementary roles in the working of the church. Thus, women are more involved in the extension-activities and social services, such as education, health, charity and a host of other activities. Besides, women are also involved in fund-raising through fairs, exhibitions, collection and sale of *khaw-kham* (literally a handful of rice) collected from the church member households, etc. Christianity, Hinduism or Islam, has been embraced by the Khasi-Pnar in varying degrees and proportions. These religions, no doubt, have a patrilineal flavour in them and this in turn influences not only the people who practice any such religion but the society at large.

In the traditional belief, ka *Niam Khasi* and *Niam-Tre*, leaders realise that it is imperative to be more organised in their religious activities. This gives rise to the organisation of *Seng-Samla Khasi* (1899), which was later retitled as *Seng-Khasi* (1901). This organisation started its youth-wings, *viz.*, *Ka Seng Samla* (1922) and *Ka Seng Pyni* (1973), which function like a Sunday school. Thus, the traditional religious institutions have become more formal and organised. The direct participation in the structure and functioning is open to women, but men are the core organisers and functionaries. Women's role and position in the indigenous, or non-indigenous religions, are becoming secondary in nature. Although women have minor duties in the traditional rites and ceremonies, their role in rituals is non-existent, especially among the Christians.

As for political sphere, women's roles are indirect and insignificant in the traditional political system (See also, Zehol in this volume). This holds true in the present day traditional institutions of the *Syiemship* among the Khasi-Pnar. Among the Khasi-Pnar, succession to the political office remains in the female line. The traditional village council (*Dorbar Shnong*) practices male suffrage. Women could not attend such council in the past. At present, women are able to make a dent in almost all village councils in urban areas and few village-councils in rural areas. Women can attend such councils and a number of the *Dorbar Shnong* in Shillong include women in the Executive Committee, or elect them as office bearers. In urban areas, women are co-opted or nominate as office bearers or executive members of the village councils; but one should note that women are not able really to penetrate or carve a place in the traditional political set-up.

Under the British rule, women were given the right to vote through the Government of India Act 1935. This Act also provides for reservation of women to the State Assembly. Thus, two women, Miss Mavis Dunn and Mrs Bonnily Khongmen, were elected to the Assam Legislative Assembly before the independence of the country from the foreign rule (Lyngdoh, 1997). In the free India Republic, the Constitution of India not only confers equal rights and opportunities for men and women in the political, economic and social spheres; but it is also very clear about discrimination against the weaker section in the society. Besides, it empowers the state to make affirmative discrimination in favour of women and children. The fact remains that representation of women in hardcore electoral politics is negligible and their presence is hardly felt. Now and then, we have one or two women MLAs or MDCs (Member of Legislative Assembly and Member of District Councils, respectively). In the 1st two state general elections held in 1952 and 1957, women had contested, but were defeated. In the ensuing elections in 1962 and 1967, no women contested the elections to the Assam Legislative Assembly. In the last three decades after Meghalaya achieved its statehood (1972), only six women were elected to the State Assembly, namely, Mrs Percylina Marak (1972), Mrs Miriam D. Shira (1978), Mrs Maysalin War (1984, 1988); Mrs Roshan Warjri (1993 and 1998), Mrs I. Lyngdoh and Mrs D. Marak (2003). Women elected to the Autonomous District Councils too were very few.

Women do participate actively in modern politics both at the regional and national levels. During election, they participate in political campaign; such as procession, public meetings, giving public speeches and other works. Women turn out in large numbers to exercise their franchise and women voters exceed that of men in some polling booths. However, if women are not elected to the State Legislature and District Councils, this would deprive them of being involved in the policy-making decision (Lyngdoh, 1997).

Concluding Remarks: Issues and Queries

The previous section highlights the traditional matrilineal structure, the rights, freedom and responsibilities of men and women as well as the constraints within it. This is followed by a brief discussion on the changing society including changing roles of men and women. If gender role and status are affected by various factors and if gender-role needs to be refocused and redefined; what would be the societal responses?

The Khasi-Pnar matrilineal society has been resilient to the religious, economic and political changes. The Khasi matriliny has its own dynamic system of descent and succession from time immemorial and has been adapting itself to the changing times. The matronymic rule and female inheritance are still the norms followed by a majority of the people till date. Inheritance of property by the converts had been challenged in the nineteenth century. During the initial stage of Christianisation, many converts were disinherited (Dutta, 1982). When the youngest daughter embraced Christianity, her rights to inheritance were opposed by family members on the ground that she no longer performed her socio-religious duties. In 1850, Lord Dalhousie passed an Act to safeguard the rights of the converts throughout India. As a result, the opposition to inheritance by the converts was gradually diminished. The Muslim Khasi, on the other hand, has reverted to Muslim law of inheritance, except a few cases (Mathur, 1979). The youngest daughter is treated at par with other daughters and she does not get any preferential treatment of ancestral property. In general, however, the traditional pattern of inheritance is followed by a majority of families, irrespective of conversion.

The 1960s witnessed the birth of an organisation known as *Ka Seng Iktiar Longbriew Manbriew*. Its main objective was to disseminate patrilineal descent, succession and inheritance. The protagonists of this movement published articles in the local papers and distributed booklets, organised seminars and discussions to propagate that matriliny is no more functional in the present context. Their movement was, however, futile. A few years later, they strived for a change in the inheritance pattern, i.e., from female to male. In 1978, the Meghalaya Youth Organisation demanded that women of Khasi-Pnar-Achik, who did not observe group endogamy, should be disinherited. In the same year, the Durbar of the *Hynniew Trep* reiterated and supported the above issue. It also demanded that the government should appoint the Inheritance Commission to investigate the existing laws of inheritance in Meghalaya. Accordingly, the government appointed the Law Commission to delve into the matter. The Commission proposed a bill, which was passed by the Meghalaya Assembly in 1984. This is known as the Meghalaya Succession to Self-Acquired Property (Khasi and Jaintia Special Provision) Act 1984. According to this act, the parents can bestow their self-acquired property to any children by the will system, but ancestral property should pass to the female line. This Act validates the traditional system of inheritance.

The various forces threatening the inheritance pattern could not have much impact on the traditional norms. At present, the ideal view is that equality should prevail in sharing the property. It is, however, a different matter with respect to the operation of this ideal. Those who have the property could distribute it to all children, but the youngest daughter gets the lion's share including parental house. Sons get a share, if the parents have the resource, but the youngest daughter and other daughters generally get a preference over the sons. Again there are many instances where the youngest daughters are deprived of the property and the other daughters inherit it. The reason for depriving of property could be marrying a person against the parents' wishes, incompatibility to stay matrilocally or other reasons. In some other cases, the youngest daughter may relinquish her rights because of many reasons, such as inability to stay with the parents because of economic factors, etc. The sons also inherit not only self-acquired property but ancestral property as well, where there is no daughter.

It should be noted that equitable distribution of property can take place if parents have less number of children. The reality is, however, very different, because the fertility rate in Meghalaya is the highest in the country (IIPS, 2000). Meghalaya is also the state where family planning method is least adopted. The questions may therefore arise: can fertility rates be reduced without family planning? Is family planning an option for equal distribution of family property at least? If family-property is equally distributed, will it reduce an inequitable distribution of economic resources in the society?

The matronymic principles have been threatened by a section of people who are inclined towards the patrilineal system. The part played by organisations like *Ka Seng Iktiar Longbriew Manbriew* has been highlighted in the preceding sections. In the 1980s, *Ka Syngkhong Rympei Thymmai* (SRT) was established and its members asseverated patrilineal principles and propagated others to follow. The members of the group follow the patronymic principles (Nongkynrih, 2005). At present one comes across few Khasi families (Khasi mother and father) who take the father's clan. Is patrilineal influence or inclination the cause? Besides, a number of Khasi families take the clan names of both parents - both among the children of Khasi parents and more so among children of the Khasi mother and non-Khasi father? In the former category, is this an acknowledgement of a father in a name? In the latter category, is it for expediency? Or is it for bridging the different cultural practices?

According to Khasi tradition, perpetuation of the clan is a vested role of woman, but men through the practice of *Tang-Jait* could (adoption of non-Khasi member into Khasi society) start a new clan for their children from a non-Khasi mother. The revival of the tradition, (i.e., incorporating new members into the society in the late part of the twentieth century) may, however, have its own reverberation in the future. The Khasi are the indigenous people of

Meghalaya and the Government of India have bestowed on them the schedule tribe status. Thus, a Khasi or Pnar has certain advantages from the government policies as well as from the cultural practices of the people. The system of adoption as practice at present is a portage for becoming a member of the Khasi community in a legitimate manner as defined within the cultural practices. In the past, this practice meted the problem of those who were not within the fold of the Khasi society. It enables such members to become part of the society by following its socio-cultural and socio-religious practices. However, this practice may raise paradoxical issues in the future.

The Khasi Lineage Bill passed by the governor in 2005 is absorbed with mixed feelings by a number of people (See, Khongsdier in this volume). People, especially Khasi men, have not taken it kindly and interpretations of the bill are many. The president of the SRT has recapitulated the organisation earlier demand that there is a need to change the matrilineal system to patrilineal one and thus the said bill should be reviewed. The president of the *Mait Shaphrang Movement* (MSM) reiterates that the said bill needs to be reviewed because custom and traditions change with the changing times. He also dwells upon the need for equitable distribution of property - both ancestral and self-acquired. Even those who are in favour of matronymic rule criticise the Bill and pointed out that it would have a negative impact on the males. The applicability or inapplicability and the interpretations of the said Bill need to be examined and discussed in the right forum.

The role and function of the clan and its council in the socio-religious arena have diminished considerably among the Khasi, whether they follow the traditional belief system or not. In modern economy and polity, the clan and its council hardly have any role to play. Without doubt, traditional economy and polity persist, but have been countermanded by the modern ones. The function of the clan in the past revolved around the whole society and the life of individual members. The change in the religious, economic and political institutions results in re-conceptualisation of the roles and duties of the individuals and the declining function of the clan in the society (Pakyntein, 1996). Migration from rural to urban areas or from one village to another in search of livelihood diminishes the kinship ties of the people. The unity and solidarity of the clan is dying. Its important function is the rule of clan exogamy, which is adhered to strictly. The question that arises is how far the Khasi-Pnar people can follow the rule of clan exogamy with matronymic rules existing side by side with that of patronymic ones? Will the matrilineal descent persist? What are the mechanisms of defining who is a marriageable partner and who is not? With the declining importance of the clan as a basic functional unit in the society, the importance of family in regulating socio-religious and socio-economic duties of its member is enhanced. Modernisation process, economic changes and modern way of life foster the growth of individualism. For example, the person who inherits the family property treats it as an individual one and this many a time leads to legal battles between family or lineage members in modern times. A combination of factors affects the unity of the clan member and diminishes the corporate life people generally. The economic hardship and loosening kinship bonds are important factors that orphanage and old-age homes have arisen at present.

A host of other factors, such as direct contact of the people with other neighbouring societies and cultures, the penetration of the global culture with the advancement in modern communication undoubtedly impinge on the perception of the individual's rights, duties, values, etc. Socio-cultural change is a process that is part and parcel of human society and culture. When human initiates change they aspire for a better future, but human innovation, initiation and invention brought about both positive and negative consequences. Therefore, as we are ready to accept the positive aspect of our ever changing world, we need to be ready to combat the negative issues that follow.

References

Das Gupta, P.K. (1984). *Life and Culture of Matrilineal Tribe of Meghalaya.* New Delhi: Inter India Publications.

Dutta, P.N. (1982). *Impact of the West on the Khasis and Jaintias. Survey of Political, Economic and Social Changes*. New Delhi: Cosmo Publications.

Gurdon, P.R.T. (1907). *The Khasis,* (Reprinted 1982). New Delhi: Cosmo Publications.

International Institute of Population Studies (IIPS)(2000). *National Family Health Survey –II (1998-99)*. Bombay: IIPS.

Lyngdoh, M.P.R. (1998). Women in Meghalaya and the Constitution 73rd Amendment Act, 1992: Problem and Expectations. In: M. N. Karna (Ed.), *Power to the People of Meghalaya*, pp. 55-68. New Delhi: Regency Publications.

Mathur, P.R.G. (1979). *The Khasis of Meghalaya: Study in Tribalism and Religion*. New Delhi: Cosmo Publications.

Mawrie, H.O. (1981). *The Khasi Milieu*. New Delhi: Concept Publishing Company.

Nakane, C. (1967). *Garo and Khasi: A Comparative Study in Matrilineal Systems*. Paris: Mouton and Co.

Nongbri, T. (1996). Problems of Matriliny: A short Review of the Khasi Kinship Structure. In: J. S. Bhandari (Ed.), *Kinship and Family in North-East India*, pp. 331-45. New Delhi: Cosmo Publications.

Nongkynrih, A.K. (2005). Avoiding Women's Empowerment in the Hindu-Kush Himalaya: A Sociological Perspective. Keynote address presented in Regional Workshop on case study sharing in Advocacy strategies for community based organisations in the Hindu-Kush Himalayas, Organised by the International Centre for Integrated Mountain Development, Kathmandu, Nepal, 18-22 April 2005.

Pakyntein, V. (1996). The Khasi Clan: Changing Religion and its effect. In: J. S. Bhandari (Ed.), *Kinship and Family in North-East India*, pp. 349-72. New Delhi: Cosmo Publications.

4

Transitions in the Traditional Institutions of a Mao Naga Village: An Ethnographic Exploration

— *Geetika Ranjan and A. Kapesa*

Introduction

India is a land of diversities - diversities in language, customs, ethnicity and tradition. Tribes form about 8.2 per cent of the population of India. Terms like 'tribes in India' or 'tribal India' may erroneously convey the impression about the term 'tribe' being a canopy term encompassing communities similar to each other. On the contrary, tribes differ from one another - linguistically, geographically, demographically and in their socio-economic systems. Each tribe is a specific entity, requiring specific addressing. Nevertheless, etymological discourses on 'tribe' do throw light on some features, which those known as 'tribes' possess and share while others do not. Broadly speaking, "a tribe in a political sense, is a group possessed of a name, a territory and a group decision-making mechanism; it usually (but not invariably) acts independently and as a unit in matters of inter-group relations, such as war, migration, alliance, treaty and land-cession" (Wallace, 1957:304). Owusu (1975:368) contends that anthropologists studying African politics lay over emphasis on 'kinship' and 'tribe' and this seems to have 'prevented a real 'scientific revolution' in the cross-cultural study of politics." However, in the case of India, there is a need to emphasise on the term 'tribe' in order to comprehensively understand how the polity of one tribe differs from the other despite these sharing a common canopy term, i.e., tribe. What is important is that the politics of a tribe or any community is seen as a dynamic reality calling for dynamic analysis. Dynamic analysis, according to Snyder (1958: 10-11), 'is process analysis. By process is meant...time plus change - change in relationships and condition...' The new dynamic concept of politics centres on such aspects as change, decision-making, resolution of conflicts, negotiation and settlement of political issues within a variety of cultural contexts, rather than the traditional view of politics as a static, well-defined integrated system (Tuden, 1969:337-338).

History of India tells that certain groups in India known as Janjati, Adivasi, Vanvasi and Girijan or in more common term - the tribes - have continued to live as almost independent and self-sufficient pockets having their own institutions of exercising control and maintaining peace in their communities, their traditions and customs forming their rule book to adjudicate. Vidyarthi (1976:26) describes that there are references to tribal communities even in the epics, Ramayan and the Mahabharata, where they are referred to as *Jana*. Thus, the traditional political institutions headed by traditional leaders were the mechanisms for regulating the different aspects of life of the tribal people. Syiemlieh (2006) states that for institutions to become traditional; a past that is somewhat long in time is required. Traditional institutions refer to all those forms of social and political authority, which have their historical origin in the pre-colonial states and societies (Crook, 2005). India goes a long way in terms of antiquity. Whether it was a tribe or a caste group – both came under the jurisdiction of their respective traditional institutions. "To say that studies of politics and leadership must go together would perhaps amount to emphasising the obvious" (Dube, 1967). Hence different types of leadership - the authority of headman, chieftains, hereditary monarchies, sacerdotal chiefs and kings, caste and village *panchayats*, village/tribal councils have been in India since ancient times.

"Traditional leadership includes those political, socio-political and politico-religious structures that are rooted in the pre-colonial period, rather than in the creations of the colonial and post-colonial states. By these key considerations, traditional leaders can include kings, other aristocrats holding offices, heads of extended families and office holders in decentralised politics, as long as their offices are rooted in pre-colonial states and other political entities" (Ray, 2003) and these pose "a special challenge to post-colonial State-makers" (Keulder, 2014). Dlungwana (2014) stated that "their primary function is to regulate and control relationship and social behaviour within a traditional community. They are in essence people oriented and not service oriented as local government structures."

The traditional political institutions continued to exist as institutions of authority to regulate social life particularly at the village level even as Indian history witnessed different regimes. Villages existed as more or less autonomous units. Empires were built and destroyed by invaders but villages have retained their identity. Charles Metcalfe wrote "The village communities are little republics, having nearly everything that they want within themselves and almost independent of any foreign relations (cited in Srinivas and Shah, 1960:1375). India's independence from the British rule opened a new era when different ethnic groups, states and principalities entered the battle of negotiations centering on terms like integration, secession and autonomy and it is regarding these talks that North-east India emerged from the margins to the centre stage. Karlsson (2005:1) writes that "autonomy or self-determination, in one form or another, is indeed on the agenda of more or less all mobilised communities in North-east India."

The present chapter brings to the fore the role of traditional institutions - the *Movuo* and the *Enulei Kotsiimei* among the Mao Naga of Manipur. Manipur is geographically divided into the hills and valleys. The hill areas are inhabited predominantly by the Nagas, Kukis, Paites, Gangtes, etc. with a sprinkling of the Nepalese in the immediate neighbourhood of the valley. The valley is inhabited by the Meiteis, (Manipuri Hindus), Pangals (Manipuri Muslims), the Nepalese and the Business communities like Marwaris, Punjabis, Biharis and so on (Choudhury, 2005). The ethnic groups of Nagas found in the state are Anal, Aimol, Chiru, Kabiu, Koireng, Mao, Maram, Maring, Thangal, Poumai, Tangkhul, Zeliangrong, etc. The Mao Naga is one of the major ethnic groups in the state and recognised as a Scheduled Tribe under the Constitution (Scheduled Tribes) order,

1950. The Mao primarily inhabits the northernmost part of the state in Senapati district. The main area of their inhabitation falls under the Tadubi Sub-Divisional Block. According to 2011 census, the total population of Mao Naga under Tadubi block is 1,16,374 (Census of India, 2011).

A Mao Naga village continues to be a politically independent unit, acquiring the term 'village state' (Singh and Maheo, 2010). Every Mao village has the institutions of the *Movuo* (Chief) and *Enulei Kotsiimei* (Council of Elders/Village Council). They together uphold the traditional practices of the Mao to run the administration of the village. *Movuo*, the Chief, also known as the King holds the exalted position as the head of the people. The office of *Movuo* is hereditary and the rule of primogeniture is followed. *Enulei Kotsiimei* is a body of representatives of each clan in the village. Generally the eldest male from each clan becomes a member of the *Enulei Kotsiimei*. The number of members in the *Enulei Kotsiimei* varies from village to village, depending on the number of clans and the size of each clan.

The present chapter is based on fieldwork carried out in the Makhel village under Tadubi block. An ethnographic exploration of the leadership scenario in a community entails consideration of the voices from different quarters. Both emic and etic perspectives are pertinent to understand the role of traditional institutions among the Mao in order to address the area of research holistically. Constraints and challenges which one encounters in such exploration are multifarious. The study of politics is the study of the political field. "A political field does not operate like clockwork, with all its pieces meshed together with finely tooled precision. It is, rather, a field of tension, full of intelligent and determined antagonists, sole and corporate, who are motivated by ambition, altruism, self-interest and by the desire for the public good and who in successive situations are bound to one another through self-interest, or idealism – and separated or opposed through the same motives" (Swartz *et. al.*, 1966).

Village Makhel

Village Makhel is located about three km from the National Highway 2 and the Tadubi sub-divisional office. There are 228 households in the village with a total population of 983 (as per data collected in January 2013) of which 517 are males and 466 females. The village is of historical importance. It is considered to be the place of origin and dispersion of the Naga. While there is lack of clarity about the migratory routes taken to reach Makhel, most of the Naga tribes believe that they belong to Makhel and regard it as their original home (Banee, 1995: 418). Hodson (1911: 13) also writes that "Makhel is regarded as the centre from which migrations took place."

As narrated by the present *Movuo* of Makhel, the origin of the *Movuo* is known through a popular myth, *N. Salew*. The first woman known as *Dziiliamosiiro* procreated three brothers mystically - Tiger, Spirit and Man at a place called *Makhriifii* or Makhel. When the mother became old and sick, a dispute broke out between the three brothers each claiming to inherit her land. To settle the dispute, the mother devised a contest among the brothers. Man being the youngest and most noble brother was favoured by his mother who made him won the contest. He inherited his mother's land. A monolith was erected at Makhel known as *Pinoumei three Kosii Tamara Tu,* meaning dispersion of the three brothers. Eventually the man had become the head of the land, known as *Movuo* or the King. This is how the institution of chieftainship started at Makhel village. The chief had executive, legislative and judicial powers in the village. The chief decided both civil and criminal cases according to customary laws.

Time passed and population increased and so did its problems. As society became more complex, it became difficult for the *Movuo* to singlehandedly manage the village affairs. The need for supporting the *Movuo* gave rise to the formation of *Enulei Kotsiimei,* which is the Council of Elders or the Village Council. Since then, *Movuo*, supported by the *Enulei Kotsiimei* has been working for maintaining peace and order of the people based on their customs and traditions.

Reflecting upon the past, the Mao Naga informed that the *Movuo* was the binding force, holding the village in the bond of unity. He was the guardian of the villagers and his word was the final word in the settlement of disputes. He was also believed to be endowed with virtues that set him apart from the ordinary Mao. Prudence, courage, oratory skill and the will to champion the cause of the Mao were the attributes that the people looked for in their leader - the *Movuo*. Thus, socio-political and religious leadership was centred in the *Movuo* - he being the supreme authority in the village.

The people reported that in the past the Angami Naga living in areas adjoining to the Mao Naga shared a strong kindred bond with the Mao. "The priests of Angami villages wait for the Chief (*Movuo*) of *Mekroma* (Angami call Makhel as *Mekroma* in their dialect) to give the word before appointing the day for celebration of any of the regular village festivals and point to the ceremonial of the Mao village of *Mekroma* as the type of Angami ceremony par excellence" (Hutton, 1969:1). *Movuo* was assisted by a helper known as *Kru-o* in carrying out his duties like performing sacrifice, rituals, announcing *gennas* and sending messages to other villages, etc. *Kru-o* was the crier of the village and was selected by the villagers from amongst themselves.

In 1891, Manipur came under British supremacy and its hill territories were kept under indirect rule (Singh and Maheo, 2010:162). "The British colonial system of indirect rule formally recognised the traditional institution of Chieftainship and the Council members and used it as an instrument of colonial establishment" (Dena, 2000:163). In addition, the British appointed a wise, literate and well informed Mao as the *Gaonbura*. He was the link between the villagers and the British administration and kept the latter informed about the affairs of the village. In return, he was paid by the British Government for his services. One of the main duties of the *Gaonbura* was to collect house tax on behalf of the British Government. Seen as the face of the British government, the *Gaonbura* was looked up with awe by the Mao villagers. So the introduction of the office of *Gaonbura* cast a shadow on the power and function of the institutions of the *Movuo* and *Enulei Kotsiimei*.

Present

With the passing of the Indian Independence Act in 1947, the State of Manipur became part of India and a series of Acts were passed for the improvement of administration in the hill areas of Manipur. The statutory body of Village Authority was constituted. The Manipur State Hill Peoples (Administration) Regulation 1947 empowers the Chiefs the right to nominate the members of the Village

Authority while the subsequent Act in 1956 imposes restrictions on this power by introducing the provision for election of the members, if not to be nominated by the Deputy Commissioner of the District. The Manipur (Village Authorities in Hill Areas) Act 1956 introduces the controversial provision for election of the members of the Village Authority on the basis of adult franchise by repealing the Manipur State Hill Peoples (Administration) Regulation 1947 (Sanga, 2012).

The Manipur (Village Authorities in Hill Areas) Act 1956 provides:

"For every village having twenty or more tax-paying houses there shall be a village Authority consisting of:

(*a*) five members, where the number of tax-paying houses in the village is not less than twenty but is not more than sixty;

(*b*) seven members, where the number of tax-paying houses in the village is more than sixty but is not more than one hundred;

(*c*) ten members, where the number of tax-paying houses in the village is more than one hundred but is not more than one hundred and fifty;

(*d*) twelve members, where the number of tax-paying houses in the village is more than one hundred and fifty."

With the introduction of the above Acts, the institutions of *Movuo* and *Enulei Kotsiimei* have been witnessing certain dynamics. In the case of *Enulei Kotsiimei* (Village Council), the change is mainly of the title rather than that of the structure. *Enulei Kotsiimei* is recognised as the Village Authority, which with time has played an important role in administrative affairs, by the sheer power of its numbers and more so because of its statutory power to receive, channelise and monitor developmental funds. According to the Act 1956, the *Movuo* has been recognised as the ex-officio Chairman of the village. The *Movuo* is also a permanent member of the Village Authority, representing his clan. The Chairman of the Village Authority is elected from among the members of the Village Authority. A unanimous decision is often taken on this with due consultation with the *Movuo*.

The institution of the *Movuo* continues to exist independent of the Village Authority in terms of observing certain traditional practices and simultaneously the *Movuo* remains a permanent member of Village Authority, thereby shouldering dual responsibility.

Among the Mao Naga it is observed that the village level politics deviates from the written word under the Manipur (Village Authorities in Hill Areas) Act 1956. As one studies, "the nature of national and local linkages in specific policy areas and the actual impact of 'macro' decisions in 'micro' structures" (Owusu, 1975: 375) in the case of Mao, one understands that the actual national and local linkages are actually quite fragile particularly with respect to written word on paper and its implementation in practice. The Manipur (Village Authorities in Hill Areas) Act 1956 states that "the election of members of the Village Authority of a village shall be on the basis of adult suffrage, that is, to say, every person who is a citizen of India and who is ordinarily resident in the village and is not less than twenty-one years of age on such date as may be fixed by rules made under this Act, shall be entitled to be registered as a vote at any such election."

The Mao do not follow the procedure of electing the Village Authority as mentioned in the Manipur (Village Authorities in Hill Areas) Act 1956, rather they continue to follow their traditional way of constituting the Village Authority. They opine that by doing so, representation of each clan in the village is ensured in the Village Authority. If the election of the Village Authority members is done through adult suffrage, there is a risk of some clans, especially those with smaller numbers, of losing out in finding a seat in the Village Authority. This would be disadvantageous for the members of that clan. The Mao feel that it is crucial to have at least one representative of each clan in the Village Authority so that the grievances and requirements of each clan are well represented and addressed by the Village Authority. Further, in the case of intra-clan disputes, the intervention of the clan representative in the Village Authority is sought to settle the issue within the clan itself. The Mao strongly believe in maintaining clan solidarity and avoid taking their clan issues outside their clan. The clan representative is expected to push the cause of the more needy members of his clan when the selection of beneficiaries is being done by the Village Authority for the allocation of developmental funds coming under different government schemes and programmes for poverty alleviation.

Functions of the *Movuo* and the Village Authority (*Enulei Kotsiimei*)

The *Movuo* continues to wield the same power as he did before the change of governments, particularly in the sphere of religious beliefs and practices. Despite the dominant influence of Christianity, the sanctity of the traditional beliefs and practices of the Mao continues to be preserved. The *Movuo* is regarded the custodian of the Mao customary practices and continues to be held in high esteem by the people. He continues to be upheld as the religious head, initiating and monitoring all the traditional religious activities in the village. Mao and Hynniewta (2011) state that the Chief (*Movuo*) of Makhel village is the supreme head of the whole Mao tribe in religious affairs. The Chief of Makhel initiates the religious rituals and thereafter the other Mao villages Chiefs follow the same. Yet, despite his exalted position, a *Movuo* is expected to be the first among the equals and not an autocrat.

The Mao believe that, for the well-being of the village, it has to be purged of all the evils and negativities. As a traditional practice, the *Movuo* performs the annual village purification ceremony. Lokho (2004:6) writes:

> "On an appointed day, the chief will declare a *genna* and call for the purification ritual. An appointed person prepares a human figure with straw and old cloths outside the village. An announcement is made that families examine themselves and find out all people, spirits that caused them harm during the year. Each family prepares a list of theft committed against them, evil spirit that caused them sickness etc. and prepares one lance (made of stick) for each of the culprits. On the appointed day, one person from the family goes near the scarecrow, hurling the lance at it and cursing the spirits of all those who caused harm to the family. From the number of participants and the number of sticks thrown, the people will judge whether their village is progressing, disciplined and living in harmony. Accordingly, the Chief will

promulgate laws to live better lives, work hard, fear God, promote harmony amongst people, etc."

Known for the knowledge of the Mao lunar calendar, the *Movuo* counts and predicts the days of *manes* or *genna*, festivals and feasts. The people have specific days kept aside for relating themselves with God every month and these days are called *mane*. On these days, they observe it as sacred like Sabbath/Sunday by the Christians (Loli, 2011:18). It is the *Movuo* who calculates the days when *mane* would 'fall'. As a ritual, he goes to a pinnacle known as *Thene Kasha Bu* and announces *genna/mane* on its eve. Once he declares a day as *mane*, his word is considered final and the whole village has to abide by his announcement and observe the day as *mane*. On this day all work-related business is put on hold and people engage in rituals of purification of the self and the community. On this day, the *Movuo* takes only ginger and rice beer and abstains from physical intercourse with his wife.

Agriculture is the mainstay of the Mao Naga in villages. It is the duty of the *Movuo* to follow the Mao Lunar Calendar, calculate the best days for the plantation of crops and guide the people to get a good harvest. As a customary practice, *Movuo* is the first to sow and the first to reap the harvest. "Generally, the process of terraced rice cultivation cycle begins in December when the village king announces *chiizhii* after which a small but some best part of the fields is repeatedly ploughed (tilling and breakage of clods) to grow paddy seedlings" (Jajou, 2013:35).

A legend says that once upon a time a Makhel Chief, named *Ma-a,* was driven away to a distant village in the far eastern part of the present Mao country, because the people considered that the rituals and *manes* announced by him were superfluous. The Mao people, as a result, forgot the planting seasons of crops and there was famine for seven consecutive years (Mao and Hynniewta, 2011:579). Experiencing such a misfortune, the people realised the importance of *Movuo*'s wisdom of calculating the days for sowing and harvesting. They realised that by disregarding the *Movuo,* they had invited divine wrath in the form of famine. The new *Movuo* then sent some village elders to the distant place where the ousted *Movuo* had settled. As the latter had become very old, he was carried on a stretcher and brought back to Makhel. It is ingrained in the psyche of the Mao that showing disrespect to the *Movuo* tantamount to the sin of disrespecting the divine. Even today the people wait for the announcement of the Chief before planting and harvesting. The *Movuo* also initiates the celebrations of any traditional festival. As per his calculations, he announces the day when a festival would fall and the people are told to start the preparations, particularly of the *ohaye* (rice beer), which is the most important food item for any kind of celebration. He performs different rituals, which are mandatory before the actual festival. He is the first to taste the *ohaye* (rice beer) prepared for the celebration. During *Chüthuni* festival, considered as the biggest festival by the Mao Naga, the villagers go to hunt birds and show case the birds in front of the *Movuo*'s house - a gesture symbolising the reiteration of acknowledging *Movuo* as the leader, the guardian of the Mao.

The *Movuo* declares yet another *genna* on *Keshi mani* when hunting and killing of any animal is prohibited. Anyone returning to the village from the journey cannot enter the village on this day and has to spend the night outside the village. On this day, the villagers are forbidden to go to agricultural field. The belief behind this *genna* is that by observing it the crops in the field are safeguarded from the attack of pests.

In the past, the *Movuo* struggled against the vagaries of nature, wild animals and also was constantly at war with his neighbouring villages (Banee, 1995: 419). He was assisted by the *Enulei Kotsiimei* (Village Council) in expediting the developmental works for the welfare of the people. These included digging wells in and around the village to get clean drinking water, constructing footpaths, bridges, etc. The Mao informed that in the olden days, people were more conscientious in leading a righteous life. There were less tensions and conflicts in the village. Yet, incidents related to land disputes, adultery, theft, etc. did come up off and on. Based on Mao customs and traditions, the *Movuo* and *Enulei Kotsiimei* together settled the disputes.

Settlement of Disputes

In the past, settlement of disputes was more private than a public affair. The *Movuo* accompanied by one or more members of the *Enulei Kotsiimei* would go to the houses of the complainant and the accused to take their statements. After deliberating on the issue with the other council elders, they would again go to the houses of the complainant and the accused to deliver the judgement. Thus, the decision taken by the *Movuo* in consultation with the *Enulei Kotsiimei* was binding on the people.

With the passage of time, *Movuo*'s house became the place for the settlement of all disputes and decision-making. Now-a-days, various cases are addressed publicly rather than in private. When there is a dispute between two persons or groups in the village; they complaint about it to their clan representatives in the Village Authority. The latter inform about it to the Chairman of the Village Authority. The Village Authority functions as the Village Court. The village authorities summon both the parties to come to the *Movuo*'s house where the *Movuo* and the Village Authority sit to settle the case. The Village Authority gives the final judgement after hearing the versions of both the parties including the witnesses.

If a dispute occurs between two persons belonging to two different villages, the case is settled through a joint sitting of the two Village Authorities. The punishment given for different types of crimes is as per the customary law of the Mao. The Mao avoid taking their issues outside their community. Cases of homicide are rare. The Mao informed that in the remote past, an incident of homicide was dealt with a heavy hand. The guilty was excommunicated from the social fold and his house and granary in the village were destroyed.

Administration of oath is a popular way of ascertaining the truth and the oath is administered by the *Muvuo*. The suspect has to take an oath on his/her own life or on his/her family or clan members. In the case of theft, the suspects are not allowed to take the oath as it is believed that a thief does not fear taking false oath. If the complainant is very sure about who has stolen his/her belonging but lacks evidence, then he/she is asked to take the oath in the name of his/her family. The Mao consider taking oath as a very serious stake as they believe that no one would risk one's own life or one's kith and kin's lives unless one is speaking the truth. If the complainant takes the oath by accusing a suspect of theft, then the *Movuo* pressurises the suspect to confess. Still, if the latter refuses to confess then the case is dropped.

In the past, if the theft took place inside the house, the guilty had to pay back seven times the price of the commodity or money stolen. If the theft took place outside the house, the guilty had to pay three times the amount of the stolen money or article. At present, the guilty has to pay a fine of eight thousand rupees for theft inside the house and five thousand rupee for theft outside the house. The Mao believe that stealing inside the house is more serious offence than stealing anywhere outside as there is more risk of human life when theft is carried out inside the house. The thief may attack the inmates in offence and defence while stealing within the confines of the house.

Administering oath for confession of truth is usually done in cases of land disputes. Conflicts over ownership of land between two parties are settled in this manner. If there is dispute over the limit of the boundary line between two adjoining plots of land, both the parties are asked by the *Movuo* to take an oath on their own lives and their clan members' lives to elicit the truth. The party which stakes the lives of a larger number of his clan's members is believed to be telling the truth about ownership of that piece of land. The Mao believes that false oath would lead to the death of all those members on whose lives the oath was taken. Divine punishment, in the case of telling a lie advertently or inadvertently, is deeply feared by the Mao.

Cases of adultery are also brought before the *Movuo* and the Village Authority. A man and a woman caught red handed in an illicit relationship are beaten up by the clan members of each other spouses; their heads are shaven and they are paraded around in the village. Public disgrace is considered the worst punishment among the Mao. The spouses of the guilty man and woman have the right to annul their marriage. In this case, the wife of the man, who is found guilty of adultery, can take back all the property she had brought with her to her husband's house at the time of marriage. Similarly, if the woman is guilty of adultery, she loses all rights over her husband and his property.

Movuo and *Enulei Kotsiimei* at Makhel Village

There are four clans in Makhel village. Each clan selects one or two of its members to represent them in the Village Authority. The number of members in the Village Authority is not fixed. The Manipur (Village Authority in Hill Areas) Act of 1956 mentions that the term of office of the members of Village Authority shall be three years from the date for its first meeting. However, at Makhel the tenure keeps changing. The phase of negotiation, networking and nexus precede the tenure of the Village Authority. When the tenure of the Village Authority ends, a general meeting of the male members of the village is summoned by the Chairman of the outgoing Village Authority to elect a new Village Authority. On that day itself, after considering the opinions of the selected representatives of each clan, the tenure of the Village Authority is decided. For example, the tenure of the Village Authority constituted in the year 2012 was only for one year. The present Village Authority selected in 2013 has tenure of two years. The Chairman, Secretary and Treasurer are selected from among the clan representatives in the Village Authority. The present Village Authority has thirteen members - four from Choroshuna clan including the *Movuo*, four from Ozhuna clan, three from Ashoya clan and two from Kapena clan.

The Village Authority works towards eliminating the village from drug peddling and abuse, gambling, theft and other crimes. Preservation of natural resources and environment is also the responsibility of the Village Authority.

Resolution of the Village Authority 2013 at Makhel village is as under:

1. A fine of rupees ten thousand is imposed on those found indulging in drug peddling and abuse.
2. Gambling is prohibited in Makhel village as well as in the adjoining area including three other villages - Shajouba, Kaibi and Tobufii - under the Makhel village area. A fine of rupees five thousand is imposed on any one found guilty of gambling.
3. The fine imposed on guilty of theft inside the house is ₹ 8,000 and for one stealing outside the house is ₹ 5,000.

Strict measures are taken by the Village Authority to minimise deforestation. It is strickly prohibited to cut more than one *thag* (one heap of logs of wood measuring approximately seven feet in height and twelve feet in length) of wood per family once in a year from the community forest land like *Kritole, Chozha, Misotsü.*

The different fines and penalties imposed are aimed at minimising the anti-social activities in the village. The Village Authority receives a token annual honorarium from the fund generated by the fines and penalties imposed. The Chairman and the Secretary of the Village Authority receive ₹ 12,000 each while the other members receive ₹ 6,000 each.

Village Administration

The Village Authority plays a key role in running the village administration. Developmental schemes implemented in the village are monitored by the Village Authority, which plays an active role in procuring various schemes from the government. An example shall elucidate this point. Mahatma Gandhi Rural Employment Guarantee Scheme (MGREGS) is a major scheme aimed at village development. The Chairman of the Village Authority in consultation with other members of the Village Authority prepares a proposal, justifying the need for infrastructure development in the village. They seek approval of the proposal from the Block Development Officer, i.e., from Mao-Maram Sub-Divisional Office at Tadubi and then the project is forwarded to the District Rural Development Agency (DRDA). Once the DRDA approves the proposal, the project fund is sanctioned in the joint account of the Chairman and the Secretary of the Village Authority. The villagers are engaged in the construction work under the scheme and are paid wages by the Village Authority. The project work is done collectively by the villagers in the village and in return the Village Authority distributes the wages to the people from the fund received from the government. Some of the developmental works of MNREGA in the village are construction and maintenance of footpaths, link roads, drainage system, minor irrigation canals in the terrace field, plantation of tree sapling, etc. Other schemes aimed at providing fund for construction of *pucca* houses, procuring agricultural implements and loan are also channelised through the Village Authority.

The implementation and monitoring of developmental schemes has increased the powers and responsibilities of the Village Authority. The role of the Village Authority or the erstwhile *Enulei Kotsiimei* has undergone a major change over time. There are diverse opinions encapsulating the role of the Village Authority. Some Mao reminisced the bygone days when the *Enulei Kotsiimei* was a simple organisation given to altruism looking after the welfare of their clan and community as a whole. They lament that the introduction of government sponsored system of administration and development has brought in the flow of money in the name of developmental funds and this is leading to latent and manifest tensions in the society. Black's work (1972:25) on Luristan highlights how local leaders use their position to control the people and to get access to limited resources. Selection of the beneficiaries and allocation of funds in different areas is a prerogative of the Village Authority. The Mao informed that the villagers try to keep the members of the Village Authority in good humour to be in their good books in order to find their names in the list of beneficiaries. Some Mao, however, accused the Village Authority of manipulating and cornering the developmental grants.

The institution of the *Movuo* continues to be upheld in reverence. Rituals related to traditional religion and agriculture are a major part of Mao worldview and *Movuo* is looked up to as the living figure of Mao's pristine past, a beholder of Mao tradition and identity. It is the seat of the *Movuo* rather than the person on it, which commands unflinching loyalty from the Mao people. The villagers opine that the institution of the *Movuo* continues to be held in deep regard as it remains 'untainted' from money. As the traditional religious head, he epitomises the face, the identity of the Mao culture.

The independence of India and the accompanying Constitutional Acts ushered in the policy of prioritising democracy and development channelled through statutory leadership. A major aspect of these statutory administrative structures is that these channelise the implementation of developmental funds. Post-independence scenario of communities and areas coming under the Panchayati Raj saw the existence of dual structures of politics – the traditional and the modern. On the one hand, there is a traditional institution of the village headman/chief and the village council which continue to exist as a matter of tradition and heredity. On the other hand, it is the elected leadership, which wields the statutory power to receive and allocate funds for development. Ranjan (2002) shows in her study of the Bhoksa tribe of Uttaranchal that the political institution, which wields the purse strings, rises in importance in the eyes of the electorate as it is the agency for the allocation of funds.

The dynamics witnessed by the traditional institutions of the *Movuo* and the *Enulei Kotsiimei* (Village Authority at present) bring to the fore the transition taking place in the Mao society as it stands in a juxtaposition between institutions, which carry the heritage of tradition and at the same time are blending with the democratic structures of governance.

References

Banee, K.S.B. (1995). The Mao Naga. In: N. Sanajaoba (Ed.), *Manipur Past and Present: The Ordeals and Heritage of Civilisation (Nagas and Kuki-Chin)*, pp. 418-439. New Delhi: Mittal Publications.

Black, J. (1972). Tyranny as a strategy for survival in 'Egalitarian' society: Luri Facts versus an Anthropological Mystique. *Man,* 7:614-34.

Chaudhury, Dipanjan Roy (2005). Autonomous District Councils and Panchayati Raj Institutions in North-East India. *Dialogue,*7(1). http://www.asthabharati.org/Dia_Jul%2005/dip.htm. Visited on 15.9.2014.

Crook, R. (2005). *The Role of Traditional Institutions in Political Change and Development*. Ghana: Policy Brief No. 4 Accra.

Dena, L. (2000). The Constitution 73rd Amendment Act, 1992 Vis-à-Vis The Hill Areas of Manipur. In: M. Horam (Ed.), *The Rising Manipur (Including other North-Eastern States),* pp.161-168. New Delhi: Manas Publications.

Dlungwana, M. Eric (2014). *Traditional Leaders and New Local Government Dispensation in South Africa.* https://halshs.archives-ouvertes.fr/halshs-00749691.Submitted on 8 Nov. 2012. Visited on 20.7. 2014.

Dube, S.C. (1967). Preface to L.P. Vidyarthi (Ed.), *Leadership in India.* Bombay: Asia Publishing House.

Hodson, T. C. (1911). *The Naga Tribes of Manipur*. Delhi: Low Price Publications.

Hutton, J. H. (1969). *The Angami Naga*. Bombay: Oxford University Press.

Jajuo, Komuha (2013). Traditional significance of paddy cultivation for Mao Naga farmers in Manipur. *Journal of Business Management and Social Sciences Research,* 2(10): 33-39.

Karlsson, B. G. (2005). Sovereignty through Indigenous Governance: Reviving traditional political institutions in North-east India. *NEHU Journal,* III(2): 1-16.

Keulder, Christian (2014). Traditional Leaders. *State, Society and Democracy.* http://www.kas.de/upload/auslandshomepages/namibia/State_Society_Democracy/chapter5.pdf.:150-170. Visited on 10.9.2014.

Lokho, Paul (2004). The Mao Nagas. *Ishani,* 1(1): 3-6.

Loli, S. (2011). *God, Man and Nature: A Philosophical Study on the Mao Naga Traditional Religion.* An unpublished Ph.D. thesis, North-Eastern Hill University, Shillong.

Mao, A. A. and M. Hynniewta (2011). Plants used as agricultural seasons indicator by Mao Naga Tribe, Manipur, India. *Indian Journal of Traditional Knowledge,* 10(3): 578-580.

Owusu, Maxwell (1975). Policy studies, development and political anthropology. *The Journal of Modern African Studies,* 13 (3): 367-381.

Ranjan, Geetika (2002). Role of elites in the development of the Bhoksa Tribe. *The Oriental Anthropologist,* 2(1): 31-35.

Ray, Donald I. (2003). Rural Local Governance and traditional leadership in Africa and the Afro-Caribbean: Policy and Research Implications from Africa to the Americas and Australasia: In: D. I. Ray and P.S. Reddy (Eds.), *Grass-roots Governance? Chiefs in Africa and Afro-Caribbean,* pp. 1-30. Calgary: University of Calgary Press.

Sanga, R. (2014). *The Manipur (Village Authority in Hill Areas) Act,1956.* http://Zogamonline.com/oldsite_2013/columns/R-Sanga/14001-the manipur-village-authority-in-hill-areas-act-1956.html. Visited on 14.7.2014.

Singh, R. K. R. and L.M. Maheo (2010). *The Mao Naga: An Ethnographic Study.* Imphal: Tribal Research Institute, Government of Manipur.

Snyder, Richard C. (1958). A Decision-Making Approach to the Study of Political Phenomena. In: Roland Young (Ed.), *Approaches to the Study of Politics,* pp. 3-37. Evanston: Northwestern University Press.

Srinivas, M.N. and A.M. Shah (1960). The myth of self-sufficiency of the Indian Village. *The Economic Weekly,* 10: 1375-1378.

Swartz, Marc J, Victor W Turner and Arthur Tuden (Eds.)(1966). *Political Anthropology.* Chicago: Aldine Publishing Company.

Syiemlieh, D. R. 2006. Traditional institutions of governance in the hills of North-East India: The Khasi experience. *Man and Society- A Journal of North-East Studies,* 3: 117-137.

Tuden, Arthur (1969). Trends in political anthropology. *Proceedings of the American Philosophical Society*, 113(5):336-340.

Vidyarthi, L.P. (1976). *Tribal Culture of India*. New Delhi: Concept Publishing Company.

Wallace Anthony F. C. (1957). Political organisation and land tenure among the Northeastern Indians, 1600-1830. *Southwestern Journal of Anthropology*, 13(4): 301-321.

5

Social and Legal Consequences of Admixture in Matrilineal Tribes of Meghalaya

— *R. Khongsdier*

Introduction

Admixture is simply an intermixture or intermarriage between individuals from different ethnic groups. It has both genetic and social implications. From the genetic point of view, it is also known as 'gene flow' because it is the major factor that spreads the genes from one population to another (although gene flow may also take place without intermarriage). It is one of the important evolutionary forces, which brings about genetic homogeneity between populations and genetic variability within populations. It increases genetic differences within populations, because new alleles are added to the gene pool of a given local population. On the other hand, it decreases the genetic differences between local populations, because it makes possible for alleles to spread from one population to another. Admixture is also increasingly recognised as a mapping tool for identifying genetic risk factors involved in complex traits or diseases between major ethnic groups (Martinez-Marignac *et. al.*, 2006).

From the social point of view, admixture is also one of the social forces that bring about certain changes in the social organisation. Earlier anthropologists suggested that intermarriage had adaptive value by creating bonds of friendship and social integration that help and protect people in times of need. It is not only an important means of economic and political alliances between groups, but it also broadens kinship networks, changes in attitude toward ethnocentrism and reduces the chances of conflict between ethnic groups. Lévi-Strauss (1963, 1969) observed exogamy as a form of intergroup social exchange in which "wife-giving" and "wife-taking" created social networks and alliances between distinct communities. It widens the human network through which "a larger number of people could pool natural resources and cultural information, including technology and other useful knowledge" (Haviland *et. al.*, 2011).

While integrating and promoting the diffusion of cultural traits from one ethnic group to another, intermarriage brings about changes in kinship organisation and descent, especially in tribal societies where kinship and descent are the essential components of social structure and ethnic identity. In this chapter, we will look into the social and legal consequences of admixture with special reference to the matrilineal tribes of Meghalaya. The data were mostly secondary based on previous published works and courts' proceedings.

Clan Organisation among the Khasis and Garos

Garo Society: The Garo society is at present divided into five exogamous matri-phratries, known as *chatchis*; namely, Sangma and Marak, Momin, Areng and Shira. Each *chatchi* is composed of a number of exogamous matri-clans known as *mahari* or *machong*, which are again segmented into different lineage groups (Nakane, 1967). The *mahari* is named after animals, birds, plants, river, hill, place, etc., which have some social significance for group identification. According to Playfair (1909), the origin of *mahari* is often totemistic, but it is a modified form of totemism that has no connection with respect, reverence or taboos. It is basically for clan identity dubbed by a family or members of the society in connection with certain event, story, place and other natural objects. It is not necessarily indicative of kinship relationship with such natural objects. The totem often serves as the name of the matri-lineage group to identify the *mahari* and its members from other *maharis* in the society. But what it is interesting among the Garos is the rule of clan exogamy, which has been subject to major changes during the last 60 years or so. Till about the middle of the twentieth century, the two major clans (*chatchis*), like Sangma and Marak, were exogamous. At present, this rule is not strictly followed by the Garos. A Sangma male can also marry a Sangma female, if both of them belong to two different sub-clans, *maharis* (say, *Manda* and *Nengminja*) of the Sangma *chatchi*. The change in rules of clan exogamy during the last 60 years or so was very fast in the Garo society. One well-known anthropologist who carried out a detail study among the Garos in 1956 and 1997, Robbins Burling (or Raben Marak as addressed by the Rengsanggri people), expressed his surprise to find about eight couples at Rengsanggri village in 1997 who shared the same *mahari* of the same *chatchi* - the practice that never existed in 1956. In the second edition of his book entitled "Rengsanggri," Burling (1997) writes as follows:

> "It did seem that a number of rules that were once quite strict have been somewhat relaxed and most startling to me was a relaxation in the rule of exogamy. In 1956, every marriage in Rengsanggri united a Marak and a Sangma. I was told about few couples in other villages where both husband and wife were Maraks or both were Sangmas, but no such marriages existed in Rengsanggri and they were not regarded as proper. In 1997, I was astonished to find no fewer than eight Rengsanggri couples, both of whom were Chambigong Maraks but who nevertheless lived together and jointly cared for their common children. These couples had never been officially married because the Garo Baptist Church will not give its blessing to marriages between people who share a lineage name, even when no literal kinship tie can be traced. Even without blessing, these Chambigong-Chambigoung relationships were regarded as marriages by their neighbours. The partners were easily referred to as "husband" and "wife" and their children were accepted as Chambigongs. People did seem mildly embarrassed by these relationships. I remember a few giggles when I showed my surprise the first time that I realised that a husband and wife were both Chambigongs. Everyone's lineage membership is so well known, however, that the impropriety cannot possibly be hidden."

Khasi Society: Unlike the Garo society, the Khasi society is divided into a large number of exogamous matri-clans (*kur or Jait*). Members of each clan are believed to be the descendants of one great ancestress known as *Iawbei-Tynrai* – the root of the clan. Each clan is again divided into different *kpohs* (sub-clans) and each *kpoh* is subdivided into various *ïng* (families). Members of each *kpoh* are the descendants of one great grandmother known as *Iawbei-Tymmen* and members of the *iing* include the young grandmother (*Iawbei-Khynraw*), her children and the children of her daughters. The descendants of the *Iawbei-Tymmen* are basically a group of *ïng* that includes the descendants of *Iawbei-Khynraw* and those of her sisters. Some clans, however, consider more generations like the descendants of the young grandmother's mother and those of her sisters as belonging to the same *kpoh*. Nevertheless, the subdivision of the clans as mentioned above is based on the degree of kinship relationship that is necessary for inheritance of property, religious practices and so on. Each clan is strictly exogamous and there are certain clans, which are considered to trace their descent from one common ancestress. Intermarriage between members of such related clans is prohibited (Gurdon, 1907). Like the Garos, some Khasi clans bear the names of animals, plants and other objects, but members of such clans do not necessarily regard such objects as totems.

Kinship Disorder and Adjustment

Both Garos and Khasis follow the matrilineal system of society in which the descent is always reckoned and accorded through the mother. These tribes are surrounded by patrilineal societies and they are not strictly endogamous. Intermarriage with other members from patrilineal societies has also taken place since time immemorial. The societal problem that arises as a result of the intermarriage between a tribal male and a female from patrilineal society is a kinship disorder in which the offshoots of such intermarriage belong to neither the mother's clan nor the father's clan, in strict sense, unless they are adopted and assimilated into the fold of a matri-clan according to customs and traditions of the society. In patrilineal societies, the children of marriage between tribal male and non-tribal female or between tribal female and non-tribal male acquire the caste of their father and the residence is always patrilocal. In matrilineal societies, on the other hand, the children of marriage between tribal male and non-tribal female belong to no clan or an adopted matri-clan and the residence is always patrilocal; whereas the children of marriage between tribal female and non-tribal male belong to the clan of the mother and the residence is always matrilocal. Since matrilineal tribes in Meghalaya are not strictly endogamous, intermarriage with non-tribal has been in existence since time immemorial and it is one factor responsible for the formation of new clans as well.

The kinship disorder due to intermarriage between tribal males and females from patrilineal societies is common in the Garo and Khasi societies. It is one of the social forces, which compels these matrilineal societies to adapt structurally through the process of clan differentiation or matri-clan adoption. Among the Khasis, the offshoot of wedlock between a Khasi male and a non-Khasi female is absorbed and assimilated into Khasi community by a form of adoption, known as *Tangjait*, which is often solemnised with naming ceremony of a new matri-clan for the siblings and descendants of such wedlock. As a matter of fact, there are a large number of clans' names started with the word *'Khar'* which owe their origin to the intermarriage between Khasi males and non-Khasi females from patrilineal societies. According to Gurdon (1907), "If the lists of the Khyriam and Cherra clans are examined, it will be seen what a large number bear the name of *'Dkhar'* or its abbreviation *'Khar.'* The word *Dkhar* is that applied by a Khasi to an inhabitant of the plains. We come across names such as 'khar-mukhi, khar sowali, the first word being an abbreviation of *dkhar* and mukhi being the common Bengali name which occurs in Chandra Mukhi, Surjya Mukhi and C Sowali (*chowali*) is the common Assamese word for a girl. The ancestresses of these tribes were plains women, carried off, no doubt, in the raids made by the Khasis over the border into Assam and Sylhet."

Among the Garos, a matri-clan adoption is also practiced by assimilating the children of marriage between a Garo male and a female from patrilineal into the fold of the matri-clan according to customs of the society. According to Marak (2014), "When a Garo man marries a non-Garo woman, another set of problems crops up – that of the clan. Will the children be called the children of the father's clan? If a Garo man marries a non-Garo woman who belongs to a patrilineal society, it logically follows that the children would become members of the father's clan. In such a scenario, unfortunately, the kinship system goes haywire. For instance, the paternal aunt (by biology) would also be the maternal aunt (by kinship). However, in many cases as in Achiksong, this problem has been solved by adopting the non-Garo wife into the folds of another clan (in most cases, the father-in-law's clan) and the children adopt the clan of the "adopted" non-Garo mother, by default, the paternal grandfather's clan."

The Garo society was primarily divided into two exogamous matri-phratries (*chatchis*), namely, Sangma and Marak, which intermarry. The third *chatchi,* Momin, was added as a result of the Garo-Muslim intermarriage after Mir Jhumla's invasion through Goalpara district in 1661 (Bareh, 1974). Later on, other matri-clans like the Areng and Shira are also regarded as the major matri-phratries or *chatchis*. In other words, the process of clan differentiation is also taking place among the Garos. For example, Areng was previously known as the *machong/mahari* of the Marak *chatchi*, but it has differentiated into a separate *chatchi*. It is beyond the scope of this chapter to deal with the factors responsible for the differentiation of matri-clans into matri-phratries.

Legal and Political Issues

The kinship disorder due to intermarriage with non-tribal female in matrilineal societies of Meghalaya is no longer *res integra*; it has also become a legal issue of individual ethnic identity as appeared in some court cases, such as *Wilson Reade v. C.S. Booth and Ors* (Election Commission, 1958); *A.S. Khongphai v. Stanley D.D. Nichols Roy* (Guahati High Court, 1965), *GLT 2008(1), Tennydard M Marak v. State of Meghalaya* (High Court of Meghalaya, 2013) and others. The petitioners have contended that the offshoots or progeny of marriage between a matrilineal tribal male and a female from patrilineal society cannot claim the status of Scheduled Tribe. For example, in A.S. Khongphai's case (*supra*), the petitioner contented that according to the Khasi custom, being a matrilineal society, every Khasi must take the *Jait* (clan) of his mother. Therefore, the respondent whose mother had no *Jait,* being an American Lady, could not be a Khasi because he was not in a position to take any *Jait*. In this case, one witness said that the matter of taking a *Jait* has, now-a-days, become a matter of choice, i.e., one can reckon the *Jait* of the father or of the mother, or he may not take any *Jait* at all. According to the witness, the contention that every person in the Khasi society, being a matrilineal society, must take the *Jait* of the mother is not wholly correct. Another witness said that there are people in the War area who are Khasis, but who have no *Jait*. The Division Bench of the Guwahati High Court in A.S. Khongphai's case (*supra*) had accepted the case of the respondent that the offshoot of marriage between Khasi male and non-Khasi female could be a Khasi.

It is clear from the above court case that the membership of an individual in matrilineal societies is not only on the basis of the purity of blood, but also on the process of enculturation or socialisation that the individual has endured as a member of the tribal community. This view was legally accepted in the case of Wilson Reade (*supra*). There is also judicial evidence that even those individuals who have no clans are regarded as members of the tribe, because they endure the same process of socialisation, suffer the same socio-economic disabilities and enjoy the same privileges and opportunities as other members of the society. What it is intriguing from the above discussion is the observation that the matter of taking a *Jait* in Khasi society is a matter of choice, which was almost common in urban areas before the year 2005, i.e., some Khasi liberals started following the clan of their father. Fortunately or unfortunately, Khasi law-makers have seen that such practice could lead to more kinship disorder in the society, thereby the Khasi Lineage Act was passed in 2005, which debars ST certificate to those individuals who follow the clan of the father. The Section 3 of the Act is extracted as follows:

(1) On or after the commencement of this Act every person born of a legal marriage.

  (a) whose parents are or were both Khasi shall be Khasi of the *Kur, Jait* or Clan of the mother, or

  (b) whose mother is or was a Khasi and the father a non-Khasi shall be a Khasi of the *Kur, Jait* or Clan of the

Khasi mother if and only if the person and his/her Khasi mother fulfill the following requirements, namely:

I. they can speak Khasi, unless prevented from knowing the language by circumstances beyond their control,

II. they observed and are governed by Khasi matrilineal system of lineage, the Khasi laws of inheritance and succession and Khasi laws of consanguinity and kinship,

III. had not, at any time, in writing or otherwise voluntarily renounced the Khasi status,

IV. have not adopted the personal law of the non-Khasi father or husband, as the case may be, or a personal law of a society incompatible with Khasi personal laws and customs, and

V. had not lost or been deprived of Khasi status by judgement or order of any competent court or by operation of any such judgement or order, or under the provisions of this Act, or

(c) whose father is or was a Khasi and the mother a non-Khasi and the Khasi father and every such person fulfilled the requirements specified in sub-clauses (I) to (V) of clause (b) of sub-section (1) of this section shall be a Khasi belonging to such Khasi *Kur, Jait* or Clan (in accordance with the prevailing Khasi customs applicable to such Khasi father or belonging to such new *Kur, Jait* or clan) as may be adopted under any prevailing Khasi customs applicable to the Khasi father or by *"Tangjait."*

Among the Garos, the writ petition filed by Tennydrad M. Marak (*supra*) in the High Court of Meghalaya has recently been in the news, perhaps, because the Chief Minister of Meghalaya happened to be a respondent. The petitioner has contended that the Garos follow the matrilineal system of society in which descent is always traced and accorded through the mother alone. If a mother belongs to the Sangma clan and a father to the Marak clan, all children should become Sangma but not Marak. It was contended that the wedlock between Garo male and non-Garo female from patrilineal society cannot claim the status of Schedule Tribe either under the customary law applicable to the Garo tribals or under the Constitution of India. The High Court of Meghalaya dismissed the writ petition (PIL) that the "petitioner has no *locus standi* to file the present PIL and/or is not an aggrieved person in the given case to file the PIL and the relief(s) sought for in the present PIL cannot be granted in the writ proceeding and the writ proceeding is not a proper proceeding for deciding the customs and also the High Court in the given case, is not the proper authority for holding enquiry as to whether the Scheduled Tribe certificate issued in favour of the respondent is correct or not and also the PIL cannot be filed for making roving enquiry." Although the writ petition in the form of PIL was not maintainable, the main contention of the petitioner is similar to that of A.S. Khongphai's case among the Khasis.

There are also a large number of litigations in other parts of India as a result of the intermarriage between tribal and non-tribal persons. One of the important judgements that may have implications for the matrilineal tribes of Meghalaya is the case of *Kendriya Vidyalaya Sangathan v. Shanti Acharya Sisingi, W.P. (C) No. 4743/ 2008*. In this case, the High Court of Delhi (2008) has held as follows:

> "III The offshoot of wedlock between Scheduled Caste/Scheduled Tribe male and a female belonging to forward community can claim Scheduled Caste/Scheduled Tribe status for Indian society is patriarchal society where the child acquires the caste of his father.
>
> IV The offshoot of wedlock between Scheduled Caste/Scheduled Tribe female and a male belonging to forward community cannot claim Scheduled Caste/Scheduled Tribe status unless he demonstrates that he has suffered the disabilities suffered by the members of the community of his mother."

The above decision of the High Court of Delhi is valid and applicable to patrilineal (patriarchal) societies. However, its applicability to matrilineal societies not only amounts to discrimination but also shatters the cultural fabric of society. In matrilineal society, the offshoot of wedlock between a Scheduled Tribe male and a female belonging to forward or backward community belongs to neither his/her father's clan nor his/her mother's clan, in strict sense, unless he/she is adopted and assimilated into the fold of a matri-clan according to customs and traditions of the society. Being adopted and assimilated into the matrilineal society, he/she becomes part and parcel of the society, suffers the same disabilities and enjoys the same privileges and opportunities as other members of the society. As mentioned earlier, in this type of marriage the residence is *patrilocal*, i.e., the type of residence in which married couple live with or near the husband's parents. The family with this type of marriage is characterised by both matrilocal and patrilocal types of residence, i.e., both son and daughter bring their spouses to live with or near their parents. In this type of family, if both son and daughter are married to non-tribals, for instance, it is discriminatory to say that the siblings of the daughter are tribals as they belong to the clan of their mother; whereas the siblings of the son are non-tribals as they belong to the adopted matri-clan, or that the latter should suffer socio-economic disabilities while the former should not. Imagine being the grandparents in such type of family. Is it possible for us to socialise our grandchildren from our son and daughter discriminately? Whereas the above decision of the High Court of Delhi is applicable to patrilineal societies, it is likely to be discriminatory in matrilineal societies.

Concluding Remarks

What it can be deduced from the above presentation and discussion is that marriage or intermarriage is not only a social institution, but also a major evolutionary force. It is also an indicator variable ranging from social to health status and a tool that can be used for understanding human biology and culture, or the interaction of the two in patterning human variation and evolution. As a tool or method, it can be used to understand not only the social organisation but also to test the differences in disease rates between populations. For example, admixture mapping is nowadays preferred to expensive and sophisticated methods like Genome-wide association scans to test the hypothesis that differences in disease rates between populations are partly because of the frequency differences in disease-causing genetic variants. It is reported that these genetic variants occur more often on chromosome segments of the individuals in hybrid populations transmitted from the ancestral population with the higher disease variant frequency (Chakraborty and Weiss, 1988; Winkler *et. al.*, 2010; Salzano and Sans, 2014).

As an evolutionary force, intermarriage brings about changes in both biological and socio-cultural aspects of human populations. It has both biological and socio-cultural consequences. It has long been recognised by evolutionists and anthropologists as the major force that reduces the genetic difference between populations, thereby enhancing the genetic fitness of the populations, although at times it may also introduce certain harmful mutations or genetic diseases into the local populations (Salzano and Callegari-Jacques, 1988). It is also the major force that differentiated the human species, *Homo sapiens*, into different local populations or hybrid populations. The intermarriage between the Khasis and the Garos, for example, has led to the formation of the hybrid groups like the Lyngngams and Megams (Gurdon, 1907; Playfair, 1909). These groups are sandwiched between Garo hills and Khasi hills (Pakyntein, 2000). The physical characteristics and ways of life of these groups appear to be the blend of the Garos and Khasis in some respects and they are different from both the Garos and Khasis in others. However, the Lyngngams are considered a sub-group of the Khasis, because they are living in the Khasi territory, thereby they are closer to the Khasis. The same is true with the Megams who are classified as a subgroup of the Garos because they are living in the Garo territory.

In the absence of constitutional law, intermarriage is likely to bring about different patterns of kinship relationship in tribal societies, especially in matrilineal tribal societies. Among the contemporary Native American populations, intermarriage of indigenous peoples with non-Indians has given rise to three categories of U.S. Indian population (Snipp, 1986). There are: (1) "American Indians" who claim to be Indian ethnically with specific tribal identification, (2) "American Indians of a multiple ancestry" who claim to be Indians but have significant non-Indian ancestry and (3) "Americans of Indian descent" who do not claim to be Indians but report an Indian component in their background. The second two categories consist of a number of individuals whose ethnic identities readily change with political, economic and social conditions. Prior to 2005, one could also broadly categorise the Khasis into three divisions: (1) Khasis whose both the parents were Khasis – although the rule of descent is through the mother, some of the Khasis under this category, especially in urban areas, followed the title of their fathers, (2) Khasis whose fathers were from patrilineal societies – Khasis under this category generally followed the clan of their mothers, perhaps because of socio-economic advantage and (3) Khasis whose mothers were from patrilineal societies. The third category is again subdivided into two groups, namely, those who followed the *Tangjait* custom and those who followed the descent of their fathers. A similar trend is recently reported among the Garos, which is one of the reasons for the demand of the Garo Lineage Act as in the case of the Khasis.

It is also evident from the above discussion that intermarriage has given rise to legal issues of individual identity as a member of the society. The issues of individual identity are in turn related to how the individual is born and brought up in a society, or as a member of the cultural group. As a member of matrilineal society, as legally contented above, the individual is supposed to follow the matrilineal rule of descent that establishes the relationship of the clan members through a common great ancestress. However, this has again become an open question whether following a clan of the mother is really an important criterion for being recognised as a member of the matrilineal society? On the basis of the Court's judgment in A.S. Khongphai's case, we can say that the rule of descent is not necessarily an essential qualification to be a member of the Khasi society. Even a person without any clan can also be treated as a Khasi, provided that person has endured the process of enculturation or socialisation like other members of the society. The point is that anthropologists have always propagated that different aspects of culture are integrated. The change in one aspect of culture is bound to affect the other, or that a number of cultural elements would have to be changed in order to accommodate the new behaviour (Ember and Ember, 1990). In the present discourse, we have highlighted that among the Garos and Khasis the kinship disorder due to intermarriage between a tribal male and a female from patrilineal society is accommodated by the practice of matri-clan adoption. But the practice of matri-clan adoption has two major consequences. First, it generates different ideas and perceptions about customs and traditions concerning clan and kinship organisation in the Khasi and Garo societies as reflected in different litigations and legal proceedings. In such situations, the courts need to examine the claims and counter-claims ranging from the very definition of customs to the implications and applicability of judgment under the Constitution of India. Second, such mode of accommodation (i.e., matri-clan adoption in the present context) tends to vary in forms if it remains unchecked at the societal level, like among the Khasis before the enactment of the Khasi Lineage Act (2005). This can also be observed in the Garo society where different forms of matri-clan adoption due to intermarriage are being followed.

References

Bareh, Hamlet (1974). *Meghalaya*. Shillong: North-Eastern India News and Feature Service.

Burling, Robbins (1997). *Rengsanggri: Family and Kinship in a Garo Village*, 2nd edition. Tura: Tura Book Room of the Garo Baptist Convention.

Chakraborty, R. and K.M. Weiss (1988). Admixture as a tool for finding linked genes and detecting that difference from allelic association between loci. *Proceedings of the National Academic of Sciences, USA*, 85:9119-23.

Election Commission (1958). Wilson Reade v. Mr. C.S. Booth and others, Election Petition No. 181 of 1957, Election Tribunal in the High Court of Judicature in Assam, Guwahati. *The Assam Gazette, Extraordinary*, 59: 363-81.

Ember, R.R. and Melvin Ember (1990). *Anthropology*, 6th edition. New Delhi: Prentice-Hall of India.

Guahati High Court (1965). A.S. Khongphai v. Stanley D.D. Nichols Roy and Anr. on 26 May, 1965, GLT 2008(1). Guwahati: Guwahati High Court.

Gurdon, P.T.R. (1907). *The Khasis*. London: Macmillan and Co.

Haviland, William A., Harald E. L. Prins, Bunny McBride and Dana Walrath (2011). *Cultural Anthropology: The Human Challenge*, 13th Edition. Belmont: Wadsworth, Cengage Learning.

High Court of Delhi (2008). Kendriya Vidyalaya Sangathan v. Shanti Acharya Sisingi, W.P. (C) No. 4743/2008. New Delhi: High Court of Delhi.

High Court of Meghalaya (2013). Tennydard M Marak v. State of Meghalaya and others, PIL No (SH) 5/2013. Shillong: High Court of Meghalaya.

Khasi Lineage Act (2005). *The Khasi Hills Autonomous District (Khasi Social Custom of Lineage) Act, 1997*. Gazette of Meghalaya, 25th February, 2005. Shillong: Government of Meghalaya.

Lévi-Strauss, C. (1963). *Structural Anthropology*. New York: Basic Books.

Lévi-Strauss, C. (1969). *The Elementary Structures of Kinship*, 2nd Edition. London: Eyre and Spottiswoode.

Marak, Q. (2014). *Food Politics: Studying Food, Identity and Difference among the Garos*. Newcastle: Cambridge Scholars Publishing.

Martinez-Marignac, V.L., A. Valladares, E. Cameron, A. Chan, A. Perera, R. Globus-Goldberg, N. Wacher, J. Kumate, P. McKeigue, D.O'Donnell, M.D. Shriver, M. Cruz and E. J. Parra (2007). Admixture in Mexico City: Implications for admixture mapping of type 2 diabetes genetic risk factors. *Human Genetics*, 120: 807-19.

Nakane, C. (1967). *Garo and Khasi: A Comparative Study in Matrilineal Systems*. Paris: Mouton and Co.

Pakyntein, V. (2000). Identity of the Lyngngam in Comparison with the Khasis and Garo in Meghalaya. In: R. Khongsdier (Ed.), *Contemporary Research in Anthropology*, pp. 99-131. New Delhi: Commonwealth Publishers.

Playfair, Major A. (1909). *The Garos* (Reprinted 1975). Guwahati: United Publishers.

Salzano, F.M. and M. Sans (2014). Interethnic admixture and the evolution of Latin American populations. *Genetics and Molecular Biology*, 37 (suppl. 1):151-170.

Salzano, F.M. and S.M. Callegari-Jacques (1988). *South American Indians: A Case Study in Evolution*. Oxford: Clarendon Press.

Snipp, C. Matthew (1986). Who Are American Indians? Some observations about the perils and pitfalls of data for Race and Ethnicity. *Population Research and Policy Review*, 5:237-52.

Winkler, C.A., George W. Nelson and Michael W. Smith (2010). Admixture mapping comes of age. *Annual Review of Genomics and Human Genetics*, 11:65-89.

6

Food Habits and Dietary Intake of Karbi Adolescent Girls of Kamrup District of Assam

— *Ritu Geu Goswami, Mini Bhattacharyya*

Introduction

Adolescence is a period which comes in everyone's life and requires utmost care and attention as this is a transition period from childhood to adulthood and involves human growth and development. The adolescent period is the most vulnerable stage from the point of view of health, food habits, nutritional care and hygiene. Rapid growth in height, weight, muscle mass and fat mass during adolescence calls for the need of balanced diet. Apart from physical changes, with the onset of puberty, there are social and psychological changes that take place among all adolescents. To live one must eat and to live healthy one should have a balanced diet with adequate nutrients. Knowledge of what to eat and in what quantities is a prerequisite to the healthy and happy life. The average nutritional requirements for different groups of people are variable depending on such measurable characteristics, such as age, sex, height, weight and degree of activity and rate of growth. Every food item whether solid or liquid from plant or animal origin has a chemical composition of nutrients and energy that are essential to the life of individuals. Good nutrition requires a satisfactory diet, which is capable of supporting the individual consuming it, in a state of good health by providing the desired nutrients in required amounts. It must provide the right amount of fuel to execute normal physical activity. If the total amount of nutrients in the diet is insufficient, a state of under-nutrition will develop. During the adolescent period, with the rapid growth, there is an increased demand for nutrients like proteins, energy, vitamins and minerals. These must be met to have a good physical and mental growth. Agarwal (2013) reported that tribal women as compared to non-tribal women were 1.3 times more likely to be underweight and anemic and were four times more likely to never/occasionally consume milk/curd or pulses/beans. It is reported that tribal people in India suffer illnesses of greater severity and duration with women and children being the most vulnerable (The World Bank in India, 2011). Given the importance of adolescents and the significant proportion of their population, the study was undertaken to understand the food habits and dietary intake among adolescent tribal girls of the Karbi community in the age group of 15-18 years living in Kamrup district of Assam.

Kamrup is one of the largest districts among 27 districts of Assam in the Northeastern region of India. Situated between 25°46' and 26°49' North Latitude and between 90°48' and 91°50' East Longitude, bounded by Udalguri and Baska District on the north; Meghalaya on the south; Darrang and Kamrup (Metro) on the east and Goalpara and Nalbari district on the west. It has a total area of 3,483.77 km. The Karbis are a tribal group scattered in North-east India with a majority of them living in Assam and are concentrated in some pockets of Kamrup district.

Methodology

This was a cross-sectional descriptive type of study conducted in two blocks of Kamrup district, namely, Chandrapur and Dimoria which were densely populated by the Karbis. Chandrapur, a semi-urban area, is located approximately 15 km from Dispur, the capital of Kamrup district. Dimoria is in the outskirt of Guwahati city and has several communities including Karbi, Tiwa, Boro, Rabha, Garo, Tea Tribes and some others. Dimoria was a rural area whereas Chandrapur was a semi-urban area. Although Chandrapur area is in close proximity to urban markets, the food habits of the people were still traditional. From the two blocks, 15 numbers of villages were selected. The sample of this study was the adolescent girls aged 15-18 years. A total of 100 adolescent girls were selected by using purposive sampling method. The adolescent girls selected were all unmarried. The primary data were collected from the individual adolescent girls by interview method. An interview schedule was prepared to elicit information on socio-economic background, food habits and dietary intake. Food intake was assessed using standard procedures (Thimmayamma, 1987; NIN, 2010) based on 24-hour recall method (Gabel and Schuster, 2006). Food consumption adequacy was compared with the Recommended Dietary Allowances (RDA) given by the National Institute of Nutrition (NIN, 2010). Statistical techniques used were averages and percentages. A code book was prepared for coding the interview schedule.

Results

Background Information

It is seen from Table 6.1 that among 100 adolescent girls, 20 per cent were matriculate, 39 per cent were under-matric and 38 per cent studied up to primary level or standard 5. About two and one per cent of the adolescent girls were illiterate and just literate, respectively. All Karbi adolescent girls were Hindus. About 52 per cent had kutcha houses, 39 per cent pucca houses and 9 per cent lived in semi-pucca houses. As for family income, about 41 and 46 per cent of the adolescent girls belonged to the families that depend on daily wage and service, respectively. Only 3 and 10 per cent of them were engaged in agriculture and business, respectively. The majority of the adolescent girls (66 per cent) belonged to the families with monthly income of ₹ 5,000 and below; whereas 28 and 6 per cent of them were respectively in the families with monthly income of ₹ 5,000 to ₹ 10,000 and ₹ 10,000 and above. As regards family type, about 77 per cent of the adolescent girls belonged to nuclear families and 23 per cent of them lived in joint families.

Table 6.1: Background of the respondents

Educational status (per cent)	
Illiterate	2.00
Just illiterate	1.00
Primary	38.00
Under matric	39.00
Matriculate	20.00
Religion (per cent)	
Hindu	100.00
House type (per cent)	
Kutcha	52.00
Semi-pucca	9.00
Pucca	39.00
Family occupation (per cent)	
Agriculture	3.00
Daily wage	41.00
Service	46.00
Business	10.00
Family income (per cent)	
Up to ₹ 5000	66.00
₹ 5000 to ₹ 10000	28.00
₹ 10000 and above	6.00
Family type (per cent)	
Nuclear	77.00
Joint	23.00

Food Habits and Food Adequacy

Table 6.2 depicts the food habits and food adequacy of the adolescent girls. It was found that all (100 per cent) of the adolescent girls were non-vegetarians. The tribal communities have more preference for non-vegetarian foods, especially the animal foods. Saikia (2012) found all the tea garden tribes in the age group 10 to 30 years preferred non-vegetarian food to vegetarian food. Another study conducted by Mittal and Srivastava (2006) revealed that all the Oraon tribes of West Bengal were non-vegetarians.

Study data shows that 29 per cent of the adolescents ate twice a day, 47 per cent ate three times/day and 24 per cent consumed food more than three times a day. The adolescents having two times meals were missing their breakfast either for school or other reasons like doing household chores, looking after the young sibling, etc. Kaur and Kaur (2011) found that 16 per cent of females consumed twice a day and missing their breakfast and about 60 per cent of them were underweight. Kotecha and colleagues (2013) found in a study that nearly 60 per cent of adolescent girls had their breakfast daily while the remaining missed to take breakfast. They also reported that the respondents were not aware of RDA.

Table 6.2: Food habits

Non-vegetarian (per cent)	100.00
Eating practices (per cent)	
2 times/day	29.00
3 times/day	47.00
More than 3 times/day	24.00
Feeding practices (per cent)	
With the family	72.00
After food is being served	11.00
Alone	17.00

Feeding Practices

Feeding practices presented in Table 6.2 reveal that 72 per cent of the Karbi adolescent girls eat food with the family, 11 per cent of them eat food after being served to the family and 17 per cent eat alone. About 17 per cent of the adolescents mentioned that they ate alone after coming from school. They eat with their mothers after the family has eaten. Gittelsohn (1997) has reported that staple food items (rice, lentil, etc.) are distributed fairly and equally, side dishes containing sources of micro nutrients (vegetables, meat, yoghurt, etc.) are often preferentially allocated to valued household members, including adult males and small children.

Consumption of Food

The staple food of Karbi was rice. In the three meals, *viz.*, breakfast, lunch and dinner; they prefer to take rice. Among the respondents, some prefer to take puffed rice and flaked rice with curd and jaggery during breakfast. Some of the respondents mentioned, if they avoid lunch, they prefer taking puffed rice *laddu* prepared with jaggery and black tea without sugar. Due to urban influence, the girls below 18 years prefer to take *chappati* or *maggi*, but the mothers were not willing to prepare it because they feel it is tedious. Cereals are one of the most important sources of energy, carbohydrates and protein. So cereals, which formed the bulk of their dietaries, were taken every day. In this study, data in Table 6.3 show that all the respondents have cereals every day. Regarding consumption of pulses, it was observed that 54 per cent of the adolescent girls consumed every day, 17 per cent had once a week and 29 per cent had only sometimes. Pulses are one of the cheap sources of protein and are required for growth and development. The Karbi girls included all types of pulses (*dals*) like red gram, green gram, black gram, lentil, etc. Qamra *et. al.* (2006) reported that the Bhil tribe of Madhya Pradesh consumed pulses as *moong* and *urad* frequently. Cooked *dal* was found to be much diluted with water, with a lot of red and green chillies. This was in contrary to what was observed among the Karbis. The *dal* prepared by them was semi-thick but not too thin. The Karbis prefer to have the *dal* as boil or they prepared with alkali (*Khar*). In the half boil *dal*, the Karbi women put vegetables like papaya, white gourd, drumstick leaves or pumpkin leaves along with *khar*. *Khar* is prepared by burning the banana stem and dipping the burnt part in water. The strained water is kept in a bottle or jar, which can be kept for many months.

Milk and milk products, which provide protein and important minerals like calcium, was included in the diet of the adolescent Karbi girls, but the study data revealed their low consumption among the Karbis. Only 35 per cent of the adolescent girls consumed milk and milk products every day, 12 per cent of them consumed once a week and 53 per cent consumed milk only sometimes.

Vegetables and fruits are known as protective foods as they are rich sources of vitamins and minerals. Vegetables are grouped into three categories *viz*., roots and tubers, green leafy vegetables and other vegetables. It was found that, roots and tubers were consumed every day by 64 per cent of the Karbi adolescent girls, 4 per cent of them consumed once a week and 32 per cent of them consumed only sometimes (Table 6.3). Under roots and tubers category all types of underground vegetables such as potatoes, onions, colocasia bulbs, carrots, raddish, beetroot, etc. are present which are rich sources of energy, carbohydrate, vitamins and minerals. The Karbis like potato and calocasia bulb (*kasu*) as it was seen very frequent in their kitchen. The meat is cooked mostly in colocasia, which is a delicacy of Karbi kitchen especially among the Karbis of Kamrup district. The vegetable groups also include green leafy vegetables which are rich sources of pro-vitamin A as well as iron and calcium. The leafy vegetable category includes dark green vegetables as amaranthus, spinach, fenugreek, colocasia leaves, etc. and light green vegetables such as cabbage, spring onions, lettuce leaves, etc. Regarding green leafy vegetables, 49 per cent of the Karbi adolescent girls consumed every day, 6 per cent consume once a week and 45 per cent of them consumed sometimes or occasionally. The Karbis prefer to eat green leafy vegetables which are grown in their homes. They go to the hilly terrain to collect such vegetables. Some of the green leafy vegetables included in their diet were unknown and their botanical names could not be identified. Some of the leafy greens leafy which Karbis include were drumstick leaves, spinach, curry leaves, *mayong sak, mesta tenga, kasidoria, semerang tenga,* etc., which are available in the hills or forest area. Similarly, other vegetables were consumed by about 25 per cent of them every day, 10 per cent of them consumed once a week and 45 per cent sometimes. The other vegetables which were covered in this category were ash gourd, bottle gourd, pumpkin, French beans, cucumber, cauliflower, brinjal, etc. These vegetables are also good sources of minerals, vitamins and fibers. The banana stem of some varieties of banana, which is called *posola* in Assamese and rich in fiber, is taken by Karbi girls. They cook the banana stem without oil with dals or putting alkali and grams. All the adolescent girls used sugar in their regular diet.

Fats and oils are instant sources of energy. They not only provide taste to the food during preparation but are an important part of dietary. About 90 per cent of the Karbi adolescent girls included fats and oils in their everyday diet and only 10 per cent did sometimes.

All the fruits are categorised under one category but their sources of nutrients differ. The yellow fruits like oranges, mango, ripe papaya, watermelon, wood apple, etc. are very good sources of pro-vitamin A. The vitamin C rich fruits include amla (Indian gooseberry), guavas, lime, berries, pears, etc. The other fruits are bananas, musk melon, grapes, apple, pomegranate, etc. that are good sources of other minerals, vitamins and fiber. The Karbis have the locally available fruits, such as wood apple, pineapple, mango, litchi, etc. All the respondents consumed fruits only sometimes.

Non-vegetarian food items such as meat, fish and poultry are good sources of protein. All the respondents mentioned whenever they have egg they prefer to have one full egg, but sometimes due to large family size they have to share it. They all prefer to have boil egg or prepared as curry. There was nothing special about preparing egg. It was seen that egg was consumed by 19 per cent of the respondents only once a week, 18 per cent twice a week and 63 per cent sometimes. The Karbis like fresh as well as dry fish. They prepared fish with bamboo shoot and green leafy vegetables (*mesta tenga pat*). Dry fish is prepared with chillies, onion, garlic and tomato. Another delicacy is dry fish prepared with alkali called *khar*. The Karbis prepare dry fish by putting it in boil water with white gourd, garlic and ginger and adding *khar* to it. They don't use turmeric while preparing delicacies with *khar*. A traditional recipe is prepared with dry fish by roasting the dry fish and making it into paste with red chillies, ginger and garlic. The chutney is very hot and it is liked by one and all. As for fish consumption, about 19 per cent Karbi adolescent girls consumed once a week, 22 per cent twice a week and 59 per cent sometimes. They mentioned that even a small piece of non-vegetarian food satisfies their satiety level and they can have enough rice without any other curries or vegetables. They cook non-vegetarian with spices and oil like the modern delicacies, but prefer boil meat prepared with vegetables like colocasia tubers, potatoes and green leafy vegetables. Boiled meat is prepared by marinating the meat mutton/pork/chicken) with ginger-garlic paste and adding to boil water. It is cooked till the meat is tender and before serving lot of chilli is added to give a hot taste. Although research reveals that all tribal population are non-vegetarians but no data were found on the frequency of the consumption of non-vegetarian foods. Qamra (2006) mentioned in a study of Bhil tribe of Madhya Pradesh that although all Bhils are non-vegetarian and extremely fond of consuming fleshes of animals and birds, yet its consumption was limited to only ceremonial and festival days. Mittal and Srivastava (2006) also mentioned that the use of non-vegetarian items among the Oraon tribes was limited to two to three times a month usually on days when they are paid for their work. The consumption of non-vegetarian items among the Karbis seems to be more frequent, despite the income level of the respondents. Consumption of meat was 20 per cent every day, 15 per cent of them consumed once a week and 65 per cent only sometimes. Kotecha *et al.* (2013) reported that nearly 80 per cent of the adolescents had consumed regular food, like dal, rice, chappati and vegetables, including green leafy vegetables.

Table 6.3: Consumption of different foodstuff

Foodstuff	*Percentage consumption per week*			
	Everyday	*Once*	*Twice*	*Sometimes*
Pulses	54.0	17.0	—	29.0
Egg	—	19.0	18.0	63.0
Fish	—	19.0	22.0	59.0
Meat	20.0	15.0	65.0	—
Milk	35.0	12.0	—	53.0
Sugar and Jaggery	100.0	—	—	—
Oils and fats	90.0	—	—	10.0
Green leafy vegetables	49.0	6.0	—	45.0
Other vegetables	25.0	10.0	—	65.0
Fruits	—	—	—	100.0

Dietary Intake

Table 6.4 shows the dietary intake of the Karbi adolescent girls. The average consumption of all the food groups was compared with the Recommended Dietary Allowances (RDA). The data revealed that the adolescent girls were adequate in cereals (103.3 per cent), green leafy vegetables (110.5 per cent) and fats and oils (102 per cent). Consumption of roots and vegetables and pulses and flesh foods was little lower than the RDA (90.6 per cent and 89.46 per cent). The adolescent girls were lacking in milk and milk products (71.84 per cent), other vegetables (55.50 per cent), fruits (62 per cent) and sugar (69.50 per cent). Alam and colleagues (2010) found in a study of the adolescent girls that consumption of staple food (rice or wheat) was by and large according to the RDA, consumptions of non-staple food items, such as meat, eggs, *dal* (lentils), fruits and leafy vegetables were not frequent in rural areas. Half of them did not eat meat and milk and 40 per cent did not eat eggs at all. A study of the adolescents of Bangladesh revealed that intake of fish, meat, eggs, milk, legumes and fruits and vegetables were lower among the female than male adolescents. Rao and colleagues (2010) found that the rural adolescents' (16-18 yrs.) intakes of pulses, milk, oils and sugar were less compared to the RDA. Intake of green leafy vegetables was more or less at par with the current study. The Study also revealed a lack of micronutrients that lead to vitamin A deficiency (4.9 per cent) and goitre (5 per cent). Dietary deficiency during adolescence adversely affects the reproductive outcome (Mailye *et. al.*, 2010). Another study of tribal adolescents (Rao *et. al.*, 2006) indicates that food and nutrient intakes were low compared to RDA and that of their rural counterparts. The prevalence of undernutrition was also relatively more among the tribal adolescents compared to their rural counterparts.

Table 6.4: Dietary intake of adolescent Karbi girls

Food groups	*Below 18 years*		
	Average intake Mean±S.D (g/day)	*Recommended intake**	*Per cent Adequacy*
Cereals	340.01 ± 39.17	330	103.03
Pulses	67.10 ± 29.73	75	89.47
Milk (ml/day)	215.51 ± 63.71	300	71.84
Roots and tubers	181.20 ± 94.49	200	90.60
Green leafy vegetables	110.50 ± 81.66	100	110.50
Other vegetables	111.00 ± 81.51	200	55.50
Fruits	62.00 ± 63.21	100	62.00
Fats and oils	25.50 ± 8.14	25	102.00
Sugar and jaggery	20.85 ± 7.42	30	69.50

* *Source:* NIN (2010).

Conclusion

The adolescent Karbi girls under the study population found to be non-vegetarian. Major sources of macro-nutrients such as cereals, pulses and fat were found to be by and large adequate among all adolescent girls. The study revealed that the food habits among Karbi adolescent girls were by and large according to the RDA and all the respondents were having balanced diet, except in milk, fruits and other vegetables. The eating pattern of two times a day has to be enhanced to three or more times a day with fruits, milk, sprouted grains and the like keeping in view their level of physical activity. Counselling on eating with the family with adequate quality and quantity for all the members of the family needs to be emphasised for good nutrition and healthy living. Nutrition education is required as a whole in the community so that modification in dietary intake and the knowledge of incorporating all food groups can be given.

References

Agarwal, S. (2013). Disadvantageous situation of tribal women and children of Odisha, India: A special reference to their health and nutritional status. *Journal of Community Nutrition and Health*, 2(1): 3-8.

Alam, A., S. W. Roy, T. Ahmed and A.M.S. Ahmed (2010). Nutritional status, dietary intake and relevant knowledge of adolescent girls in rural Bangladesh. *Journal of Health, Population and Nutrition*, 28 (1): 86-94.

Gabel, C. and Ellen Schuster (2006). Individual 24-Hour Dietary Recall Protocols. Adapted from Texas A and M University and Iowa State University, 8/06.

Gittelsohn, J., M. Thapa and L. Landman (1997). Micronutrient sufficiency in rural Nepali Households. *Social Science and Medicine*, 44(11):1739-49.

Kaur, I.P. and S. Kaur (2011). A comparison of nutritional profile and prevalence of anaemia among rural girls and boys. *Journal of Exercise Science and Physiotherapy*, 7(1): 11-18. Kotecha, P. V., S.V. Patel, R.K. Baxi, V.S. Mazumdar, M. Sobha, K.G. Mehta, D. Mansi and M. Ekta (2013). Dietary pattern of schoolgoing adolescent in urban Baroda, India. *Journal of Health, Population and Nutrition,* 4:490-96.

Mailye, C.H., P.R. Deshmukh, S.S. Gupta, S. Kaur, A.M. Mehendele and B.S. Garg (2011). Nutrient intake amongst rural adolescent girls of Wardha. *Indian Journal of Community Medicine*, 35(13):400-02.

Mittal, P.C. and S. Srivastava (2006). Diet, nutritional status and food related traditions of Oraons tribe of new Mal (West Bengal), India. *Rural and Remote Health*, 6:385. http://rrh.dreakin.edu.au. Visited on 02.04.2016.

National Institute of Nutrition (NIN)(2010). *Dietary Guidelines for Indians: A Manual National.* Hyderabad: Institute of Nutrition.

Qamra, S. R., J. Roy and D.K. Mishra (2006). Food consumption pattern and associated habits of the Bhil tribe of Dhar district of Madhya Pradesh.

Proceedings of National Symposium on Tribal Health, pp. 211-219. Jabalpur: ICMR.

Rao, M.R., N. Balakrishna, N. Arlappa, A. Laxmaiah and G.N.V. Brahmam (2010). Diet and nutritional status of women in India. *Journal of Human Ecology*, 29(3): 165-70.

Saikia, S. (2012). Food pattern of tea-tribes of two selected tea garden, Dibrugarh. *Basic Applied and Social Sciences*, 2:300-03.

The World Bank in India (2011). Innovations in Development. Improving health services for tribal populations. Karnataka, Rajasthan, Tamil Nadu. Ministry of Finance, Issue 4, p. 4. New Delhi: Department of Economic Affairs.

Thimmayamma, B.V.S. (1987). *Schedules and Guidelines in Socio-Economic and Diet Surveys*. Hyderabad: National Institute of Nutrition.

7

Nutritional Status and Blood Pressure among the Ageing Tiwas of Morigaon District, Assam

— *Barnali Das and Chandana Sarmah*

Introduction

Ageing is a natural process. It begins from the very birth of an individual and continues till death. Old age is usually a period of declining physical health. Physical parameters during ageing are the outcome of many factors, such as hereditary factors, personal temperament, child births, metabolic characteristics, vicissitude of living, nutrition level, infections, intoxication, gluttony, occupational influences, internal responsibilities, endocrine disorders and other environmental factors (Kashyap and Sidha, 2011).

Nutritional status of a population is an important tool to study the health status of any population. Proper nutrition keeps human healthy and fit whereas inadequate or improper nutrition reduces fitness and causes susceptibility to various diseases. The health and nutritional status of the tribal population is often reported as poor. The tribal population is at a higher risk of undernutrition because of their dependence on primitive agricultural practices and irregularity of food supply (Kapoor *et. al.*, 2009). Anthropometry is considered one of the most reliable parameters for the assessment of nutritional status. Body mass index (BMI) is widely accepted as one of the best indicators of nutritional status.

The people's need for food and nutrition are determined by the ecology and culture in which they live. Proper nutrition as part of an active and healthy life style is a key to successful ageing. The nutritional status of women in India, especially those belonging to the tribal groups are found to be poor. Rao and colleagues (2010), while analysing the National Family Health data collected during 1998–99 and 2005–06 on diet and nutritional status of tribal and rural population in nine states of India, stated that the tribal women were particularly vulnerable to undernutrition compared to women in rural areas. The prevalence of chronic energy deficiency was higher (56.0 per cent) among tribal women compared to rural women (36.0 per cent).

Studies on ageing are relatively less in North-east India, especially those relating to nutritional status and blood pressure. Sarmah (2014) reported the nutritional status in relation to ageing among three communities of Lakhimpur district living under similar ecological conditions. The prevalence of malnutrition was found to be high. It was found that females were more prone to malnutrition than males. Borah and Sarmah (2012) undertook a study on the nutritional status and blood pressure among 256 Adult Karbi women of Kamrup district, Assam. They found that the prevalence of undernutrition was high (35.97 per cent). Hypertension was about 15.63 per cent among women and the occurrence of hypertension increased with increasing age. Das and Das (2011) also reported the disease prevalence among the Kaibarta males (aged 55-75 years) of Barpeta town in relation to their age, socio-economic and nutritional status. The results showed that the Kaibarta males suffered from various types of disease, such as hypertension (34.8 per cent), gastrointestinal disease (42.4 per cent), tuberculosis and asthma (26.8 per cent) and arthritis/body pain (40.0 per cent).

Borah and Sarmah (2012) undertook a study on nutritional status and blood pressure among the adult Karbi women of Kamrup district, Assam. About 256 women aged 20 to 70 years were selected for the study. The prevalence of undernutrition was found to be high (35.97 per cent). The prevalence of hypertension was 15.63 per cent among women and it increased with the increase in age. Das and Das (2011) reported the nutritional status and disease of the Kaibarta aged males of Barpeta town in the age group 55 to 75 years. They examined the disease prevalence in relation to their age, socio-economic background and nutritional status. The results showed that the Kaibarta males suffered from various types of disease. The frequencies are: hypertension (34.8 per cent), gastrointestinal disease (42.4 per cent), tuberculosis and asthma (26.8 per cent) and arthritis/ body pain (40.0 per cent).

Blood pressure is a dynamic physiological measure, which is influenced by a number of biological and socio-cultural factors. The level of blood pressure is affected by climate, degree of urbanisation, work schedule, activity pattern and dietary behaviour (Bassey, 1992). Waldrom and colleagues (1982) analysed the relation between blood pressure and cultural characteristics and found that "slopes of blood pressure with age were greater in groups which had greater involvement in a money economy, more economic competition, more contact with people of different culture or beliefs and more unfulfilled aspirations for a return to traditional beliefs and values."

Many studies of blood pressure in relation to different variables have been carried out across the globe. However, there are still limited numbers of such studies in North-east India. There are a number of tribes and communities living in this region. Each community has their unique culture, food habits, cultural practices and adaptation process to their ecology. Hazarika and colleagues (2004) found the overall prevalence of hypertension as 33.3 per cent among the native rural population of Assam. The gender specific prevalence was 33.2 per cent in men and 33.4 per cent in women. They also found a significant increase in the prevalence of hypertension with increasing age in both the sexes. In another study, Hazarika *et al.* (2003) reported the high prevalence of hypertension (63.63 per cent) among the elderly population of Assam. It was also found to be higher in males (64.2 per cent) than in females (62.89 per cent). It was also reported that only 26.90 per cent of the persons with hypertension were aware of their increase in blood pressure.

The nutritional assessment of a community is very important to map the magnitude and geographical distribution of malnutrition as a public health problem (Jelliffe, 1966). In North-east India, very few studies have been done at the community level relating to the nutritional status and blood pressure of the ageing population. The present study was carried out to examine the nutritional status and blood pressure among the ageing Tiwas of Morigaon District in Assam.

Methodology

The present study was conducted among the ageing Tiwas of Morigaon district. It is a cross-sectional study consisting of 262 respondents, 130 males and 132 females, who were aged 50 years and above. The respondents were briefed about the study and a verbal consent was obtained. Only those who consented to be part of the study were included.

For the assessment of nutritional status, height and body weight were measured. Height was measured using the anthropometric rod and weight with the help of weighting machine. The BMI (weight in kg/height in meter squared) was used for estimating the nutritional status of the individuals, following the cut-offs suggested for Asian populations (WHO, 2000). Blood pressure was measured using a digital blood pressure monitor in the sitting posture after the subject had rested for at least 15 minutes. The blood pressure was recorded in the right arm using a cuff of standard size with instrument at the level of the individual's heart. Three readings were recorded and the average of the three readings was used for data analysis. In assessing the blood pressure, the individuals who are using medication for blood pressure were not considered. The blood pressure measures of the population were classified into different categories according to American Heart Association (2005). Data on the social variables were collected with the help of a structured schedule. The income group was classified on the basis of the Planning Commission poverty estimates for 2011-12 (released in July 2013) calculated as per Tendulkar Committee Methodology (Planning Commission, 2009). Following this methodology, families with an annual income less than 49,000 rupees were categorised as below the poverty line.

Study Area and People

The study was conducted in two villages, namely, Sidhabari and Buragaon. The villages are located close to the town of Morigaon.

Sidhabari is a heterogeneous village inhabited predominantly by the Tiwas. There are a few Boro and Assamese caste families living in the village. The village Buragaon is also heterogeneous, inhabited dominantly by the Tiwas, although Nepalis, Boros, Bengalis and Assamese caste families also live in the village.

The Tiwas were originally known as Lalungs. They are believed to have migrated from Tibet and settled in Assam. They are of Mongoloid origin. They are mainly found in the district of Nagaon in Central Assam. They are spread in Kapili, Mayang, Morigaon, Bhurbandha, Kathiatali and Kamrup development block areas of Nagaon district. There are also a few Tiwa villages in Dhemaji areas of Dhemaji, Lakhimpur district, Titabar areas of Jorhat and Sonapur areas of Kamrup district.

Agriculture is the primary means of subsistence of the Tiwas. Those who do not have agricultural land, work as wage earners in agricultural fields, or are involved in other semi-skilled jobs like masonry, carpentry, electrician, pulling rickshaw, etc. Women are predominantly housewives. The educational level of the people is low, especially among the ageing population. Most of them are illiterates.

The Tiwas of the study area are patrilineal, though there is also a matrilineal faction of the Tiwas. Their social organisation is based on a twelve clan structure. As for marriage, they follow clan exogamy and tribe endogamy. The staple food of the Tiwas is rice. Their two major meals consist of rice and vegetables. Meat, fish and eggs are also included in their menu. Fowl and Pork are their delicacies. They take locally brewed rice beer (*zu*) in their day-to-day life.

Nutritional Status

The nutritional status of the population was assessed by using BMI. Table 7.1 shows the prevalence of chronic energy deficiency (CED) was 30.53 per cent among the ageing Tiwas. About 52.67 per cent of them had normal body weight and 16.79 per cent were overweight. The overall prevalence of CED was 30.53 per cent and it was higher in females (34.85 per cent) than in males (25.16 per cent). Similarly, the prevalence of overweight was slightly higher in males

(19.23 per cent) than in females (14.39 per cent). However, the chi-square test shows that gender difference in nutritional status was not statistically significant.

Table 7.1: Nutritional status according to BMI among the ageing Tiwas

Gender	*Underweight (< 18.5 kg/m²)*	*Normal bodyweight (18.5-22.9 kg/m²)*	*Overweight (≥ 23.0 kg/m²)*
Male (n = 130) per cent	34 26.15	71 54.62	25 19.23
Female (n = 132) per cent	46 34.85	67 50.76	19 14.39
χ^2 value	2.332	0.392	1.095

The nutritional status was examined against a few social variables for both males (Table 7.2) and females (Table 7.3). Age though a biological variable becomes highly social in ageing as roles and functions are largely determined by this constantly changing variable. The males and females have been discussed separately for better understanding of the subject. Among the males, CED is found to be highest among the highest age category, i.e. among those who are above 70 years of age. Among the overweight males, the percentage is found to be highest in the youngest age group. In the case of women, the prevalence of CED is much higher than men in all the age groups and it is highest in the oldest age group. Thus, it can be said that the prevalence of CED in females increased with the increase in age, although it was not statistically significant. It also suggests that the prevalence of overweight was higher in the lower age group.

Being predominantly involved in agriculture as their main occupation, the ageing individuals do not have any saving other than their agricultural land. With advancing age, they are no longer able to be work in cultivating land and become dependent on their sons. About 31.54 per cent of the families of the ageing males fall below the poverty line and 36.36 per cent of the ageing females fall in this category. The prevalence of CED or underweight is found to be higher significantly among the ageing males who fall below the poverty line (Table 7.2). On the other hand, the prevalence of overweight is relatively higher in the economically better Tiwa males and females, despite the absence of significant differences. Socio-economic condition is said to be related to nutritional status in terms of access to proper food and medical facilities.

Table 7.2: Nutritional status of Tiwa males according to social variables

Categories	*Nutritional Status according to BMI*		
	Underweight (<18.5 kg/m²)	*Normal body weight (18.5-22.9 kg/m²)*	*Overweight (≥23.0 kg/m²)*
Age group (years)			
50-59 (n=70)	16 (22.86)	39 (55.71)	15 (21.43)
60-69 (n=33)	7 (21.21)	21 (63.64)	5 (15.15)
≥70 (n=27)	11 (40.74)	11 (40.74)	5 (18.52)
χ^2 value	3.828	3.221	0.551
Income groups			
Low (n=41)	16 (39.02)	19 (46.34)	6 (14.63)
Higher (n=89)	18 (20.22)	52 (58.43)	19 (21.35)
χ^2 value	5.143*	1.652	0.811
Marital Status			
Never married (n=2)	—	1 (50.00)	1 (50.00)
Married (n=105)	27 (25.71)	59 (56.19)	19 (18.10)
Widowed/separated (n=23)	7 (30.43)	11 (47.83)	5 (21.74)
χ^2 value**	0.215	0.534	0.166
Family types			
Nuclear (n=59)	13 (22.03)	32 (54.24)	14 (23.73)
Extended/joint (n=71)	21 (29.58)	39 (54.93)	11 (15.49)
χ^2 value	0.949	0.006	1.842

Figures within parentheses indicate percentage. *Significant at 5 per cent.

The marital status is another significant social variable in ageing. Having another person to share and take care of makes a significant difference to both mental and physical health of a person. It is found that around 4.0 per cent of the ageing persons remained unmarried and the proportion is higher in females. About 81.0 per cent of men as compared to 53.0 per cent of women currently have a surviving spouse. About 18 per cent of men and 40.0 per cent of women have no longer a surviving spouse. The prevalence of CED malnutrition is found to be high among men and women who no longer have a surviving spouse. The prevalence is, moreover, relatively higher in women than in men. The difference in the prevalence of undernutrition among the married and widowed women was statistically significant at 5.0 per cent level, although it was not significant in males. The prevalence of CED is also high among the women who have remained unmarried.

Living arrangement means with whom the elderly person resides. Study of living arrangement is important in the study of ageing. This is a reflection of the social support and care that is available to the ageing persons, which is also related to the life satisfaction level among the elderly. Unlike in urban areas, no elderly Tiwa individual was found to be living alone. The proportion of elderly living with only their spouse is also low (2.67 per cent). These couples do not have children, or they have only daughters. They continue to live in this way as long as it is physically possible for them. The Tiwas have the tradition of having a resident son-in-law, in case, they do not have a male child or if they have large landed property. A few resident son-in-laws are still found in the villages. But the tradition is slowly dying and as a result those ageing Tiwa couples, who have only daughters, are now living alone after the latter's marriage. Extended or joint family is the predominant type of family (62.59 per cent). For those ageing persons living in nuclear families, the marital status appears to have some influence. The persons, who do not have a surviving spouse, show a higher prevalence of CED. It is also found that CED is more prevalent in those males who live in extended or joint families. Overweight males are more in nuclear families. In the case of females, the family type does not appear to exert much influence.

Under nutrition is found to be high among the ageing Tiwa population. Age, gender, marital status and economic condition can be said to have certain influence on the prevalence of malnutrition. Women who longer have a surviving spouse appear to be more vulnerable. Such women who live in nuclear families single-handedly have the additional responsibility of their children.

Table 7.3: Nutritional status of the Tiwa females according to social variables

Categories	*Nutritional Status according to BMI*		
	Under weight (<18.5 kg/m^2)	*Normal body weight (18.5-22.9 kg/m^2)*	*Over weight (≥ 23.0 hg/m^2)*
Age group (years)			
50-59 (n=73)	23 (31.51)	40 (54.79)	10 (13.70)
60-69 (n=37)	12 (32.43)	19 (51.35)	6 (16.22)
$\geq$70 (n=22)	11 (50.00)	8 (36.36)	3 (13.64)
χ^2 value	2.674	2.310	0.138
Income groups			
Low (n=48)	20 (41.67)	23 (47.92)	5 (10.42)
Higher (n=84)	26 (30.95)	44 (52.38)	14 (16.67)
χ^2 value	1.348	0.243	0.969
Marital Status			
Never married (n=9)	2 (22.22)	4 (44.44)	2 (22.22)
Married (n=70)	19 (27.14)	40 (57.14)	11 (15.71)
Widowed/separated (n=53)	25 (47.17)	23 (43.40)	5 (9.43)
χ^2 value	5.437*	2.280	1.052
Family types			
Nuclear (n=39)	14 (35.90)	19 (48.72)	6 (15.38)
Extended/joint (n=93)	32 (34.41)	48 (51.61)	13 (13.98)
χ^2 value	0.027	0.094	0.044

Figures within parentheses indicate percentage. *Significant at 5 per cent.

Blood Pressure

Table 7.4 shows the prevalence of prehypertension and hypertension among the ageing Tiwas. It may be noted that no individual in the present study was detected with low blood pressure or hypotension. It is seen from Table 7.4 that about 36.0 per cent of the individuals have normal blood pressure levels, 44.57 per cent of them are pre-hypertensive and 19 per cent hypertensive. Women by and large had normal blood pressure levels, but a majority of men were in the pre-hypertensive category. The gender difference in the prevalence of pre-hypertensive blood pressure is found to be statistically significant. The prevalence of hypertension is, however, lightly higher in females, despite the absence of statistical difference.

Table 7.4: Distribution of blood pressure measure among the ageing Tiwas

Gender	*Normal*	*Pre-hypertension*	*Hypertension*
Male (n=127) per cent	32 25.19	74 58.27	21 16.54
Female (n=131) per cent	62 47.38	41 31.20	28 21.37
χ^2 value	12.965*	18.982*	0.981

*significant at 1 per cent level.

If we look at the prevalence of hypertension among men, it shows a positive relation with age (Table 7.5). The proportion of men having hypertension increases with increasing age. The finding is similar for the ageing women but the proportions are relatively higher in women. The ageing Tiwa men are predominantly in the pre-hypertensive stage and their proportions are highest in the youngest age group. These men have the possibility of developing hypertension as they grow older. The age differences in the prevalence of pre-hypertension among males are statistically significant.

The blood pressure in relation to the income group is shown in Tables 7.5 and 7.6. It is seen that the prevalence of hypertension is slightly higher in men who fall below the poverty line. The finding is contrary in case of women (Table 7.6). Hypertension is more prevalent among women whose families have a better economic condition. The prevalence of pre-hypertension stage is found to be higher among the economically better off. It is also significantly higher in men.

Marital status appears to have some influence on the prevalence of hypertension among the ageing Tiwa males. The males who no longer have a surviving spouse show a much higher prevalence of hypertension. The difference in the prevalence of hypertension between the married men and the widowers is statistically significant (Table 7.5). In case of the ageing women, the never married women showed the highest occurrence of hypertension relative to the others. They are followed by the women who no longer have a spouse.

The living arrangement does not appear to have much influence on the prevalence of hypertension. The prevalence of hypertension is slightly higher in both ageing men and women who live in nuclear families. The difference is however not significant.

The prevalence of hypertension in relation to nutritional status, based on BMI, is found to be highest among the overweight men and women. In the case of men, the occurrence increases with an increase in nutritional grades from underweight through normal to overweight. It holds true for the prevalence of pre-hypertension. Among women, the prevalence of hypertension according to nutritional grades is statistically significant. The women with overweight show the highest prevalence of normal blood pressure.

Conclusion

Thus, from the study, it can be said that prevalence of CED malnutrition is high among the ageing Tiwas. Women are more vulnerable to malnutrition. Age is another factor, which influences the occurrence of malnutrition, as the prevalence of CED malnutrition is highest in the oldest age group. Marital status has a greater significant effect on the occurrence of undernutrition in women than men. The prevalence of malnutrition is significant among the ageing males who economically fall below the poverty line. Hypertension prevalence is not very high, but what is noteworthy is that the prevalence of hypertension is higher in women. Age and nutritional status have a greater influence on the occurrence of hypertension in the ageing men and women than the other social factors.

Table 7.5: Blood pressure measures among the Tiwa males according to bio-social variables

Categories	*Blood Pressure Measures*		
	Normal	*Pre-hypertension*	*Hypertension*
Age group (years)			
50-59 (n=67)	14 (20.89)	45 (67.16)	8 (11.94)
60-69 (n=29)	7 (24.13)	17 (58.62)	5 (17.24)
≥70 (n=31)	11 (35.48)	12 (38.71)	8 (25.81)
χ^2 value	2.412	7.053*	2.960

(Contd...)

Income groups Low (n=40) Higher (n=87)	 11 (27.50) 21 (24.14)	 21 (52.50) 53 (60.92)	 8 (20.00) 13 (14.94)
χ^2 value	0.164	0.801	0.439
Marital Status Never married (n=1) Married (n=103) Widowed/separated (n=23)	 1 (100) 27 (26.21) 4 (17.39)	 — 63 (61.17) 11 (47.83)	 — 13 (12.62) 8 (34.78)
χ^2 value	1.110	1.383	6.663*
Family types Nuclear (n=59) Extended/joint	 14 (23.73) 18 (26.47) (n=68)	 33 (55.93) 38 (55.88)	 12 (20.34) 12 (17.65)
χ^2 value	0.127	0.000	0.151
Nutritional status (BMI) Underweight (n=33) Normal body weight (n=70) Overweight (n=24)	12 (36.36) 16 (22.86) 4 (16.67)	17 (51.52) 42(60.00) 15 (62.5)	4 (12.12) 12 (17.14) 5 (20.83)
χ^2 value	3.312	1.209	0.809

Figures within parentheses indicate percentage. *Significant at 5 per cent.

Table 7.6: Blood pressure measures among the Tiwa females according to bio-social variables

Categories	*Blood Pressure Measures*		
	Normal	*Pre-hypertension*	*Hypertension*
Age group (years) 50-59 (n=71) 60-69 (n=38) ≥70 (n=22)	 34 (47.89) 18 (47.37) 10 (45.45)	 24 (33.80) 12 (31.58) 5 (22.73)	 13 (18.31) 8 (21.05) 7 (31.82)
χ^2 value	0.040	0.964	1.832
Income groups Low (n=47) Higher (n=84)	 27 (57.45) 35 (41.67)	 11 (23.41) 30 (35.71)	 9 (19.14) 19 (22.62)
χ^2 value	3.016	2.124	0.217

(Contd...)

Marital Status			
Never married (n=9)	1 (11.11)	4 (44.44)	4 (44.44)
Married (n=69)	33 (47.83)	25 (36.23)	11 (15.94)
Widowed/separated (n=53)	28 (52.83)	12 (22.64)	13 (24.53)
χ^2 value	0.300	2.610	1.400
Family types			
Nuclear (n=39)	19 (48.71)	11 (28.21)	9 (23.08)
Extended/joint (n=92)	43(46.74)	30 (32.61)	19 (20.65)
χ^2 value	0.044	0.249	0.097
Nutritional status (BMI)			
Underweight (n=46)	22 (47.83)33	11 (23.91)	13 (28.26)
Normal body weight (n=66)	33 (50.00)	25 (37.88)	8 (12.12)
Overweight (n=19)	7 (47.33)	5 (26.32)	7 (36.84)
χ^2 value	1.030	2.717	7.373*

Figures within parentheses indicate percentage. *Significant at 5 per cent.

References

American Heart Association (2005). Blood pressure measurement in humans: Statement for the sub-committee of professional and public education of the American Heart Association Council in high blood pressure research. *Hypertension*, 45:142-161.

Bassey, E.J. (1992). Physiological aspect of activity and ageing. In: N.G. Norgan (Ed.), *Physical Activity and Health,* pp.121-28. Cambridge: Cambridge University Press.

Bharadwaj, S. and S. Kapoor (2007). Nutritional anthropometry and health status: A study among Dhanka Tribals of Rajasthan. *Anthropologist,* 9(3): 211-214.

Borah, M.P. and C. Sarmah (2012). Nutritional status and blood pressure among the adult Karbi women of Kamrup District. *Bulletin Department of Anthropology, Guwahati University*, XIII: 91-109.

Das, S. and R. Das (2010). Food, nutritional status and disease of the aged male Kaibartas of Barpeta Town, Assam. *Bulletin of the Department of Anthropology Guwahati University*, XII: 74-81.

Hazarika, N. C., K. Narain, D. Biswas, H.C. Kalita and J. Mahanta (2004). Hypertension in the native rural population of Assam. *The National Medical Journal of India,* 17(6): 300-304.

Hazarika, N.C., D. Biswas and J. Mahanta 2003. Hypertension in the elderly population of Assam. *Journal of the Association of Physicians of India,* 51: 567-573.

Jelliffe, D.B. (1966). *The Assessment of the Nutritional Status of the Community.* Geneva: World Health Organisation.

Kapoor, A.K., M. Dhall and R. Tyagi (2010). Nutritional status and ageing among Car Nicobarse and Molia males of India. *The Open Anthropology Journal*, 3:155-160.

Kapoor, S., R. Tyagi, K. Chaturvedi and A.K. Kapoor (2009). Nutritional profile and socio-economic status of Saharia: A primitive tribe of India. *The Open Anthropology Journal,* 2:58-63.

Kashyap, S. and R. Sidhu (2011). A study of health and subjective well being of the aged. *Indian Journal of Gerontology*, 25:111-122.

Rao, K.M., N. Balakrishna, N. Arlappa, A. Laxmaiah and G.N.V. Brahmam (2010). Diet and nutritional status of women in India. *Journal of Human Ecology*, 29(3):165-170.

Sarmah, C. (2014). Ageing and nutritional status among three communities of Lakhimpur District, Assam. *Indian Journal of Gerontology*, 28(1): 51-69.

Sarmah, C. and A.F.G.I. Barbhuiya (2011). Nutritional status of the adult Dimasa Kacharis of Cachar district, Assam. In: T. Baruah (Ed.), *People of Contemporary North-East India*, pp. 59-67. Guwahati: Pratisruti Publication.

Thakur, G.C.S. (1985). The Lalungs (Tiwas): A monograph on one of the major plains tribes of Assam. Guwahati: Tribal Research Institute, Assam Guwahati.

Waldrom, I., M. Nowatarski, M. Freimer, J.P. Henry, N. Post and C.Witten (1982). Cross-cultural variation in blood pressure: A qualitative analysis of the relationships of blood pressure to cultural characteristics, salt consumption and body weight. *Social Science Medicine,* 16(4):419-430.

8

The Effects of the Interaction of Household Income with Age and Sex on BMI among the Pnars of Nangbah Village in Jaintia Hills of Meghalaya

—*Abigail Lalnuneng and R. Khongsdier*

Introduction

Body mass index (BMI) calculated as weight (kg) divided by height squared (m^2) is one of the anthropometric indices that is considered a good indicator of the nutritional status at the individual and population levels. It is widely used to monitor underweight and overweight or obesity (WHO, 2000). According to the World Health Organisation (WHO, 1995), BMI ranges of 25-30 and > 30 kg/m^2 are considered to be indicative of overweight and obesity, respectively. The BMI < 18.5 kg/m^2 is widely used as a practical cut-off point for classifying the chronic energy deficiency (CED), i.e., a "steady" underweight in which an individual is in energy balance irrespective of a loss in body weight, or body energy stores (Khongsdier, 2005). Such a "steady" underweight is likely to be associated with different types of morbidity, or other physiological and functional impairments (WHO, 1995). On the other hand, overweight and obesity are ranges of weight gain that are indicative of excess body fat in individuals with sedentary lifestyles, but not in athletes and persons involved in high physical activity. It is well-established that overweight and obesity are the major risk factors for different types of morbidity, including diabetes, cardiovascular diseases, some types of cancer and musculoskeletal disorders (NCD Risk Factor Collaboration, 2016). In the last two decades or so, overweight and obesity were the common health and nutritional problems only in developed countries, but they are now dramatically increasing in developing countries, particularly in urban settings (WHO, 2015).

According to WHO (2015), obesity has reached epidemic proportions globally with 39 per cent of adults (36.0 per cent of men and 40.0 per cent of women) over the age of 18 years being overweight or obese in 2014. In developing countries including India, the situation is more complex, because the problem of CED still continues along with an emerging problem of overweight and obesity (Caballero, 2005; Mendez *et. al.*, 2005; Caballero, 2007; Wang *et. al.,* 2009; WHO, 2014; Pradeepa *et. al.*, 2015; WHO, 2015).

It is obvious from the above snapshot that BMI is very important anthropometric indicator, which is linked not only to nutritional status but also to different types of health problems. In addition, BMI is also considered a good indicator of the socio-economic status (SES) of populations in developing countries (Nube *et al.*, 1998; Khongsdier, 2002). Many earlier studies suggest that BMI is higher in the higher SES of populations in low- and middle-income countries, whereas in the high-income countries the relationship between SES and BMI is found to reversed (Sobal and Stunkard, 1989; Subramanian *et al.*, 2006; Subramanian, 2009; Dinsa *et al.*, 2012). It is suggested that such a reversed relation between SES and BMI in developing countries may be due to sedentary lifestyle and consumption of high calorie food among the individuals with higher SES; whereas the individuals with higher SES in developed countries may respond with healthy eating and regular exercise (Pampel *et al.*, 2012; Bhurosy and Jeewon, 2014). In the meanwhile, other studies have revealed that the relation between SES and BMI is actually inconsistent and contentious across developed and developing countries (Sobal and Stunkard, 1989; Monteiro *et al.,* 2004; Wang, 2007; Khandelwal and Reddy, 2013). It is likely that the relation between SES and BMI may be associated with different compounding factors.

In the present study, an attempt has been made to understand the effects of the interaction of household income with age and sex on

BMI among the Pnars of Nangbah Village in West Jaintia Hills District of Meghalaya.

Materials and Methods

The present study is preliminary. It was conducted among the adult Pnars of Nangbah Village in West Jaintia Hills District of Meghalaya. Meghalaya is a hilly state in North-east India (25°02' to 26°06' North latitude and 89°48' to 92°50' East longitude). Nangbah village is one of the oldest villages in Jaintia Hill District, Meghalaya. It is located in the northeast of Jowai town on the J.N.K.K. Road (Jowai Nartiang Kdiap Khanduli Road), which is about 13 km from Jowai towards Khanduli.

According to Census of India (2011), Nangbah village has a population of 6965 individuals (3422 males and 3543 females) and is predominantly populated by the Pnars, also known as Jaintias. The Pnars are one of the Khasi sub-groups, who follow the matrilineal system of society and speak the Mon-Khmer language of Austro-Asiatic language family. Although they still maintain their unique religion called *Niam-Tre*, a majority of the Pnars of Nangbah village have embraced Christianity. Unlike other areas of Jaintia Hills District where coal mining is widely practised, the Pnars of Nangbah village is mainly engaged in agriculture and business. Rice is their staple food and they consume different varieties of vegetables, fish and meat.

A cross-sectional sample of 229 individuals (67 males; 162 females) aged 20 to 70 years was included in the present study. Data on height and body weight were measured following the standard techniques described in Weiner and Lourie (1981) and Sen (1994). Data on household monthly income were collected directly from the heads of households, using structured schedule for household economic conditions. The per capita monthly income of the households was arbitrarily classified as follows: Above 75th percentile (₹ 1600) as high income group (HIG); 50th to 75th percentile (₹ 1250 to ₹ 1600) as middle income group (MIG); and below 50th percentile (below ₹ 1250) as low income group (LIG).

BMI was calculated to assess the nutritional status of the participants. The presence of underweight and overweight was evaluated using the WHO Asian cut-off points (WHO, 2000) by which the adult individuals with BMIs of <18.5 kg/m^2, 18.5 - 22.9 kg/m^2 and $\geq$ 23 kg/m^2 were categorised as underweight, normal and overweight and/or obese, respectively. Both t-test and chi-square test were used to test the differences between means and proportions, respectively. Analysis of variance was carried out to find the effects of the interaction of household income with age and sex on BMI. SPSS software was used for all statistical analysis.

Results

Table 8.1 shows the baseline characteristics of the participants in the present study. There were 67 males and 162 females who were on an average aged 32 and 37 years, respectively. The mean age was significantly higher in females than in males ($t = 2.32$, $p < 0.02$). The table also shows that about 51.0 per cent, 25.0 per cent and 24.0 per cent of both males and females belonged to the LIG, MIG and HIG, respectively. As normally expected, males were significantly heavier ($t = 5.81$, $p < 0.0001$) and taller ($t = 12.32$, $p < 0.0001$) than their female counterparts. However, the difference between the sexes in respect of BMI was not statistically significant ($t = 0.57$, $p > 0.05$). Thus, the present findings are in consistent with the general observation that the BMI cut-off points for classifying the nutritional status of adults should be the same for both males and females (WHO, 1995).

Table 8.1: Baseline characteristics of participants

Characteristics	*Mean/Percentage*
Age (Mean ± SD years)	31.88±13.37
Males (n=67)	36.60±14.3
Females (n=162)	
Income groups (per cent)	
Lower Income Group (n = 116)	50.66
Middle Income Group (n = 57)	24.89
Higher Income Group (n = 56)	24.45
Anthropometric characteristics for males (Mean ± SD)	
Body weight (kg)	54.97±7.94
Height (cm)	159.44±6.59
BMI (kg/m^2)	21.60±2.86

(Contd...)

Anthropometric characteristics for females (Mean ± SD)	
Body weight (kg)	48.62±7.34
Height (cm)	149.14±5.38
BMI (kg/m^2)	21.85±3.06

Table 8.2: Nutritional status according to BMI for both males and females

Nutritional status according to BMI categories	*Males (n=67)* Frequency (per cent)	*Females (n=162)* Frequency (per cent)	*Total (n=229)* Frequency (per cent)
Underweight (≤18 kg/m^2)	7(10.45)	17(10.49)	24(10.48)
Normal (18.5 – 22.9 kg/m^2)	39(58.21)	93(57.41)	132(57.64)
Overweight/Obese (≥ 23 kg/m^2)	21(31.34)	52(32.10)	73(31.88)
Overweight/Obese (≥ 25.0 kg/m^2)	10(14.93)	25(15.43)	35(15.28)

χ^2 for sex difference in overweight (≥ 23 kg/m^2) = 0.9111, d.f. = 1, $p > 0.05$.

Nutritional Status

Table 8.2 shows the nutritional status of the Pnar adults based on BMI categories recommended by the WHO for Asian populations (WHO, 2000). The prevalence of underweight was more or less similar in both males (10.45 per cent) and females (10.49 per cent). Females (32.0 per cent) have slightly higher prevalence of overweight compared to males (31.0 per cent). In general, it shows that the major nutritional problem among the Pnar adults is at present tilting towards that of overweight (32.0 per cent) compared to underweight (11.0 per cent). It may be noted that even if the international cut-off of 25.0 kg/m^2 is taken into consideration (WHO, 1995), the prevalence of overweight (15.28 per cent) was higher than that of underweight (14.93 per cent). Although our study had limited sample size, it suggests that the present population is facing the nutritional problem of both under- and over-nutrition, or the double burden of malnutrition.

Table 8.3 shows the mean and SD of body weight, height and BMI according to income groups. On average, it shows that body weight and BMI were higher in the HIG as compared with the MIG and LIG for both males and females. However, the analysis of variance shows that the differences between income groups in respect of weight and height is not statistically significant for both the sexes. But the differences in BMI between income groups is statistically significant for both males ($F = 3.99$, $p < 0.02$) and females ($F = 3.29$, $p < 0.04$). This indicates that household income had significant effects on the BMI of both adult males and females of the present study. However, it is not clear whether household income has an interaction with either one or all the variables, such as age and sex. In order to understand this problem, we have carried out analysis of variance on the effects of the interaction of household income with age and sex on BMI. The results are shown in Table 8.4.

Table 8.3: Body weight, height and body mass index (BMI) according to income groups

Income Groups	*Weight (kg.)*		*Height (cm.)*		*BMI (kg/m²)*	
	SD	*Mean*	*SD*	*Mean*	*SD*	*Males*
Mean						
LIG (n=39)	53.72	7.10	159.98	5.86	20.97	2.38
MIG (n=14)	53.93	6.38	158.36	7.85	21.60	3.00
HIG (n=14)	59.21	10.31	159.02	7.50	23.37	3.36
F-statistics	2.74, p > 0.05		0.340, p > 0.05		3.99, p < 0.02	
Females						
LIG (n=77)	48.17	5.99	149.70	5.38	21.48	2.39
MIG (n=43)	47.58	7.38	148.82	5.86	21.50	3.20
HIG (n=44)	50.50	9.17	148.44	4.87	22.88	3.78
F-statistics	1.98, p > 0.05		0.84, p > 0.05		3.29, p < 0.04	

Table 8.4: Results of the analysis of variance on the effects of age, sex and household income on BMI

Source of Variation	*Sum of squares*	*df*	*Mean sum of squares*	*F-value*	*P-level*	*Eta²*
Age	28.69	2	14.35	1.69	0.19	0.014
Sex	10.64	1	10.64	1.25	0.27	0.005
Income	60.52	2	30.26	3.55	**0.03**	0.029
Age*Sex	29.23	2	14.61	1.72	0.18	0.014
Age*Income	101.96	4	25.49	2.99	**0.02**	0.050
Sex*Income	28.53	2	14.26	1.68	0.19	0.014
Age*Sex*Income	37.23	4	9.31	1.09	0.36	0.018
Error	1796.97	211	8.52			
Total	**2051.78**	**228**				

It is seen from Table 8.4 that the effects of income is significant even after controlling the effects of age and sex ($F = 3.55$, $p < 0.05$). The eta^2 shows that about 0.029 or 2.9 per cent of the variance was accounted for by household income, whereas age and sex accounted for about 1.4 per cent and 0.5 per cent of the variance, respectively. Table 8.4 further shows that the interaction between household income and age (Age* Income) accounted for about 5 per cent of the variance in BMI. The F-statistics also shows that it was statistically significant ($F = 2.99$, $p < 0.05$). On the basis of these results, we may suggest that the effect of the interaction between household income and age on BMI is more important than the individual main effects of either household income or age of persons. Although age had no significant effect on BMI, it appears that its interaction effect with household income on BMI of the participants in the present study cannot be totally ignored. To have a better understanding of this problem, an attempt has been made to show the nature of variation in BMI due to

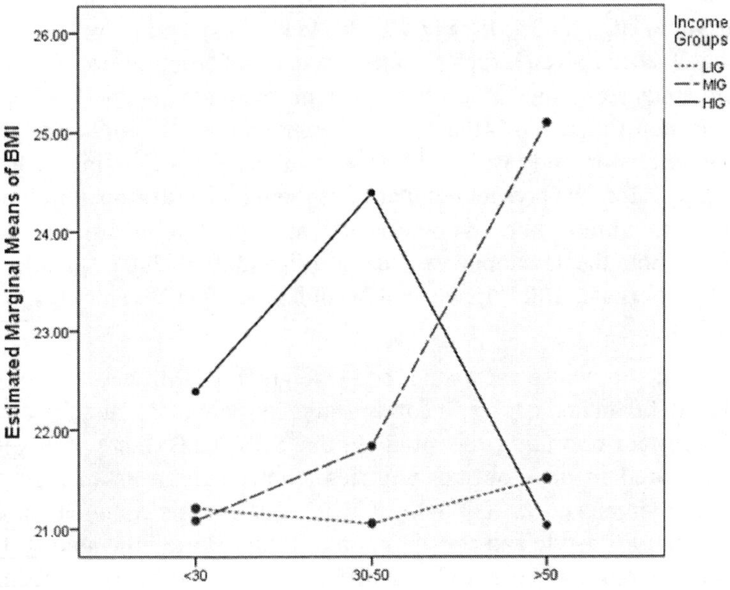

Age-group (years)

Figure 8.1: Interaction effect of age and household income on BMI

the interaction between household income and age. It is seen from Figure 8.1 that BMI in the HIG was higher than the lower income groups (MIG and LIG) when the individuals are in the age group 30-50 years; thereafter the BMI was higher in the LIG and MIG. This indicates that the individuals in the higher income group are more aware of how to control their weight gain when they crossed 50 years of age.

Concluding Remarks

The present study indicates that the prevalence of underweight was more or less similar in both the sexes. The prevalence of overweight is also similar in both the sexes but slightly higher among females. The prevalence of overweight was higher than that of underweight even if the international cut-off of 25.0 kg/m^2 is taken into consideration (WHO, 1995). May studies have suggested that the upsurge in obesity prevalence could be linked to acculturation resulting from westernisation with alterations in diet and activity patterns and overall lifestyles (Popkin, 1994; Popkin, 2002; WHO, 1998; WHO, 2003; Misra *et. al.*, 2011; Bhurosy and Jeewon, 2014; WHO, 2015). Even if such a conjecture may not be entirely applicable, our study suggests that the nutritional problem among the Pnars is at present tilting towards that of overweight compared to underweight. Although our study was preliminary and had limited sample size, it suggests that the present population is facing the nutritional problem of both under- and over-nutrition as reported in populations throughout the developing world (Garrett and Ruel, 2005; Caballero, 2005; Fernald, 2007; Lewis and MacPherson, 2012; Pampel *et. al.*, 2012).

Our study also shows that body weight and BMI were higher in the HIG than in the lower income groups for both males and females, thereby corroborating other findings that SES and BMI are positively correlated in developing countries (Subramanian *et. al.*, 2006; Subramanian *et. al.*, 2009; Dinsa *et. al.*, 2012). This could be due to sedentary lifestyle and consumption of high calorie food among the Pnars belonging to the HIG. The differences in BMI between income groups were statistically significant for both males and females. Even after controlling the effects of age and sex, the effect of income was significant thus indicating that household income had significant effects on the BMI of both males and females.

The present study also suggests that the effect of the interaction between household income and age on BMI is more important than the individual main effects of either household income or age. Although age had no significant effect on BMI, it appears that its interaction effect with household income on BMI of the participants in the present study cannot be totally ruled out. The nature of variation in BMI due to the interaction between household income and age shows that BMI in the HIG was higher than in the MIG and LIG when the individuals are in the age group 30-50 years; thereafter the BMI was higher in the lower income groups. In other words, there is evidence that the individuals in the HIG are more aware of how to control their weight gain when they crossed 50 years of age as compared to those in the lower income groups.

References

Bhurosy, T. and R. Jeewon (2014). Overweight and obesity epidemic in developing countries: a problem with diet, physical activity, or socioeconomic status? *The Scientific World Journal*, 2014, Article ID 964236, doi:10.1155/2014/964236.

Caballero, B. (2005). A nutrition paradox: Underweight and obesity in developing countries. *New England Journal of Medicine,* 352(15):1514-1516.

Caballero, B. (2007). The global epidemic of obesity: An overview. *Epidemiologic Reviews,* 29(1):1-5.

Census of India (2011). http://www.censusindia.gov.in. Retrieved on 09.05.2012.

Dinsa, G., Y. Goryakin, E. Fumagalli and M. Suhrcke (2012). Obesity and socioeconomic status in developing countries: A systematic review. *Obesity Reviews*, 13:1067-1079.

Fernald, L. (2007). Socio-economic status and body mass index in low-income Mexican adults. *Social Science and Medicine*, 64: 2030-2042.

Garrett, J. and M.T. Ruel (2005). The coexistence of child undernutrition and maternal overweight: Prevalence, hypotheses and programme and policy implications. *Maternal and Child Nutrition,* 1:185-196.

Khandelwal, S. and S. Reddy (2013). Eliciting a policy response for the rising epidemic of overweight-obesity in India. *Obesity Reviews*, 14:114-125.

Khongsdier, R. (2002). Body mass index and morbidity in adult males of the War Khasi in North-east India. *European Journal of Clinical Nutrition*, 56:484-489.

Khongsdier, R. (2005). BMI and morbidity in relation to body composition: A cross-sectional study of a rural community in North-East India. *British Journal of Nutrition*, 93:101-107.

Lewis, M.J. and K.L. MacPherson (2012). *Health Transitions and the Double Disease Burden in Asia and the Pacific*. London: Routledge.

Mendez, M.A., C.A. Monteiro and B.M. Popkin (2005). Overweight exceeds underweight among women in most developing countries. *American Journal of Clinical Nutrition*, 81: 714-721.

Misra, A., N. Singhal, B. Sivakumar, N. Bhagat, A. Jaiswal and L. Khurana (2011). Nutrition transition in India: Secular trends in dietary intake and their relationship to diet-related noncommunicable diseases. *Journal of Diabetes*, 3:278-292.

Monteiro, C.A., E.C. Moura, W.L. Conde and B.M. Popkin (2004). Socio-economic status and obesity in adult populations of developing countries: A review. *Bulletin of World Health Organisation,* 82:940-946.

NCD Risk Factor Collaboration (2016). Trends in adult body-mass index in 200 countries from 1975 to 2014: A pooled analysis of 1698 population-based measurement studies with 19.2 million participants. *Lancet*, 387:1377-1396.

Nube, M., W.K. Asenso-Okyere and G.J.M. van den Bloom (1998). Body mass index as an indicator of standard of living in developing countries. *European Journal of Clinical Nutrition*, 77:1186-1191.

Pampel, F.C., J.T. Denney and P.M. Krueger (2012). Obesity, SES and Economic Development: A test of the reversal hypothesis. *Social Science and Medicine*, 74:1073-1081.

Popkin, B.M. (1994). The nutrition transition in low income countries: An emerging crisis. *Nutrition Review*, 52:285-298.

Popkin, B.M. (2002). The shift in stages of the nutritional transition in the developing world differs from past experiences! *Public Health Nutrition*, 5:205-214.

Pradeepa, R., R.M. Anjana, S.R. Joshi, A. Bhansali, M. Deepa, P.P. Joshi, V.K. Dhandania, S.V. Madhu, P.V. Rao, L. Geetha, R. Subashini, R. Unnikrishnan, D.K. Shukla, T. Kaur, V. Mohan and A.K. Das (2015). Prevalence of generalised and abdominal obesity in urban and rural India - The ICMR-INDIAB Study (Phase-I) (ICMR-INDIAB-3). *Indian Journal of Medical Research*, 142:139-150.

Sen, T. (1994). *A Guide to Anthropometry*. Kolkata: The World Press Pvt. Ltd.

Sobal, J. and A.J. Stunkard (1989). Socioeconomic status and obesity: A review of the literature. *Personality and Social Psychology Bulletin*, 105:260-275.

Subramanian, S.V. and G.D. Smith (2006). Patterns, distribution and determinants of under- and overnutrition: A population-based study of women in India. *American Journal of Clinical Nutrition*, 84:633-640.

Subramanian, S.V., J.M. Perkins and K.T. Khan (2009). Do burdens of underweight and overweight coexist among lower socioeconomic groups in India? *American Journal of Clinical Nutrition*, 90:369-376.

Wang, Y., H.J. Chen, S. Shaikh and P. Mathur (2009). Is obesity becoming a public health problem in India? Examine the shift from under to over-nutrition problems over time. *Obesity Review*, 10:456474.

Wang., Y. and M.A. Beydoun (2007). The obesity epidemic in the United States – gender, age, socioeconomic, racial/ethnic and geographic characteristics: A systematic review and meta-regression analysis. *Epidemiology Review*, 29:6-28.

Weiner, J.S. and J.A. Lourie (1981). *Practical Human Biology.* New York: Academic Press.

World Health Organisation (1995). *Physical Status:The Use and Interpretation of Anthropometry. Report of a WHO Expert Committee,Technical Report Series No. 854.* Geneva: WHO.

World Health Organisation (1998). *Obesity: Preventing and Managing the Global Epidemic. Report of a WHO Consultation.* Geneva: WHO.

World Health Organisation (2000). *The Asia Pacific Perspective: Redefining Obesity and Its Treatment.* Geneva: WHO.

World Health Organisation (2003). *Diet, Nutrition and the Prevention of Chronic Diseases. Report of a Joint WHO/FAO Expert Consultation.* Geneva: WHO.

World Health Organisation (2014). *Global Status Report on Non-Communicable Diseases 2014.* Geneva: WHO.

World Health Organisation (2015). *World Health Statistics 2015.* Geneva: WHO.

9

Somatotype Components and Body Mass Index: A Case Study of the Adult Bhoi Males

— *Sudipta Ghosh and Thepuvekho Dawhuo*

Introduction

Body composition and/or physique are the product of continuous and complex interaction of biological or indigenous and environmental or exogenous factors. Biological factors influencing these characteristics, among other, are heredity or genetics, age and sex of an individual. Exogenous factors, on the other hand, include both environmental and socio-cultural factors, such as nutrition, altitude, climate, socio-economic status, religious practices, physical activity, cultural believes and mode of subsistence. Therefore, all the anthropometric traits related to body composition are the result of the influence of either genetic or environmental factors, or combinations of both (Susanne, 1975).

Somatotyping is an effective technique for the study of anthropometric variations and body composition in adult subjects (Buffa *et. al.*, 2005). Anthropometric somatotyping is basically the modified and developed version of Sheldon's technique but it has gained impetus since the last two decades following the introduction of a simplified method for somatotyping by Heath and Carter (Heath and Carter, 1967). Because of its uniqueness, it has been used for studying, among others population variation, age changes and sex differences. Anthropometric somatotyping has been applied in a variety of ways from measuring the effects of nutrition on physique to the description of many different groups and individuals including children, athletes and adults (Heath and Carter, 1967). The method of somatotyping is used as a means of assessing body shape and composition, independent of size (Bailey *et al.,* 1982).

In addition, anthropometry is the single most portable, easily applied, inexpensive and non-invasive method of assessing body composition, which reflects both health and nutrition (Ismail *et al.*, 1995). Anthropometric measurements like body mass index (BMI) have long been used by the anthropologists as one of the measures of health status, as it has proved to be a good estimator of body fatness. It is widely known that distribution of body fat is an important indicator of nutritional and health status.

Previous investigators suggested that adults' physique and body dimension are influenced by various factors, such as occupation (Singh and Singh, 2006; Heath and Carter, 1967), age (Gakhar and Malik, 2002; Bhasin and Jain, 2007), sex (Ghosh and Malik, 2007; Heath *et al.,* 1961; Prakash and Malik, 1989; Kalichman and Kobliansky, 2004), high altitude (Malik *et al.,* 1986; Singh *et al.,* 2007), nutrition (Malik *et al.,* 1986; Chakrabarty *et al.*, 2009), physical activity (Ghosh and Malik, 2010; Singh *et al.,* 2013), socio-economic differences (Singh and Singh, 2006; Singh, 2011), disease (Singh, 2007). However, such studies from North-east India are very few and far in between, especially on the adult somatotype characteristics.

Like the rest of the country, North-east India is also facing the double burden of under and over-nutrition. In other words, in countries like India, which are typically known for high prevalence of under-nutrition, significant proportions of overweight and obese individuals now coexist with the undernourished. Most of the earlier studies suggested the prevalence of under-nutrition among different social groups of Eastern and Northeastern India for generations, where tribal populations are the most vulnerable section (NFHS II, 1998-99; ICMR, 2010; Chakrabarty and Bharati, 2010; Ghosh and Bharati, 2006; Bisai and Bose, 2009; Ghosh and Malik, 2007;

Khongsdier, 2002, 2005). However, obesity and diabetes are also increasing in North-east India and even among tribal populations like the Tangkhul Naga (Mungreiphy, 2011) or Ao Naga (Longkumer, 2013). On the other hand, there is hardly any study from North-east India associating nutritional status with somatotype characteristics, especially among adult tribal populations.

Keeping these issues in mind, the present study aims to investigate the effects of age and socio-economic factors on somatotype characteristics and BMI for Bhoi males of Ri-Bhoi district of Meghalaya with special emphasis on the factors influencing these biological characteristics.

Materials and Methods

A cross-sectional sample of 250 adult Bhoi males was collected from nine localities of Umden area of Ri-Bhoi district, Meghalaya. The investigated cohort includes the Bhoi males, aged 18-60 years (mean 32.3 years). All the relevant variables for this study were derived from this sample.

Meghalaya, essentially is a tribal state, attained its statehood on the 21st of January 1972. Initially, it was part of Assam and had only two districts. Presently, there are seven districts, namely, Jaintia Hills, East Khasi Hills, West Khasi Hills, Ri-Bhoi, East Garo Hills, West Garo Hills and South Garo Hills. The people of Umden area earlier resided at Umsohklong Umtong, the old capital of Raid Nongtluh, which is now known as Nongbah. However due to a plague outbreak in the old capital, they left their old settlement and shifted to Umden, approximately 200 years ago. The people living in Umden belong to the Bhoi group of Khasi tribe and share the tribal status with the other Khasi sub-groups, like the Pnars, Wars and Lyngngams. Like all other Khasi sub-groups, the Bhois follow the matrilineal system of society.

Anthropometric somatotyping

In accordance with internationally accepted standards ten body measurements were taken on each subject (Tanner *et al.*, 1969; Heath and Carter, 1967; Martin and Saller, 1957). These were: (1) Height vertex; (2) Body weight, (3) Bicondylar humerus, (4) Bicondylar femur, (5) Mid upper arm circumference, (6) Calf circumference, (7) Skinfold at triceps, (8) Skinfold at subscapula, (9) Skinfold at suprailliac and (10) Skinfold at calf. Anthropometric measurements were taken following standardised protocols and all the measurements were taken on the right side of the subject, using anthropometric rod and sliding caliper. Circumferences were measured with the help of a steel tape. All the skinfold measurements were taken on the left side of the subject (Tanner *et al.*, 1969). Skinfold measurement in the present study was taken with the Holtain skinfold caliper in mm, with the dial marked in division of 0.2 mm.

Anthropometric somatotyping was calculated using Heath and Carter's method (1967, 1980). Three somatotype components, i.e., Endomorphy, Mesomorphy and Ectomorphy were plotted on somatocharts, after calculating 'X' and 'Y' values. Individual somatotypes of Bhoi males were classified into thirteen categories following Carter's classification (1980). A One-way Analysis of Variance (ANOVA) was computed to examine age differences in somatotype components and BMI.

BMI was calculated as body mass (kg)/stature (m^2). The World Health Organisation (WHO) regional office for Western Pacific Region along with the International Association for the Study of Obesity (IASO) and the International Task Force (IOTF) has recommended a BMI of 23.0 kg/m^2 as the cut-off point for defining overweight in Asian populations. This BMI classification was used in the present study (WHO, 2000). All the statistical computations were carried out using SPSS 15.0 and STATA 11.1 for Windows. Linear regression technique was used to assess the effect of various factors on somatotype characteristics and BMI for Bhoi males. Categorical or nominal variables like physical activity, economic status, smoking and drinking habits were incorporated into regression model by means of dummy variables.

Major Findings

Descriptive statistics of weight and other fat-mass or soft tissue related measurements like circumferential and skinfolds of adult Bhoi males suggest a trend of steady increment with advancing age, except height and other linear measurements like bicondylar humerus

(Table 9.1). As expected weight and fat-mass related measurements showed greater variations as compared to linear measurements, i.e., as evident from the standard deviations.

Table 9.1: Descriptive statistics (mean ± sd) of anthropometric and somatotype characteristics by age for the Bhoi males

	≥ 30 years (n = 134)	*31-40 years (n = 50)*	*≥ 41 years (n = 66)*	*All Males (n = 250)*	*F-ratio*
Height (cm)	162.82 ± 5.40	163.53± 6.43	163.94 ± 6.19	163.28 ± 5.87	0.693
Weight (kg)	57.35 ± 7.74	58.02 ± 7.70	61.59 ± 10.88	58.63 ± 8.82	5.2578
Bicondylar Humerus (cm)	6.50 ± 0.34	6.68 ± 0.51	6.80 ± 0.74	6.62 ± 0.53	7.092*
Bicondylar Femur (cm)	8.90 ± 0.65	9.03 ± 0.48	9.18 ± 0.66	9.01 ± 0.63	3.731*
Mid-upper arm circum. (cm)	25.85 ± 2.65	26.05 ± 2.02	26.60 ± 2.64	26.10 ± 2.52	1.952
Mid - calf circum. (cm)	33.60 ± 2.57	33.39 ± 2.71	34.57 ± 3.08	33.81 ± 2.78	3.468*
Skinfold at triceps (mm)	7.63 ±3.25	7.46 ± 3.13	8.57 ± 4.19	7.84 ± 3.51	2.067
Skinfold at subscapula (mm)	12.70 ± 4.89	13.32 ± 5.22	16.48 ± 7.80	13.84 ± 6.06	9.309*
Skinfold at suprailiac (mm)	9.15 ± 3.90	10.06 ± 4.69	10.59 ± 5.31	9.74 ± 4.52	2.347
Skinfold at calf (mm)	7.58 ± 3.43	6.40 ± 3.06	7.62 ± 4.73	7.31 ± 3.76	3.120*
BMI	21.64 ± 2.78	21.63 ± 1.98	22.84 ± 3.28	21.96 ± 2.80	2.651*
Endomorphy	2.97 ± 1.08	3.09 ± 1.10	3.52 ± 1.52	3.14 ± 1.23	2.467*
Mesomorphy	4.11 ± 0.98	4.26 ± 1.00	4.66 ± 1.15	4.29 ± 1.05	3.094*
Ectomorphy	2.53 ± 1.22	2.48 ± 0.90	2.11 ± 1.13	2.41 ± 1.14	2.319*

*Significant at 5 per cent.

In somatotype characteristics adult Bhoi males were predominantly mesomorphic. The common prevalence of mesomorphic component among the Bhoi males is also apparent from the somatochart (Figure 9.1). Moreover, this trend is noticeable across age groups (Table 9.1). One of the important factors behind this could be hard work, necessary for survival in harsh conditions. The Bhoi people use primitive technology for terrace cultivation in a hilly land that requires more physical labour than cultivation in plains land. As a consequence, these compel them to do a lot of hard work to sustain their livelihood that may result in muscular body physique.

Of the other two components of somatotype, endomorphy was more common than ectomorphy, especially after 30 years of age (Table 9.1). Variation, as evident from the standard deviation, indicates less variation in all the three somatotype components across

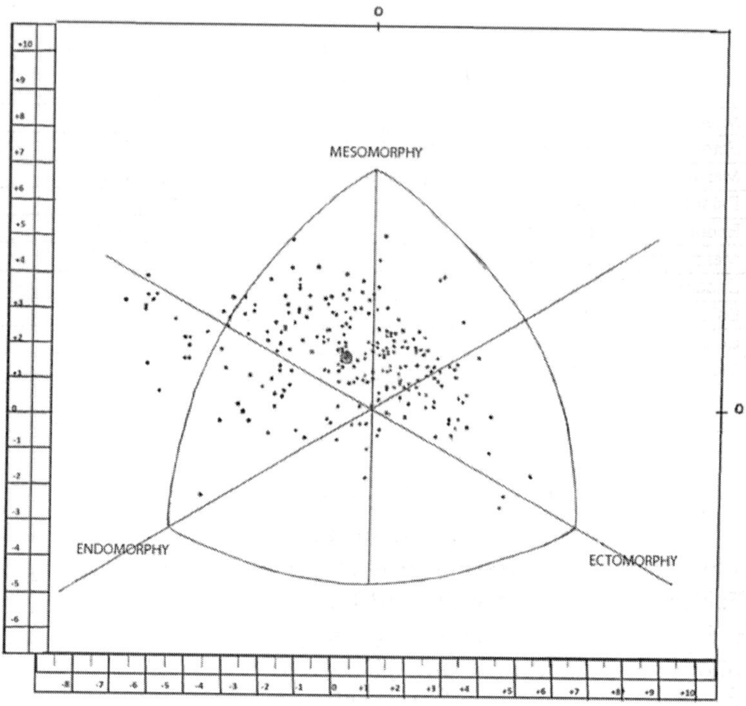

Figure 9.1: Somatochart of Bhoi males.

age groups. This homogeneity among the Bhoi males in their body physique suggests that they are by and large similar in physique. Considering that the Bhoi males have high mesomorphy but small range of variation in their somatotype components, it seems reasonable to infer that most of them are muscular, which perhaps is a prerequisite for surviving in harsh environmental conditions. Except for ectomorphic component, the other two somatotype components increased with advancement of age. This phenomenon is further confirmed by the ANOVA results, where age group differences were statistically significant in endomorphic and mesomorphic components but not in ectomorphic component (Table 9.1).

Table 9.2: Incidence of occurrence of the Bhoi males in 13 somatotype categories

Somatotype category	*Frequency*	*Percentage of occurrence*
Mesomorph-Ectomorph	26	10.40
Ectomorphic-Mesomorph	30	12.00
Mesomorphic-Ectomorph	11	4.+40
Balanced Mesomorph	46	18.40
Endomorphic-Mesomorph	70	28.00
Mesomorph-Endomorph	28	11.20
Endomorpic-Ectomorph	2	0.80
Balanced Ectomorph	6	2.40
Ectomorphic-Endomorph	0	0.00
Mesomorphic-Endomorph	18	7.20
Balanced Endomorph	4	1.60
Endomorph-Ectomorph	3	1.20
Central	6	2.40
Total	**250**	**100.00**

The distribution of various somatotype categories indicates a substantial concentration around mesomorphic components (Table 9.2). Ghosh and Malik (2010) reported that the occurrence of Endomorphic-Mesomorph among the Santhals were 28.0 per cent, followed by Balanced Mesomorph (18.4 per cent) and Ectomorphic-Mesomorph (12.0 per cent). A sizable number of them were either Mesomorph-Endomorph (11.2 per cent) or Mesomorph-Ectomorph (10.4 per cent). This suggests that in general the Bhoi males are either fatty-muscular or muscular or linear-muscular in their physique.

Nutritional status, as evaluated from body mass index (BMI), suggests that the Bhoi males are generally normal in body weight (21.96±2.80) in their BMI with similar trend across the age groups (Table 9.1). A marginal increment in BMI is, however, observed with advancing age, which is in accordance with their gain in body weight, especially after 40 years of age. The one-way analysis of variance (ANOVA) further revealed that these age group differences in BMI were statistically significant at 5 per cent probability level (Table 9.1). The BMI classification further confirmed that the majority (67.2 per cent) of the Bhoi males were under the BMI category of normal weight (Table 9.3). A similar trend was also observed across age groups. About 4.8 per cent of men were underweight in this population. On the other hand, the prevalence of overweight was fairly high (28.0 per cent). This trend was more apparent after 40 years of age (39.4 per cent).

The relations between somatotype components and nutritional status are presented in Table 9.4. It is observed that endomorphic and mesomorphic components increased gradually with increasing BMI level. On the other hand, ectomorphic component decreased with the increase in BMI level. The association between somatotype characteristics and BMI was statistically significant at one per cent probability level for all the three somatotype components.

It is perhaps interesting to note here that the overweight Bhoi males showed a greater mesomorphic component over endomorphic component. This is in contradiction to the general expectation that overweight and obese people would have endomorphic component dominating over the other two somatotype components. This observation suggests that, on average, the Bhoi males possessed a higher muscle mass and less fat mass. As a result, when they show high BMI due to the possession of low fat-mass but not fat-free mass. This could happen because BMI contains both fat-mass and fat-free mass (Durnin and Womersley, 1974).

The selection of predictor variables for linear regression model was based on the result of univariate analysis calculated on each predictor variable for all the three somatotype components and BMI. Parameters used in regression model are those which have shown significant relation with the dependant variables in univariate analysis (Table 9.5). The specification of the linear regression model in this paper includes age.[2] Through this variable we observed the effect on change in the somatotype components and BMI due to change in age.

In the present study, age was significantly associated with both endomorphic and ectomorphic somatotype components but not with mesomorphic component. With advancement in age, endomorphy increased and ectomorphy decreased as evident from the positive and negative β co-efficients respectively. These two somatotype components were significantly influenced by smoking habits and alcohol intake. It is observed in the regression model that smokers in this population were notably more ectomorphic and less endomorphic as compared to their non-smoker counterparts, which was statistically significant at one per cent probability level. Alcoholics, on the other hand, were considerably more endomorphic and less ectomorphic in their physique as compared to those who had never consumed alcohol.

Physical activity in the present study was based on primary occupation, in which the Bhoi males engaged in occupations like teaching or business were categorised as 'Moderate activity' and those engaged in occupations like labour work or cultivation as 'Vigorous activity,' following WHO STEPS Surveillance (WHO, 2008). Physical activity is found to play a crucial role in influencing on endomorphic component among the Bhoi males. It is observed that the Bhoi males with vigorous physical activity had a significantly lower endomorphy than those with moderate physical activity ($\beta = -0.662$, $p < 0.001$). Income status, on the other hand, was associated with mesomorphic component, but not with the other two somatotype components. The regression analysis suggests that males from higher income group (HIG) were significantly more mesomorphic than their counterparts from lower income group (LIG). This could be due to the fact that person belonging to HIG can afford to have a regular protein intake, which helps in building muscle mass in body, than those belonging to LIG.

BMI in this population is found to be notably influenced by age, physical activity and smoking-drinking habits, which is statistically significant at five per cent probability level (Table 9.5). It is evident that among the Bhoi males BMI increases gradually with advancing age. However, during old ages they have a tendency to develop comparatively low BMI as compared to the younger age groups. In accordance with endomorphic component of body physique, BMI was significantly higher among the Bhoi males with 'moderate physical activity' as compared to their counterparts with 'vigorous physical activity' in their day-to-day life ($\beta = -0.924$, $p < 0.04$). Smokers had considerably lower BMI than non-smokers in this population, which was statistically significant at five per cent probability level. On the other hand, males consuming alcohol on regular basis had significantly greater chance of developing higher BMI as compared to those who never consumed alcohol (Table 9.5).

Table 9.3: Nutritional status among the Bhoi males by age groups

Nutritional status	*Age groups (years)*							
	≤ 30 (n = 134)		*31-40 (n = 50)*		*≥ 41 (n = 66)*		*Total (n = 250)*	
	N	*Per cent*	*N*	*Per cent*	*N*	*Per cent*	*N*	*Per cent*
Underweight								
Normal weight	8	6.0	0	0.0	4	6.1	12	4.8
Overweight	93	69.4	39	78.8	36	54.5	168	67.2
	33	24.6	11	22.0	26	39.4	70	28.0

Table 9.4: Mean and standard deviation of somatotype characteristics according to nutritional status

Nutritional status	*Endomorphy*	*Mesomorphy*	*Ectomorphy*
Underweight (12)	2.04 ± 0.30	3.05 ± 1.53	4.80 ± 0.82
Normal weight (168)	2.75 ± 0.89	4.11 ± 0.85	2.80 ± 0.66
Overweight (70)	4.28 ± 1.30	4.94 ± 1.05	1.06 ± 0.54
F-ratio	65.129, $p < 0.001$	29.602, $p < 0.001$	271.282, $p < 0.001$

Number of subjects in each category is given in parenthesis.

Table 9.5: Results of linear regression: effects of factors on somatotype characteristics and BMI for Bhoi males

Dependent Variables	*Parameters*	*β Co-efficients*	*t-value*	*p-level*
	Age	0.134	3.39	0.001
	Age2	-0.001	2.63	0.009
	Level of	0.094	1.14	0.256
Endomorphy	education	-0.662	3.70	0.000
	Physical activity	0.245	1.42	0.158
	Income level	-0.525	2.72	0.007
	Smoking habit	0.341	2.08	0.039
	Drinking habit	0.756	1.11	0.270
	Constant			
	Age	0.041	1.06	0.291
	Age2	-0.000	0.56	0.576
	Level of	-0.060	0.86	0.393
Mesomorphy	education	0.099	0.61	0.545
	Physical activity	0.323	2.02	0.045
	Income level	-0.240	1.47	0.143
	Smoking habit	0.191	1.29	0.198
	Drinking habit	3.327	5.25	0.000
	Constant			

(Contd...)

Ectomorphy	Age Age2 Level of education Physical activity Income level Smoking habit Drinking habit Constant	-0.127 0.001 0.045 0.296 -0.191 0.616 -0.326 4.363	3.21 2.75 0.57 1.62 1.05 3.41 2.00 6.32	0.002 0.006 0.568 0.107 0.295 0.001 0.046 0.000
BMI	Age Age2 Level of education Physical activity Income level Smoking habit Drinking habit Constant	0.245 -0.002 0.065 -0.924 0.329 -1.548 1.073 17.870	2.65 2.11 0.33 2.08 0.74 3.07 2.59 10.72	0.008 0.036 0.742 0.039 0.463 0.002 0.010 0.000

Discussion

The Bhoi males are, on an average, mesomorphic in their physique. Such characteristics of muscular and strong built might be due to the vigorous physical labour required for sustaining their livelihood. The subsistence pattern of the Bhois demands a lot of muscular activity in their day-to-day life. The Bhoi Khasis live in hilly terrain and practice terrace cultivation, as a majority of them are cultivators or agricultural labourers. As a consequence, they have developed strong muscle mass as evident from the predominance of mesomorphic component over the other two components in somatotype. Similar kind of physique is also observed among the Santhals (Ghosh and Malik, 2010). However, we need more studies from other Khasi populations, like War and Pnar, to have a holistic idea about the physique of the Khasi tribe.

As regards the nutritional status, the Bhoi males were 'normal' in their BMI across age groups, unlike the War Khasi who had lower BMI values (Khongsdier, 2002, 2005). The greater BMI among the present population, however, is due to greater muscle mass or fat-free mass and low fat-mass. This phenomenon is further confirmed by the predominance of mesomorphic component over the other two somatotype components in their physique. In addition, the association between BMI and somatotype components further indicates the same.

Socio-economic determinants of physique and nutritional status suggests that apart from age and physical activity, smoking and drinking habits play crucial roles in defining the body dimensions of the adult Bhoi males. However, mesomorphic component of somatotype is not influenced by any of the above mentioned exogenous factors. This could be due to the fact that mesomorphy has a greater degree of hereditary and genetic component than the other two somatotype components and thereby less influenced by environmental factors. This observation is consistent with almost all the previous investigations in this aspect (Sanchez-Andres, 1995; Peters *et al.,* 2003; Katzmarzyk *et al.,* 2000).

Succinctly, adult Bhoi males are strong and muscular built, which is their significant adaptive mechanism to cope up with the harsh environment that they live in. It is observed that socio-economic factors significantly influence both endomorphic and ectomorphic components but not with mesomorphic component. Age, physical activity and smoking-drinking habits play important roles in determining the nutritional status of the adult Bhoi males.

References

Bailey, D.A., J.E.L. Carter and R.L. Mirwald (1982). Somatotypes of Canadian men and women. *Human Biology*, 54(4): 813-828.

Bhasin, M. K. and S. Jain (2007). Biology of the tribal groups of Rajasthan, India: 4. Age changes in Somatotype. *Anthropologist*, 9(4): 257-265.

Bisai, S. and K. Bose (2009). Under-nutrition in the Kora Mudi tribal population, West Bengal, India: A comparison of body mass index and mid-upper-arm circumference. *Food and Nutrition Bulletin*, 30(1): 63-67.

Buffa, R., V. Succa, D. Garau, E. Marini and G. Floris (2005). Variations of somatotype in elderly Sardinians. *American Journal of Human Biology*, 17(4): 403-411.

Carter, J.E.L. (1980). *The Heath and Carter Somatotype Method*, 3rd edition. San Diego: State University Syllabus Service.

Chakrabarty, S. and P. Bharati (2010). Adult body dimension and determinants of chronic energy deficiency among the Shabar tribe living in urban, rural and forest habitats in Odisha, India. *Annals of Human Bioliolgy*, 37(2): 149-167.

Chakraborty, R., K. Bose and S. Bisai (2009). Relationship of family income and house type to body mass index and chronic energy deficiency among urban Bengalee male slum dwellers of Kolkata, India. *Journal of Comparative Human Biology*, 60: 45-57.

Durnin, J.V.G.A and J. Womersley (1974). Body fat assessed from total body density and its estimation from skinfold thickness measurements of 481 men and women aged from 16-72 years. *British Journal of Nutrition*, 32: 77-97.

Gakhar, I. and S.L. Malik (2002). Age changes and sex differences in somatotypes among Jats of Delhi. *Anthropologist* (Special Issue), 1: 115-125.

Ghosh, R. and P. Bharati (2006). Women's status and health of two ethnic groups inhabiting a periurban Habitat of Kolkata City, India: A Micro-Level Study. *Health Care for Women International*, 26: 194-211.

Ghosh, S. and S.L. Malik (2007). Parent-offspring correlation in body measurements, physique and physiological variables among Santhals of West Bengal. *Journal Exercise Science Physiotherapy*, 3(1): 26-43.

Ghosh, S. and S.L. Malik (2010). Variations of body physique in Santhals: An Indian Tribe. *Collegium Antropologicum*, 34 (2): 467-472.

Heath, B.H. and J.E.L. Carter (1967). A modified somatotype method. *American Journal of Physical Anthropology*, 27: 57-74.

Heath, B.H., C.E. Hopkins and C.D. Miller (1961). Physiques of Hawaii-born young men and women of Japanese ancestry, compared with college men and women of the United States and England. *American Journal of Physical Anthropology*, 19: 173-184.

Indian Council of Medical Research (ICMR, 2010). Nutrient Requirements and Recommended Dietary Allowances for Indians. New Delhi: Indian council of Medical Research.

Ismail, M.N., H. Zawiah, S.S. Chee and K.K. Ng (1995). Prevalence of obesity and chronic energy deficiency (CED) in adult Malaysians. *Malaysian Journal of Nutrition*, 1: 1-9.

Kalichman, L., G. Livshits and E. Kobyliansky (2004). Association between somatotypes and blood pressure in an adult Chuvasha population. *Annals of Human Biology*, 31(4): 466-476.

Katzmarzyk, P.T., R.M. Malina, L. Perusse, T. Rice, M.A. Province, D.C. Rao and C. Bouchard (2000). Familial resemblance for physique: Heritabilities for somatotype components. *Annals of Human Biology*, 27(5): 467-477.

Khongsdier, R. (2002). Body mass index and morbidity in adult males of the War Khasi in North-east India. *European Journal of Clinical Nutrition*, 56: 484-489.

Khongsdier, R. (2005). BMI and morbidity in relation to body composition: A cross-sectional study of a rural community in North-East India. *British Journal Nutrition*, 93:101-107.

Longkumer, T. (2013). Physical activity and somatotypes among Ao Naga Boys. *Anthropologist*, 17(2): 669-675.

Malik, S.L., O.G. Eiben, M. Parkash and M. Mittal (1986). Impact of high altitude on body shape. *Anthropologiai Kozlemenyek*, 30: 203-208.

Martin, R. and K. Saller (1957). *Lehrbuch der Anthropooigie*. Stuttgart: Gustav Fischer Verlag.

Mungreiphy, N. K., S. Kapoor and R. Sinha (2011). Association between BMI, Blood Pressure and Age: Study among Tangkhul Naga tribal males of North-east India. *Journal of Anthropology, Article ID 748147*. http://dx.doi.org/10.1155/2011/748147.

National Family Health Survey (NFHS-II, 1999). *National Family Health Survey* (NFHS-II). Mumbai: International Institute for Population Science.

Parkash, M. and Malik, S.L. (1989). Anthropometric somatotypes among Santhals of district Midnapur, West Bengal. In: S.C. Tiwari (Ed.), *Changing Perspectives of Anthropology in India*, pp. 237-255. New Delhi: Today and Tomorrow's Printers and Publishers.

Peters, M.W., M.A.Thomis, A.L. Claessens, R.J. Loos, H.H. Maes, R. Lysens, Eynde, B. Vanden, R. Vlietinck and G. Beunen (2003). Heritability of somatotype components from early adolescence into young adulthood: A multivariate analysis on a longitudinal twin study. *Annals of Human Biology*, 30(4): 402-418.

Sanchez-Andres, A. (1995). Genetic and environmental influences on somatotype components: Family study in a Spanish population. *Human Biology*, 67: 727-738.

Singh, A. P. and S.P. Singh (2006). Somatotypic variations: An analysis of some traditional occupations. *Journal of Human Ecology*, 19(4): 249-25.

Singh, A., S.P. Singh and J. Sekhon (2013). Occupational impact on body physique and health status: An Anthropometric Analysis of carpenters. *Human Biology Review*, 2(1): 12-23.

Singh, L. D. (2011). Somatotype of the affluent and non-affluent Meitei boys of Manipur, India. *Anthropologist*, 13(1):9-16.

Singh, S. P. (2007). Somatotype and disease. *Anthropologist*, 3: 251-261.

Singh, S. P., S. Pritpal, P. Malhotra and L.S. Sidhu (2007). Somatotypes of high altitude Spitian boys. *Journal of Human Ecology*, 22(2): 129-133.

Susanne, C. (1975). Genetic and environmental influences on morphological characteristics. *Annals of Human Biology*, 2(3): 279-287.

Tanner, J.M., J. Hiernaux and S. Jarnan (1969). Growth and physique studies. In: J.S.Weiner and J.A.Lourie (Eds.), *Human Biology- A Guide to Field Methods,* pp. 315-340. Oxford: Blackwell Scientific Publication.

WHO (2008). Stepwise approach to surveillance (STEPS): Typical Physical Activities. The STEPS Instrument, Section 3. http://www.who.int/chp/steps/en/. Visited on 4.4.2016.

WHO/IASO/IOTF (2000). *The Asia-Pacific Perspective: Redefining Obesity and Its Treatment*. Melbourne: Health Communications Australia.

10

Growth Study among the Ahom Children of Upper Assam

— *Dali Dutta and Sarthak Sengupta*

Introduction

Growth is a natural process and the common property of life and dynamic system including somatic, biological, psychological and social process of individuals with continuous interaction and adaptations to the environment. Growth is a progressive increase in volume, weight and a number of other measurable attributes. It is not just an increase in proportion to age. It is a harmonious development of all the organs. The growth differentiation and development of the body structure begins with the formation of the zygote and the processes continue until the stage of full adult maturity is reached. Growth starts at the womb of the mother and ends at the tomb.

Growth studies help to understand the relationship between man and environment. It reveals certain important fundamental biological facts that reflect the image of health and nutritional status of a particular group of children living in a particular region.

The present study is a modest attempt to assess the growth status in terms of anthropometric characters of Ahom boys and girls of 6 to 20 years of age inhabiting in the rural areas of upper Assam.

The Ahoms are one of the numerically dominant major Mongoloid populations of upper Assam. They belong to the Tai family and came to Assam from Myanmar through Patkai range in 1228 A.D. Linguistically the Ahoms belong to the Siamese Chinese branch of the Sino Tibetan language family.

Material and Methods

In the present study, cross-sectional anthropometric data of 1741 children (842 boys and 899 girls) aged 6 to 20 years of Ahom children of Upper Assam were collected. Ages of the children were collected on the basis of school records and cross-checked by their parents. Six anthropometric measurements are used for the present study. These are height, body weight, head circumference, mid upper arm circumference and skin fold measurement at biceps and triceps. All anthropometric measurements were taken following standard anthropometric techniques as proposed by Martin and Saller (1957), Weiner and Lourie (1981) and Lohman *et al.* (1988). The skin-fold measurement was observed using a Holtain skin-fold calliper calibrated to exert a constant pressure of 10 g/mm^2 on the left side of each subject to the nearest 0.20 mm.

The data were compared with International Standards of References, i.e., the growth references of the U.S. National Centre for Health Statistics (NCHS, 2000; Kuczmarski *et al.,* 2000), Indian Standards of References (ICMR, 1972) and available data from various population groups of North-east India (Choudhury, 1979; Devi, 1985; Khongsdier, 1995; Government of India, 1998; Singh and Singh, 2000; Mukherjee, 2002; Tsopo, 2003; Singh, 2008).

Results and Discussion

Table 10.1 shows the mean values of stature of Ahom boys and girls according to age groups with standard deviation and other relevant statistical derivatives. The mean values show a gradual increase from 6 to 20 years of age in both Ahom boys and girls. The differences between the mean values at each age group with regard to stature, however, suggest that the increments are not uniform over the entire period.

The Ahom boys are taller than the Ahom girls at the age group of 6 to 9, 11 years and 13 years onwards, whereas the latter are taller than the former from 10 to 12 years of age. The bisexual differences

Table 10.1: Statistical constants of stature

Age (in Years)	*Boys*					*Girls*					*t-value*
	N	*Mean*	*S.D*	*Absolute Growth*	*Growth Gradient*	*N*	*Mean*	*S.D*	*Absolute Growth*	*Growth Gradient*	
6	67	109.68	5.01	-	65.42	57	107.28	5.50	-	68.72	2.53*
7	53	119.66	6.20	10.00	71.37	60	117.96	5.60	10.68	75.56	1.53
8	54	123.26	5.64	3.60	73.52	54	121.83	5.37	3.87	78.04	1.35
9	55	129.30	5.96	6.04	77..12	64	128.70	5.92	6.87	82.44	0.55
10	53	131.49	5.96	2.19	78.43	69	131.72	5.71	3.02	84.38	0.21
11	54	137.71	5.19	6.22	82.14	65	139.72	8.16	8.00	89.50	1.63
12	59	144.14	8.35	6.43	85.98	70	144.36	6.15	4.64	92.47	0.17
13	53	148.73	8.30	4.59	88.71	56	147.77	6.36	3.41	94.66	0.68
14	55	156.43	9.79	7.70	93.31	51	151.29	4.14	3.52	96..91	3.57*
15	60	163.65	8.16	7.22	97.61	63	152.32	5.65	1.03	97.57	8.99*
16	61	164.18	5.45	0.53	97.93	59	154.05	5.11	1.73	98.68	10.44*
17	57	165.97	6.27	1.79	98.99	61	154.68	4.67	0.63	99.08	11.07*
18	58	166.74	5.62	0.77	99.46	62	154.74	5.27	0.06	99.12	12.00*
19	51	166.97	5.67	0.20	99.58	53	155.31	7.48	0.57	99.49	8.95*
20	52	167.65	5.88	0.71	100.00	55	156.11	4.97	0.80	100.00	10.89*

*indicates probability level < 0.05.

with regard to stature are found to be statistically significant at 6 and 14 to 20 years of age. It is observed that the maximum increase in height occurs between 13 and 14 years for boys (7.70 cm) and 10 and 11 years for girls (8.00 cm). Thus, the adolescent growth spurt with regard to stature occurs earlier in girls (11 years) than in boys (14 years).

As for weight, the means with standard deviation and other statistical constants for both Ahom boys and girls against their age groups are shown in Table 10.2. It is observed that the Ahom girls are slightly heavier than the boys at 10, 11, 13 and 14 years of age whereas at 6 to 9 and from 15 to 20 years of age boys are relatively heavier than the girls. The t-test of significance indicates that the Ahom girls are having higher mean values of weight and significantly apart from that of the boys at 13 years of age, while the boys are significantly heavier than girls at 6, 11, 12 and 15 to 20 years of age (Table 10.2). The rate of growth per year in Ahom girls is greater than the boys at 7 to 11, 13, 16 and 18 years. At age groups 8 and 12 to 20 years, the rate of growth of Ahom boys surpasses the girls. The adolescent growth spurt in weight took place earlier in girls than in boys. The values of growth gradients indicate that the girls attain maturity level earlier than boys do from 6 to 18 and 20 years while the boys attain maturity level earlier than the girls only at 19 years of age.

The statistical constants of the head circumference for both Ahom boys and girls are given in Table 10.3. It is observed that the head circumference of the Ahom boys is larger than girls from 6 to 10 years of age and again from 15 to 20 years of age, while the girls surpass the boys at 11 to 14 years of age. However, the t-values as detailed in Table 10.3 shows that the differences between the sexes are significant at 7, 13 and 17 to 20 years of age. The highest increment for girls is 1.39 cm at the age of 11 years and that of boys is 1.09 cm at 15 years. The values of growth gradients show that the Ahom girls attain the maturity level at 20 years slightly faster than the boys.

Table 10.2: Statistical constants of weight

Age (in Years)	*Boys*					*Girls*					*t-value*
	N	*Mean*	*S.D*	*Absolute Growth*	*Growth Gradient*	*N*	*Mean*	*S.D*	*Absolute Growth*	*Growth Gradient*	
6	67	17.05	2.18	-	28.61	57	15.91	2.16	-	32.57	2.92*
7	53	20.33	3.32	3.28	34.11	60	19.98	3.06	4.07	40.90	0.58
8	54	21.42	2.99	1.09	35.94	54	20.53	2.44	0.55	42.03	1.68
9	55	24.73	4.31	3.31	41.49	64	24.20	3.39	3.67	49.54	0.74
10	53	25.74	3.82	1.01	43.19	69	25.93	3.87	1.73	53.08	0.27
11	54	28.51	3.17	2.77	47.84	65	31.58	6.21	5.65	64.65	3.49*
12	59	32.63	6.00	4.12	54.75	70	34.66	5.13	3.08	70.95	2.05*
13	53	36.18	7.79	3.55	60.70	56	38.92	6.18	4.26	79.67	2.03*
14	55	41.78	8.10	5.60	70.10	51	42.49	4.92	3.57	86.98	0.55
15	60	49.20	8.59	7.42	82.55	63	44.27	6.96	1.78	90.61	3.50*
16	61	50.11	5.57	0.91	84.08	59	45.98	4.01	1.71	94.12	5.36*
17	57	55.08	6.56	4.97	92.42	61	46.02	5.03	0.04	94.21	8.39*
18	58	55.67	7.21	0.59	93.41	62	46.84	5.98	0.82	95.88	7.24*
19	51	58.02	6.75	2.35	97.35	53	47.12	6.78	0.28	96.46	8.20*
20	52	59.60	7.09	1.58	100.00	55	48.85	7.53	1.73	100.00	7.62*

*indicates probability level < 0.05.

Table 10.3: Statistical constants of head circumference

Age (in Years)	*Boys*					*Girls*					*t-value*
	N	*Mean*	*S.D*	*Absolute Growth*	*Growth Gradient*	*N*	*Mean*	*S.D*	*Absolute Growth*	*Growth Gradient*	
6	67	49.07	4.73	-	85.55	57	48.92	4.13	-	87.14	0.19
7	53	51.60	1.37	2.53	89.96	60	50.75	2.54	1.83	90.40	2.18*
8	54	51.64	3.69	0.04	90.03	54	50.80	3.78	0.05	90.49	1.18
9	55	52.52	1.88	0.88	91.56	64	52.35	1.59	1.55	93.25	0.53
10	53	52.95	1.35	0.43	92.31	69	52.42	3.20	0.07	93.37	1.20
11	54	53.46	1.42	0.51	93.20	65	53.81	1.60	1.39	95.85	1.25
12	59	53.62	1.59	0.16	93.48	70	53.98	1.49	0.17	96.15	1.38
13	53	54.04	1.77	0.42	94.21	56	54.76	1.86	0.78	97.54	2.06*
14	55	54.66	1.73	0.62	95.29	51	54.82	1.39	0.06	97.65	0.57
15	60	55.75	1.92	1.09	97.19	63	55.49	1.50	0.67	98.84	0.81
16	61	55.84	1.35	0.09	97.35	59	55.55	1.40	0.06	98.95	1.21
17	57	56.43	1.40	0.59	98.38	61	55.74	1.89	0.19	99.29	2.16*
18	58	56.73	1.35	0.30	98.90	62	56.01	1.58	1.19	99.77	2.77*
19	51	56.95	1.57	0.22	99.28	53	56.09	1.66	0.08	99.91	2.69*
20	52	57.36	1.46	0.41	100.00	55	56.14	3.12	0.05	100.00	2.60*

* indicates probability level < 0.05.

The statistical constants of the mid-upper arm circumference of both Ahom boys and girls are shown in the Table 10.4. It is observed that the mid-upper arm circumference is greater in girls than in boys from 11 to 16 years of age. Although the growth pattern is more or less similar at the age group of 6 to 10 years while in the rest of the ages the boys' mid-upper arm circumference is relatively more. The maximum increment occurs at 11 years for Ahom girls and in the case of boys it takes place at 14 years of age. The growth gradients show that the Ahom girls reached the maturity level earlier than that of the boys.

Table 10.5 shows the statistical constants of skin fold thickness at biceps. The mean values show that the girls exhibit a greater skin fold thickness at biceps throughout all the ages. The t-test of significance indicates that the Ahom girls are having statistically significant higher mean values than the boys at 8, 11 to 15, 17 and 18 years of age. At 8 and 20 years, both the sexes have almost similar skin fold thickness at biceps. It is also observed that at 7, 10 and 15 years the fat accumulation at biceps among boys decelerated, whereas in girls it accelerated at 7, 14 and 16 years. The growth gradients show that the girls attain maturity level earlier than their male counterparts.

The statistical constants of the skin fold thickness at triceps for both Ahom boys and girls are shown in Table 10.6. It is observed from the table that in the age groups 6 and 9 years both the sexes have almost similar mean values of fat accumulation at triceps while in the rest of the age groups the fat accumulation at triceps in girls are more. In the age groups 7, 8 and from 10 to 16, 18 and 20 years, girls are statistically significantly different from boys in this regard. The increment rate is higher in girls than in boys at several age groups and these are 8, 10, 12, 13, 15 and 19 years. The boys have higher acceleration rate at 9, 11, 14, 16, 17 and 20 years of age. Growth deceleration occurs in case of boys at ages 7 and 10 and on the other hand in the case of girls deceleration takes place only at 7 years.

Ahom boys have higher growth gradients in the early ages *i.e.* 6 and 9 years. Both the sexes have similar growth gradients at 10 and 11 years and in the later ages the girls have higher growth gradients than the boys.

Table 10.4: Statistical constants of mid-upper arm circumference

Age (in Years)	Boys					Girls					t-value
	N	Mean	S.D	Absolute Growth	Growth Gradient	N	Mean	S.D	Absolute Growth	Growth Gradient	
6	67	16.83	1.70	-	62.38	57	16.55	1.24	-	64.75	1.08
7	53	17.71	4.28	0.88	65.64	60	17.40	1.54	0.85	68.08	0.50
8	54	17.82	1.28	0.11	66.05	54	18.08	3.29	0.68	70.74	0.54
9	55	18.02	1.68	0.20	66.79	64	18.29	1.42	0.21	71.56	0.96
10	53	18.22	1.28	0.20	67.53	69	18.46	1.41	0.17	72.22	1.00
11	54	18.96	1.24	0.74	70.27	65	19.77	1.87	1.31	77.35	2.89*
12	59	19.62	1.65	0.66	72.72	70	20.58	1.44	0.81	80.52	3.69*
13	53	20.22	2.31	0.60	74.94	56	21.77	2.08	1.19	85.17	3.69*
14	55	21.90	2.22	1.68	81.17	51	22.70	2.03	0.93	88.81	1.95
15	60	23.43	2.00	1.53	86.84	63	23.18	1.86	0.48	90.69	0.69
16	61	23.69	2.01	0.26	87.81	59	24.40	1.64	1.22	95.46	2.03*
17	57	24.83	2.22	1.14	92.03	61	24.54	2.09	0.14	96.01	0.74
18	58	25.46	2.38	0.63	94.37	62	25.02	2.34	0.48	97.89	1.00
19	51	26.06	3.05	0.60	96.59	53	25.30	2.52	0.28	98.98	1.38
20	52	26.98	2.83	0.92	100.00	55	25.56	2.65	0.26	100.00	2.68*

* indicates probability level < 0.05.

Table 10.5: Statistical constants of skin fold thickness at biceps

Age (in years)	*Boys*					*Girls*					*t value*
	N	*Mean*	*S.D*	*Absolute growth*	*Growth gradients*	*N*	*Mean*	*S.D*	*Absolute growth*	*Growth gradients*	
6	67	3.47	0.85	-	69.68	57	3.58	0.86	-	70.20	0.74
7	53	2.89	0.72	-0.58	58.03	60	3.34	0.84	-0.13	65.49	1.03
8	54	3.00	0.70	0.11	60.24	54	3.47	1.08	0.13	68.04	2.58*
9	55	3.36	0.69	0.36	67.47	64	3.48	0.95	0.01	68.24	0.81
10	53	3.32	0.70	-0.04	66.67	69	3.61	1.01	0.13	70.78	1.87
11	54	3.35	0.71	0.03	67.27	65	3.87	1.09	0.26	75.88	3.02*
12	59	3.43	0.87	0.08	68.88	70	4.05	1.09	0.18	79.41	3.65*
13	53	3.58	0.95	0.15	71.89	56	4.59	1.06	0.54	90.00	5.26*
14	55	3.74	0.88	0.16	75.10	51	4.50	0.99	-0.09	88.24	4.13*
15	60	3.70	1.05	-0.04	74.30	63	4.73	1.14	0.23	92.75	6.17*
16	61	3.80	1.50	0.10	76.30	59	4.00	1.00	-0.73	78.43	0.87
17	57	4.00	1.60	0.20	80.32	61	4.84	1.20	0.84	94.90	3.26*
18	58	4.20	1.80	0.20	84.34	62	4.92	1.80	0.08	96.47	2.17*
19	51	4.90	1.88	0.70	98.39	53	5.02	2.20	0.10	98.43	0.30
20	52	4.98	1.98	0.08	100.00	55	5.10	2.60	0.08	100.00	0.27

* indicates probability level < 0.05.

Table 10.6: Statistical constants of skin fold thickness at triceps

Age (in years)	*Boys*					*Girls*					*t value*
	N	*Mean*	*S.D*	*Absolute growth*	*Growth gradients*	*N*	*Mean*	*S.D*	*Absolute growth*	*Growth gradients*	
6	67	5.34	1.41	-	76.29	57	5.29	1.19	-	64.12	0.21
7	53	4.25	1.13	-1.09	60.71	60	4.76	1.31	-0.53	57.70	2.17*
8	54	4.27	0.98	0.02	61.00	54	4.85	1.40	0.09	58.79	2.52*
9	55	4.87	1.33	0.60	69.57	64	4.94	1.47	0.09	59.88	0.28
10	53	4.40	0.95	-0.47	62.86	69	5.18	1.37	0.24	62.79	3.77*
11	54	4.60	1.36	0.20	65.71	65	5.33	1.49	0.15	64.61	2.87*
12	59	4.89	1.39	0.29	69.86	70	6.09	1.67	0.76	73.82	4.48*
13	53	5.13	1.56	0.24	73.29	56	6.45	1.75	0.36	78.18	4.24*
14	55	5.24	1.23	0.11	74.86	51	6.47	1.83	0.02	78.42	3.95*
15	60	5.25	1.63	0.01	75.00	63	6.77	1.78	0.30	82.06	5.02*
16	61	5.60	1.80	0.35	80.00	59	7.00	2.30	0.23	84.85	3.70*
17	57	6.20	2.00	0.60	88.57	61	7.50	2.01-	0.50	90.91	1.51
18	58	6.28	1.98	0.08	89.71	62	7.58	2.58	0.08	91.88	3.10*
19	51	6.50	2.20	0.22	92.86	53	8.00	2.87	0.42	96.97	1.42
20	52	7.00	2.28	0.50	100.00	55	8.25	3.00	0.25	100.00	2.44*

* indicates probability level < 0.05.

Comparisons of Growth Pattern

The mean value of height of the Ahom boys at the age of 6 years is 109.68 cm, which increases to 167.65 cm, at the age of 20 years. When Ahom boys are compared with the pooled data of Assamese, Indian and NCHS references it is seen that the Ahom boys are taller than the Indian boys reported by ICMR, Assamese pooled data and in most of the ages of 10th percentile of NCHS references but shorter than 25th and 50th percentile of NCHS references at all ages (Table 10.7).

Table 10.7: Comparisons of stature of Ahom boys with NCHS, Indian and Assamese references

Age (in Years)	*NCHS 10th*	*NCHS 25th*	*NCHS 50th*	*Indian (ICMR)*	*Assam (pooled)*	*Present Study*
6	108.66	111.73	115.12	107.40	109.00	109.68
7	114.64	117.88	121.51	113.20	115.10	119.66
8	120.37	123.78	127.63	118.60	120.80	123.26
9	125.54	129.18	133.29	123.00	125.70	129.30
10	130.11	134.01	138.41	128.10	130.70	131.49
11	134.48	138.62	143.31	132.40	134.50	137.71
12	139.45	143.83	148.79	137.40	139.40	144.14
13	145.79	150.49	155.76	143.50	144.60	148.73
14	153.03	158.05	163.53	148.30	149.20	156.43
15	159.32	164.35	169.74	153.10	152.20	163.65
16	163.46	168.25	173.40	157.50	155.20	164.18
17	165.72	170.28	175.24	160.40	156.60	165.97
18	166.84	171.27	176.13	162.00	158.20	166.74
19	167.39	171.76	176.59	162.40	160.10	166.94
20	167.65	172.01	176.81	162.90		167.65

The comparison of stature of Ahom boys with other population groups of North-east India shows that the Ahom boys are taller than the Khynriam Khasi, War Khasi and Lotha Naga boys of North-east India. The Rabha and Sonowal Kachari boys have a higher mean value particularly at 11, 13 and 14 years of age in respect of stature.

The Rabha boys exceeds in stature at the age group of 6 years also (Table 10.8).

Table 10.8: Comparisons of stature of Ahom boys with other population groups of North-east India

Age (in years)	*Meitei*	*Khynrim Khasi*	*War Khasi*	*Lotha Naga*	*Rabha*	*Sonowal Kachari*	*Present Study*
6		103.21	107.98		110.15	106.66	109.68
7		108.69	113.86		116.97	114.58	119.66
8		113.61	118.96		120.08	119.93	123.26
9		119.20	124.20	119.49	125.98	126.12	129.30
10		122.76	127.52	124.07	129.86	131.32	131.49
11		126.13	132.44	130.60	138.06	137.77	137.71
12	136.40	129.22	137.75	134.84	141.36	143.28	144.14
13	139.70	136.94	142.85	145.06	149.63	150.49	148.73
14	146.45	140.64	149.87	151.77	154.54	160.19	156.43
15	155.70	144.25	153.11	156.43	158.88	162.23	163.65
16	159.20	146.78		160.24	161.33	162.94	164.18
17	163.05	150.27		162.37	161.33	163.41	165.97
18	164.25	154.65		162.79	161.41	164.06	166.74
19						164.93	166.94
20						165.96	167.65

The mean stature of Ahom girls when compared with the NCHS, Indian and Assamese references, show that the mean value of height at 6 years of age is 107.28 cm, which increases to 156.11 cm. at 20 years of age (Table 10.9). The Ahom girls are taller than the Indian girls reported by ICMR and Assamese pooled data at all ages considered in the present study. However, they are below the 25th and 50th percentile of NCHS references. Although the Ahom girls are above the 10th percentile of NCHS references at some age groups, a reverse trend occurs at 6 and 13 through 16 years of age.

Table10.9: Comparisons of stature of Ahom girls with that of NCHS, Indian and Assamese references

Age (in years)	*NCHS 10th*	*NCHS 25th*	*NCHS 50th*	*Indian (ICMR)*	*Assam (Pooled)*	*Present Study*
6	108.05	111.01	114.42	106.30	109.00	107.28
7	114.40	117.57	121.22	111.90	114.80	117.96
8	120.09	123.47	127.35	117.20	120.70	121.83
9	124.97	128.58	132.71	122.20	125.70	128.70
10	129.39	133.31	137.77	126.70	130.60	131.72
11	134.49	138.82	143.69	131.20	134.40	139.72
12	141.34	145.88	150.89	136.70	138.50	144.36
13	148.00	152.26	156.96	141.50	143.20	147.77
14	151.84	155.85	160.30	145.30	146.00	151.29
15	153.60	157.52	161.82	147.70	147.90	152.32
16	154.24	158.16	162.53	149.60	149.10	154.05
17	154.60	158.53	162.90	150.10	150.20	154.68
18	154.81	158.74	163.12	150.00	150.20	154.74
19	154.93	158.87	163.25	150.50	150.80	155.31
20	155.01	158.96	163.34	150.70		156.11

The comparison of stature of Ahom girls with other population groups of North-east India shows that the Ahom girls are taller than the Meitei, Khynriam Khasi, Rabha and War Khasi population at all age groups (Table 10.10). The only exception to it is seen at age 6 when the Rabha girls are taller than the Ahom girls. The Sonowal Kachari girls are taller than the Ahom girls at 10 to 15 and 18 to 20 years of age. The Lotha Naga girls on the other hand are taller than the Ahom girls at the ages 16 to 18 years.

Comparison of weight of Ahom boys with that of NCHS, Indian and Assamese references shows that at the age of 6 years, the mean value of weight is 17.05 kg, which increases to 59.60 kg at the age of 20 years (Table 10.11). The Ahom boys are heavier than the Indian boys reported by ICMR (1972), but they are above the 25th and 50th percentile of NCHS (2000) references. The Ahom boys are below the 10th percentile of NCHS references particularly

Table 10.10: Comparisons of stature of Ahom girls with other population groups of Northeast India

Age (in years)	*Khynriam Khasi*	*War Khasi*	*Lotha Naga*	*Rabha*	*Meitei*	*Sonowal Kachari*	*Present Study*
6	103.43	107.24		109.78	104.89	105.96	107.28
7	108.65	111.23		115.17	108.61	113.78	117.96
8	114.19	116.02		119.91	113.61	119.86	121.83
9	118.87	121.27	119.08	127.40	120.73	126.03	128.70
10	122.63	127.15	124.75	131.77	125.27	132.67	131.72
11	126.24	133.17	132.21	138.49	131.23	139.84	139.72
12	135.09	139.80	138.14	141.64	136.19	146.81	144.36
13	137.80	142.36	143.81	147.14	143.97	149.79	147.77
14	142.22	143.42	148.40	148.92	146.87	152.94	151.29
15	143.72	144.38	151.92	148.93	148.13	153.12	152.32
16	145.84		154.61	149.90	151.41	153.74	154.05
17	146.89		156.25	149.94	152.09	154.39	154.68
18	147.20		156.73	150.28	153.49	155.11	154.74
19					154.67	155.58	155.31
20					154.67	156.55	156.11

at 6, 10 and 11 years of age. The Assamese pooled boys are heavier than the Ahom boys at 6, 10, 11 and 13 years of age.

Table 10.11: Comparisons of weight of Ahom boys with that of NCHS, Indian and Assamese references

Age (in years)	*NCHS 10th*	*NCHS 25th*	*NCHS 50th*	*Indian (ICMR)*	*Assam (Pooled)*	*Present Study*
6	17.49	18.83	20.58	15.90	17.20	17.05
7	19.38	20.91	22.96	17.60	19.20	20.33
8	21.40	23.14	25.53	19.30	21.50	21.42
9	23.57	25.61	28.42	21.10	24.50	24.73
10	25.99	28.41	31.78	23.10	27.10	25.74

(Contd...)

11	28.76	31.68	35.72	25.10	29.20	28.51
12	32.06	35.52	40.27	27.80	32.20	32.63
13	35.96	39.96	45.37	31.00	36.60	36.18
14	40.42	44.85	50.78	33.70	39.20	41.78
15	45.11	49.81	56.07	37.10	43.10	49.20
16	49.51	54.32	60.75	41.20	45.50	50.11
17	53.09	57.93	64.44	43.90	47.60	55.08
18	55.62	60.51	67.11	45.80	48.40	55.67
19	57.31	62.32	69.05	46.40	50.20	58.02
20	58.39	63.60	70.55	47.90		59.60

The comparison of mean weight of Ahom boys with other population groups of North-east India shows that the Ahom boys are heavier than the Khynriam Khasi, War Khasi and Lotha Naga in all the age groups with only exception at 6 years of age (Table 10.12). The mean weight of Ahom boys when compared with Rabha and

Table 10.12: Comparisons of weight of Ahom boys with other population groups of North-east India

Age (in years)	*Meitei*	*Khynriam Khasi*	*War Khasi*	*Lotha Naga*	*Rabha*	*Sonowal Kachari*	*Ahom (Present Study)*
6		17.10	17.83		17.93	16.17	17.05
7		18.11	19.69		20.17	18.71	20.33
8		20.65	21.25		21.59	20.67	21.42
9		23.04	23.48	22.47	23.96	23.90	24.73
10		24.59	25.40	24.39	25.70	26.23	25.74
11		26.98	27.71	28.36	29.86	29.94	28.51
12	29.27	28.86	30.36	31.33	32.02	33.44	32.63
13	32.52	34.00	33.67	36.89	38.61	38.89	36.18
14	37.49	37.30	37.26	41.49	41.82	45.83	41.78
15	44.46	41.67	40.49	44.78	45.40	48.53	49.20
16	47.05	43.29		49.11	49.16	50.35	50.11
17	50.75	47.63		51.11	51.04	51.17	55.08
18	51.96	48.88		51.95	51.08	53.13	55.67
19						54.32	58.02
20						54.98	59.60

Sonowal Kachari population groups of Assam shows that at 6, 8, 11, 13 and 14 years, the Ahom boys are lighter than the Rabha boys, but the Sonowal Kachari boys surpass the Ahom boys at 10 to 14 years of age. The Lotha Naga and Meitei boys are lighter than the Ahom boys in all the ages.

The comparison of mean weight of Ahom girls with that of NCHS, Indian and Assamese references shows that the mean value of weight of Ahom girls is 15.91 kg at age 6, which reaches 48.85 kg at 20 years of age (Table 10.13). The Ahom girls are heavier than the Indian girls reported by ICMR (1972) at all age groups considered in the present study. They are lighter than the 25th and 50th percentile but heavier than the 10th percentile of NCHS references. However, exception is limited in the age group of 6, 8 and 17, 18 years. The Ahom girls are heavier than the Assamese pooled data except in the age group 6 as well as 8 to 10 years.

Table 10.13: Comparisons of weight of Ahom girls with that of NCHS, Indian and Assamese references

Age (in years)	*NCHS 10th*	*NCHS 25th*	*NCHS 50th*	*Indian (ICMR)*	*Assam (Pooled)*	*Present Study*
6	16.98	18.32	20.14	15.40	17.00	15.91
7	18.89	20.48	22.65	17.20	18.80	19.98
8	20.96	22.87	25.50	18.80	21.40	20.53
9	23.32	25.65	28.84	20.80	24.30	24.20
10	26.08	28.88	32.72	22.50	26.60	25.93
11	29.26	32.53	37.02	24.50	29.20	31.58
12	32.75	36.42	41.46	27.30	32.00	34.66
13	36.33	40.25	45.66	30.60	35.90	38.92
14	39.69	43.68	49.23	33.50	38.60	42.49
15	42.54	46.45	51.95	35.40	41.00	44.27
16	44.71	48.48	53.82	37.90	42.70	45.98
17	46.19	49.86	55.09	39.30	44.40	46.02
18	47.17	50.87	56.14	39.60	44.70	46.84
19	47.89	51.77	57.26	39.90	45.70	47.12
20	48.37	52.46	58.20	42.00		48.85

The mean body weight for the Ahom girls and other population groups of North-east India records that in all the stages, the Ahom girls are heavier than the Khynriam Khasi, War Khasi and Lotha Naga in most of the age groups (Table 10.14). On the other hand, the Rabha, Meitei and Sonowal Kachari girls have higher mean values in respect of weight at different ages.

Table 10.14: Comparisons of weight of Ahom girls with other population groups of North-east India

Age (in years)	*Meitei*	*Khynriam Khasi*	*War Khasi*	*Lotha Naga*	*Rabha*	*Sonowal Kachari*	*Ahom (Present Study)*
6	17.89	17.74	17.00		16.81	15.51	15.91
7	19.65	18.69	18.82		19.07	18.73	19.98
8	22.75	20.41	20.27		20.97	20.19	20.53
9	24.41	22.68	22.65	22.50	24.50	23.73	24.20
10	25.73	24.72	24.74	22.92	26.51	26.25	25.93
11	26.81	26.99	27.98	29.15	30.69	31.74	31.58
12	30.09	30.87	31.58	31.82	34.66	38.29	34.66
13	33.83	33.08	33.54	35.97	39.69	42.42	38.92
14	37.33	37.27	35.38	40.23	42.81	44.23	42.49
15	42.29	41.12	37.22	43.86	43.05	45.40	44.27
16	44.45	43.17		47.51	46.90	46.88	45.98
17	46.75	44.67		49.31	46.96	48.34	46.02
18	49.01	44.38		49.81	47.19	49.82	46.84
19	49.03					51.27	47.12
20	49.05					52.48	48.85

In case of head circumference, the Ahom boys have larger head circumference. When they are compared with Khynriam Khasi, War Khasi, Lotha Naga and Sonowal Kachari population groups of North-east India, only exception is seen at age group 6 in the case of War Khasi and Sonowal Kachari boys (Table 10.15).

The Ahom girls possess relatively more head circumferences than the Khynriam Khasi, War Khasi, Lotha Naga and Sonowal Kachari at all ages, exception is seen at age 6 in the case of Sonowal Kachari girls (Table 10.16).

Table 10.15: Comparisons of head circumference of Ahom boys with other population groups of North-east India

Age (in years)	*Khynriam Khasi*	*War Khasi*	*Lotha Naga*	*Sonowal Kachari*	*Ahom (Present Study)*
6	48.49	49.37		50.38	49.07
7	49.06	49.89		50.56	51.60
8	49.47	50.13		51.37	51.64
9	50.13	50.71	49.90	51.77	52.52
10	50.52	51.16	50.27	52.49	52.95
11	50.36	51.62	50.46	52.50	53.46
12	51.25	51.96	51.18	52.99	53.62
13	51.77	52.94	52.77	53.99	54.04
14	52.01	54.16	53.66	54.69	54.66
15	52.33	54.57	53.79	54.98	55.75
16	52.89		53.98	55.28	55.84
17	53.65		54.24	55.40	56.43
18	54.05		54.45	55.74	56.73
19				55.89	56.95
20				56.15	57.36

Table 10.16: Comparisons of head circumference of Ahom girls with other population groups of North-east India

Age (in years)	*Khynriam Khasi*	*War Khasi*	*Lotha Naga*	*Sonowal Kachari*	*Ahom (Present Study)*
6	48.81	48.68		49.24	48.92
7	49.28	49.08		50.00	50.75
8	49.35	49.68		50.27	50.80
9	49.93	50.41	50.14	50.93	52.35
10	49.74	50.86	50.29	51.59	52.42
11	50.18	51.70	51.43	52.66	53.81
12	51.00	52.88	52.44	53.26	53.98
13	51.45	53.27	52.86	53.92	54.76
14	51.88	53.64	53.24	54.13	54.82
15	52.49	54.00	53.47	54.49	55.49
16	52.89		53.75	54.78	55.55
17	52.94		53.97	54.89	55.74
18	53.22		54.18	55.03	56.01
19				55.13	56.09
20				55.28	56.14

Comparison of mid-upper arm circumference of Ahom boys with other population groups of North-east India shows that the Ahom boys have greater mid-upper arm circumference than the Rabha, Khynriam Khasi, Lotha Naga and War Khasi boys with exception of the Rabha at 13 years of age (Table 10.17). The Sonowal Kachari boys also show higher values of mid-upper arm circumference at 13 to 16 years in comparison to the Ahom boys.

Table 10.17: Comparisons of mid-upper arm circumference of Ahom boys with other population groups of North-east India

Age (in years)	*Rabha*	*Khynriam Khasi*	*War Khasi*	*Lotha Naga*	*Sonowal Kachari*	*Ahom (Present Study)*
6	15.00	15.19	16.10		15.49	16.83
7	15.51	15.51	16.44		15.78	17.71
8	16.09	15.78	16.86		16.32	17.82
9	16.75	16.25	17.38	16.08	16.77	18.02
10	17.32	16.80	17.97	16.28	17.46	18.22
11	18.04	17.45	18.67	16.61	18.40	18.96
12	18.81	17.59	19.28	17.22	19.05	19.62
13	20.28	18.61	20.29	19.58	20.70	20.22
14	20.99	19.04	21.52	20.79	22.54	21.90
15	21.69	19.99	22.14	21.69	23.51	23.43
16	22.94	20.46		22.49	23.82	23.69
17	23.94	21.45		23.08	24.09	24.83
18	24.26	22.17		23.87	24.99	25.46
19					25.55	26.06
20					25.81	26.98

Mid-upper arm circumference of Ahom girls are relatively greater than the Khynriam Khasi, War Khasi, Lotha Naga and Sonowal Kachari girls at all age groups (Table 10.18). At 15 and 16 years of age, the Rabha girls have higher mid-upper arm circumference.

With respect to fat accumulation at biceps, the Ahom boys have lower biceps skin fold than all the other three populations like the Lotha Naga, Rabha and Sonowal Kachari boys (Table 10.19). The Ahom boys have greater biceps thickness than the Rabha boys at 14, 15, 17 and 18 years of age. Similarly, at the age of 9 years, the Ahom boys have more biceps skin fold than the Lotha Naga does. On the

Table 10.18: Comparisons of mid-upper arm circumference of Ahom girls with other population groups of North-east India

Age (in years)	*Rabha*	*Khynriam Khasi*	*War Khasi*	*Lotha Naga*	*Sonowal Kachari*	*Ahom (Present Study)*
6	15.08	14.88	15.63		15.28	16.55
7	15.63	15.33	16.50		16.06	17.40
8	16.30	15.80	16.97		16.31	18.08
9	17.41	16.34	17.83	15.76	17.29	18.29
10	18.02	16.87	18.23	16.02	17.67	18.46
11	19.11	17.28	19.05	17.64	19.18	19.77
12	20.50	18.07	20.25	18.72	20.72	20.58
13	21.77	18.66	20.89	19.62	21.91	21.77
14	23.00	19.08	21.16	20.40	22.34	22.70
15	23.61	19.85	21.69	21.27	22.89	23.18
16	24.41	20.54		22.08	23.74	24.40
17	24.41	20.88		22.78	23.94	24.54
18	24.59	20.96		22.92	24.14	25.02
19					24.45	25.30
20					24.65	25.56

Table 10.19: Comparisons of skin fold thickness at biceps of Ahom with other population groups of North-east India

Age (in years)	*Boys*				*Girls*			
	Rabha	*Lotha Naga*	*Sonowal Kachari*	*Ahom*	*Rabha*	*Lotha Naga*	*Sonowal Kachari*	*Ahom*
6	3.81		5.17	3.47	3.85		5.34	3.58
7	3.89		4.48	2.89	3.86		5.29	3.34
8	4.10		4.32	3.00	3.85		4.67	3.47
9	3.82	3.29	3.82	3.36	3.84	4.41	4.69	3.48
10	3.86	3.44	3.94	3.32	3.89	4.22	5.27	3.61
11	3.75	3.82	4.19	3.35	4.00	4.48	5.65	3.87
12	3.69	4.10	4.46	3.43	4.87	4.68	7.11	4.05
13	3.78	3.78	4.50	3.58	5.44	5.32	8.98	4.59
14	3.54	4.27	4.44	3.74	5.49	6.08	9.52	4.50
15	3.43	4.38	4.50	3.70	6.74	6.23	8.95	4.73
16	3.89	4.55	4.41	3.80	6.62	6.68	8.44	4.00
17	3.82	4.50	4.07	4.00	6.67	6.59	7.03	4.84
18	3.60	4.90	4.13	4.20	6.18	7.19	7.51	4.92
19			3.96	4.90			7.27	5.02
20			4.34	4.98			5.85	5.10

other hand, the Ahom boys have greater skin fold thickness at biceps than the Sonowal Kachari boys only from 18 years and above. Contrary to the above, the Ahom girls shows relatively lower skin folds at biceps in comparison with all the population groups like the Lotha Naga, Rabha and Sonowal Kachari girls of North-east India.

The mean values of the fat accumulation at triceps of Ahom boys have relatively less skin fold thickness at triceps than the Lotha Naga and Sonowal Kachari boys at all age groups (Table 10.20). However, exception is seen in the case of Rabha boys from 17 years onwards when the Ahom boys have more triceps skin fold than the former. On the contrary, the Ahom girls have lower triceps skin fold than the Rabha, Lotha Naga and Sonowal Kachari girls across ages.

Table 10.20: Comparisons of skin fold thickness at triceps of Ahom with other population groups of North-east India

Age (in years)	*Boys*				*Girls*			
	Rabha	*Lotha Naga*	*Sonowal Kachari*	*Ahom*	*Rabha*	*Lotha Naga*	*Sonowal Kachari*	*Ahom*
6	5.44		7.19	5.34	5.85		7.81	5.29
7	5.05		6.62	4.25	5.72		8.08	4.76
8	5.19		6.59	4.27	5.73		7.19	4.85
9	5.11	5.75	6.11	4.87	6.18	7.15	8.24	4.94
10	5.29	5.99	6.59	4.40	6.28	6.92	8.90	5.18
11	5.32	6.28	7.05	4.60	7.19	7.21	10.04	5.33
12	5.36	6.60	7.57	4.89	9.19	7.99	13.22	6.09
13	5.66	6.29	7.43	5.13	10.56	8.29	15.68	6.45
14	5.72	6.71	7.48	5.24	12.02	10.53	16.88	6.47
15	5.42	6.76	8.11	5.25	13.56	10.60	17.25	6.77
16	5.66	6.91	8.14	5.60	14.44	10.94	16.49	7.00
17	5.74	6.79	6.73	6.20	13.75	10.87	15.51	7.50
18	6.01	7.18	7.43	6.28	12.92	11.22	15.61	7.58
19			7.14	6.50			14.91	8.00
20			7.39	7.00			14.15	8.25

Based on the comparison presented in the preceding paragraphs, it is apparent that the physical growth pattern of the Ahom children is largely comparable to the 10th and 25th percentiles of the NCHS growth references in respect of weight and height. They are taller and heavier than the Indian children reported by the ICMR (1972) and the Assamese children (pooled data of twenty two districts, Department of Women and Child Development, Ministry of Human Resource Development, Government of India), particularly after the pre-adolescent period. The physical growth of the Ahom children is also better than the other population groups of North-east India, like the Rabhas and Sonowal Kachari of Assam, Meiteis of Manipur, Khynriam Khasi and War Khasi of Meghalaya, Lotha Naga of Nagaland particularly in higher age groups.

References

Choudhury, B. (1979). *A Cross Sectional Study of Growth of Some Somatometric Characters of Rabha Boys of Kamrup District, Assam.* Unpublished Ph.D. Thesis, Guwahati University.

Devi, S. (1985). *The Physical Growth in the Meitei Kshatriya and Muslim Girls of Imphal, Manipur.* Unpublished Ph.D. Thesis, Guwahati University.

Government of India (1998). *India Nutrition Profile.* Department of Women and Child Development, Ministry of Human Resource Development, Government of India.

Indian Council of Medical Research (ICMR)(1972). *Growth and Physical Development of Indian Infants and Children.* Indian Council of Medical Research Technical Report Series No. 18. New Delhi: Indian Council of Medical Research.

Khongsdier, R. (1995). *A Study on Nutrition and Health Status in Relation to Some Bio-Social Factors among the War Khasi of Meghalaya.* Unpublished Ph.D. Thesis, North-Eastern Hill University, Shillong, Meghalaya.

Kuczmarski, R.J., C. L. Ogden, L.M., Grummer-Strawn, K.M. Flegal., S.S. Guo, R. Wei, Z. Mei, L.R. Curtin, A.F. Roche and C.L. Johnson (2000). *Growth Charts: United States. Advance Data from Vital and Health Statistics. Revised.* Hyattsville, Maryland: National Centre for Health Statistics.

Lohman, T.G., A.F. Roche and R. Martorell (1988). *Anthropometric Standardisation Reference Manual.* Chicago: Human Kinetics Books.

Martin, R. and K. Saller (1957). *Lehrbuch der Anthropologie*, Vol. I and II. Stugart: Gustav Fisher Verlag.

Mukherjee, N. (2002). *Studies on Demography and Growth Pattern among the Khasi Children of Shillong, Meghalaya.* Unpublished Ph.D. Thesis, North-Eastern Hill University, Shillong, Meghalaya.

National Centre for Health Statistics (NCHS)(2000). *CDC Growth Charts for the United States: Methods and Development.* Series Report 11, No. 241. Hyattsville, Maryland: National Centre for Health Statistics.

Singh, J. (2008). *A Study on Growth and Nutritional Status of the Sonowal Kachari of Dibrugarh District, Assam.* Unpublished Ph.D. Thesis, Dibrugarh University, Dibrugarh.

Singh, L.D. and T.S. Singh (2000). Physical growth among the affluent and non-affluent Meitei boys of Manipur. *Man in India,* 80 (3-4): 295-307.

Tsopoe, T. (2003). *Nutritional Status and Physical Growth of Lotha Children of Wokha District, Nagaland.* Unpublished Ph. D. Thesis, North-Eastern Hill University, Shillong, Meghalaya.

Weiner, J. S. and J.A. Lourie (1981). *Practical Human Biology*. London: Academic Press.

11

Influence of Socio-Economic Factors on Infant and Child Mortality among the Pnars of Jaintia Hills District, Meghalaya

— *Dhruba Kumar Limbu and*
Happystone Syngkon

Introduction

Infant mortality may be defined as "mortality or death during the first year of life" and child mortality may be defined as "mortality or death during the age of 1 to 4 years" (Kabir *et al.*, 1995). The study of child mortality is important for a number of reasons. It has a substantial positive impact on fertility (Mahadevan, 1979; Bhuyan *et al.*, 1996), which is strongly influenced by many biological and socio-economic factors. The biological determinants of child mortality have been studied extensively (Scrimshaw *et al.*, 1968; Mata, 1978; Jelliffe and Jelliffe, 1984). The important social determinants of child mortality include education, income and wealth (Das Gupta, 1990).

The child mortality rate has been recognised as a good summary index of the level of living and socio-economic development of a country. This recognition has inspired international organisations as well as national governments to intensify their efforts to lower the level of mortality and raise the level of child survival (Jain and Visaria, 1988). Most of the meaningful researches on mortality, particularly on infant and child mortality have been carried out since the 1980s. They have been doing mostly at macro level. It is proved beyond doubt that there are marked variations in mortality patterns and rates between various countries and between various populations, even within one country. It is also reported that there are lots of variations in respect of infant and child mortality patterns and rates between different ecological zones. Recent researches on mortality have shown that child mortality patterns and rates are influenced by various types of bio-social factors.

Infant and child mortality rates reflect a country's level of socio-economic development and quality of life and used for monitoring and evaluating population and health programmes and policies. Many earlier findings have suggested that biological as well as social factors, such as women's age, age at marriage, age at menarche, age at first child birth, age at menopause, types of marriage, education, income, religious attitudes, adoption of contraceptive devices and others that have an effect on infant and child mortality (Caldwell, 1979; Lee 1979; Elamin and Bhuyan, 1999; Reddy *et al.*, 2006). The aim of the present study is to investigate the influence of age and socio-economic factors such as age of mother, age at marriage, mother's education, religion, household income, family type, family size and place of residence on infant and child mortality.

Land and People

The Pnars are one of the five sub-groups of the Khasi tribe who occupy the Jaintia Hills lying on the eastern side of Meghalaya. According to historians, the Pnars are the stock of Mon-Khmer people of Mongoloid race and they are Austric by their linguistic affiliation. The Pnars are short in stature, with a muscular body (Majumdar and Ray, 1984). The Pnars are generally endogamous within the tribe but exogamous as far as the clans are concerned. Traditionally, they practiced visiting husband system - after marriage, the husband visits his wife only after dark and does not stay there. It is after sometime; in most cases after the couples have children that the husband and wife live together under the same roof. In Jowai town, the visiting husband system still prevails among the Non-Christians whose parent's house is nearby. However, the Christians living in Jowai town and Sanaro village do not practice the visiting husband system (Singh, 1994).

In the rural areas of Jaintia Hills, the primary occupation of the people is agriculture. Those people possessing no land property are working as day labourers. But with the rapid growth of education and construction of roads, even the rural folks have started migrating to the urban centres and district headquarters like Jowai and Shillong and others. Many rural people have migrated to these urban centres for white collar jobs or petty business. There are also quite a few civil servants, engineers, medical practitioners and lawyers, especially in the urban areas (Singh, 1994).

Materials and Methods

The fieldwork for the present study was conducted among the Pnar of Jowai town and Sanaro village of Jaintia Hills district, Meghalaya. On the basis of the above, a house to house survey was conducted to collect data on infant and child mortality and socio-economic variables. Such data were collected by interviewing 276 ever-married women aged 15-49 years from Jowai town and 157 from Sanaro village with the help of interview schedule for the purpose of the present study.

Data were collected on mother's age at marriage, education, household income, family type and place of residence as suggested by Mahadevan (1986). Mortality records included numbers of dead children, their date of birth, age at death, etc.

Table 11.1: Infant and child mortality by urban-rural setting

Urban-rural setting	*Number of mothers*	*Live-births*	*Infant mortality*	*Child mortality*
Urban	276	962	28(2.91)	16(1.66)
Rural	157	875	123(14.06)	156(17.83)
Total	433	1837	151(8.22)	172(9.36)
χ^2-value			75.44, $p < 0.05$	88.02, $p < 0.05$

Figures in parentheses indicate percentages.

Table 11.2: Infant and child mortality by mothers' age at marriage

Age at marriage (years)	*Number of mothers*	*Number of live-births*	*Infant mortality*	*Child mortality*
Urban				
= 19	67	282	16(5.67)	2(0.71)
= 20	209	680	12(1.76)	14(2.06)
χ^2 -value			10.77, $p < 0.05$	2.22, $p > 0.05$
Rural				
= 19	138	763	112(14.68)	133(17.43)
= 20	19	112	11(9.82)	23(20.54)
χ^2 -value			1.90, $p > 0.05$	0.46, $p > 0.05$

Figures in parentheses indicate percentages.

Results

This study has highlighted on the socio-economic factors that influence the infant and child mortality. The present study was restricted only to the Pnar of Sanaro village (Rural) and Jowai town (Urban) with a view to understanding the influence of rural-urban settings on infant and child mortality.

Table 11.1 shows the percentage frequencies of infant and child mortality by two different places of residence, i.e., Jowai town and Sanaro village representing urban and rural settings, respectively. Significant differences were observed between the two places of residences, i.e., urban and rural settings in respect of infant ($\chi^2 = 74.44$, df = 2, $p < 0.05$) and child ($\chi^2 = 88.02$, df = 2, $p < 0.05$) mortality.

Table 11.2 shows the percentage frequencies of infant and child mortality by mother's age at marriage which is divided into two age groups, i.e., upto19 years and 20 years and above. The percentages of infant mortality among the mothers who had married by 19 years were 5.67 per cent and 14.68 per cent in the urban and rural study areas, respectively. These frequencies were respectively 1.76 per cent and 9.82 per cent among the mothers who married at 20 years and above. Unlike the infant mortality, the child mortality rates were higher among the mothers whose age at marriages were 20 years and above in both rural and urban areas. The prevalence of child mortality observed among those mothers who had married on or before 19 years were 0.71 per cent and 17.43 per cent in the urban and rural areas, respectively and 2.06 per cent and 20.54 per cent, respectively among the mothers who married at 20 years and above. The χ^2 test indicates that mothers' age at marriage was significantly associated with infant mortality only in the urban area ($\chi^2 = 10.77$, df = 1, $p < 0.05$).

The percentage frequency of infant and child mortality by mother's education is shown in Table 11.3. In the rural area, there were 110 mothers who were illiterate, 41 of them completed upto primary and only 6 of them studied upto secondary level. All the urban mothers included in this study were literate. The infant mortality rate in rural area was inversely associated with the mother's education ranging from 6.82 per cent among the secondary and higher level to 15.02 per cent among the illiterate mothers. The percentage of child mortality in the same area was highest among the illiterate mothers (19.12 per cent), followed by mothers with secondary level of education (15.91 per cent). The lowest rate was recorded among those who studied upto primary level (13.37 per cent). In the urban area, the infant mortality rates varied between 6.21 per cent among primary educated mothers and 2.19 per cent among the mothers with higher secondary and above and the child mortality varied between 3.11 per cent and 1.31 per cent respectively. Therefore, mother's education is likely to be an important factor in regulating the infant mortality in the urban area. However, the χ^2 test for the difference between educational groups of mothers in respect of infant mortality was significant only in urban area ($\chi^2 = 7.43$, df = 2, $p < 0.05$).

The percentage frequencies of infant and child mortality by monthly household income are given in Table 11.4. The amount for income groups in the two study areas were calculated separately as their monthly income varies within them. The income groups were divided into three groups, *viz.*, Low Income Group (LIG), Middle Income Group (MIG) and High Income Group (HIG). For the rural area households with monthly income of below ₹ 1500, ₹ 1500 up to ₹ 3,000 and above ₹ 3,000 were categorised as LIG, MIG and HIG respectively. For the urban, these amounts were ₹<19,000, ₹ 19,000 upto ₹ 29,000 and above ₹ 29,000 for LIG, MIG and HIG, respectively.

Table 11.3: Infant and child mortality by mother's education

Educational level	*Number of mothers*	*Number of live-births*	*Infant mortality*	*Child mortality*
Urban				
Illiterate	0	0	0 (0.00)	0 (0.00)
Primary	36	161	10 (6.21)	5 (3.11)
Secondary and above	240	801	18 (2.25)	11 (1.37)
χ^2-value			7.43, $p < 0.05$	2.45, $p > 0.05$
Rural				
Illiterate	110	659	99 (15.02)	126 (19.12)
Primary	41	172	21(12.21)	23 (13.37)
Secondary and above	6	44	3 (6.82)	7 (15.91)
χ^2-value			2.91, $p > 0.05$	3.20, $p > 0.05$

Figures in parentheses indicate percentages.

Table 11.4 further shows that in both the study areas, the percentages of infant and child mortality are inversely associated with the household income; however, they are not statistically significant. In rural area, the percentages of infant mortality declined from 16.94 per cent for the LIG to 11.93 per cent for the HIG; whereas the child mortality rates varied between 19.87 per cent and 14.20 per cent. In urban area, the percentages of infant mortality among the LIG, MIG and HIG were 2.99 per cent, 1.56 per cent and 4.22 per cent, respectively and child mortality were 2.56 per cent, 0.78 per cent and 0.84 per cent, respectively. The χ^2 tests for the differences between income groups in respect of infant and child mortality were, however, not statistically significant in both rural and urban areas.

Table 11.5 shows the percentage frequencies of infant and child mortality in rural by family types which are found to be higher in nuclear families than in joint families. The infant mortality rates in this study area were 14.47 per cent and 10.34 per cent in the nuclear and the joint families, respectively and the child mortalities were 18.15 per cent and 14.94 per cent, respectively. Unlike in rural area, the infant and child mortality rates in urban study area were higher in joint families. The percentages of infant mortality in this area were 2.36 per cent in the nuclear families and 3.98 per cent in the joint families. The child mortality rates in the same study area were 1.57 per cent and 1.83 per cent, respectively. However, the χ^2 tests were not statistically significant in both rural and urban areas.

Table 11.4: Infant and child mortality by monthly household income

Income Groups	*Number of mothers*	*Number of live-births*	*Infant mortality*	*Child mortality*
Urban				
LIG (₹ 19,000)	133	469	14(2.99)	12(2.56)
MIG (₹ 19,000-29,000)	73	256	4(1.56)	2(0.78)
HIG (₹ 29,000)	70	237	10(4.22)	2(0.84)
χ^2-value			3.09, $p > 0.05$	4.49, $p > 0.05$
Rural				
LIG (₹ 1500)	63	307	52(16.94)	61(19.87)
MIG (₹ 1500-3000)	68	392	50(12.76)	70(17.86)
HIG (₹ 3000)	26	176	21(11.93)	25 (14.20)
χ^2-value			3.31, $p > 0.05$	2.46, $p > 0.05$

Figures in parentheses indicate percentages.

Table 11.5: Infant and child mortality by family type

Family types	*Number of mothers*	*Number of live-births*	*Infant mortality*	*Child mortality*
Urban				
Nuclear	179	635	15(2.36)	10(1.57)
Joint	97	327	13(3.98)	6 1.83)
χ^2-value			1.98, $p > 0.05$	0.09, $p > 0.05$
Rural				
Nuclear	135	788	114 (14.47)	143 (18.15)
Joint	22	87	9 (10.34)	13 (14.94)
χ^2-value			3.41, $p > 0.05$	0.54, $p > 0.05$

Conclusion

The present study reveals a significant variation between the urban and rural populations in respect of infant and child mortality, perhaps due to better socio-economic conditions and medical amenities in urban area. The effects of socio-economic factors like age at marriage and mother's education on infant and child mortality were clearly perceptible, especially in urban areas. We hope that future studies will shed more light on the factors influencing infant and child mortality among the Pnars of Jaintia Hills in Meghalaya.

References

Bhuyan, K. C., A. K. Majumder and K. Choudhury (1996). Differential fertility among adopter and non-adopter couples of different social status and mobility pattern in rural Bangladesh. *Journal of Family Welfare*, 42: 51-60.

Caldwell, J. C. (1979). Education as a factor in mortality decline, an examination of Nigerian data. *Population Studies,* 33 (3): 395-413.

Census of India (2001).*Census Highlights*. New Delhi: Census of India.

Das Gupta, M. (1990). Death clustering, mother's education and the determinants of child mortality in rural Punjab, India. *Population Studies*, 44: 489-505.

Elamin, M. and K. C. Bhuyan (1999). Differential fertility in North-Eastern Libya. *The Journal of Family Welfare*, 45 (1): 12-22.

Jain, K. A. and P. Visaria (1988). *Infant Mortality in India: Differentials and Determinants.* New Delhi: Sage Publication.

Jelliffe, D. B. and E.F.P. Jelliffe (1984). *Advances in International and Child Health.* Oxford: Oxford University Press.

Kabir, M., R. I. Chowdhury and R. Amin (1995). Infant and child mortality levels and trends in Bangladesh. *Journal of Bio-social Science,* 27 (2): 179-192.

Lee, R. B. (1979). *The Kung San.* Cambridge: Cambridge University Press.

Mahadevan, K. (1979). *Sociology of Fertility - Determinants of Fertility Differentials in South India.* New Delhi: Sterling Publishers.

Mahadevan, K. (1986). *Mortality, Biology and Society: Analytical Framework and Conceptual Model.* New Delhi: Sage Publication.

Majumdar, D. N. and B. Datta Ray (1984). *Tribal Occupational Mobility.* Calcutta: Research India Publications.

Mata, L. J. (1978). *The Children of Santa Maria Couque: A Prospective Field Study of Health and Growth.* Cambridge: Mass.

Reddy, B. K. and C. S. Reddy (2006). Demographic profile of Yadavas: A backward caste population of Andhra Pradesh. *Anthropologist*, 8 (3): 167-169.

Scrimshaw, N. S., G.E. Taylor and J.E. Gorden (1968). Interactions of nutrition and infection. WHO *Monograph Series*, No. 57. Geneva: WHO.

Singh, K. S. (1994). *People of India: Meghalaya.* Volume XXXII. Calcutta: Seagull Books.

12

Of Gods and Goddesses: Agricultural Rituals of the Garos of Meghalaya, India

— *Queenbala Marak*

Introduction

Rituals are techniques for interacting with and influencing the supernatural beings and are interwoven with different activities. In every society there is a common element of meaning underlying different ritual context (Radcliffe-Brown, 1952). Among all religious rituals, agricultural rituals are one of the oldest. These are conducted specifically to improve crops, animals and do away with drought and famine. The aim of rituals is to garner favour with deities and spirits; this is done by forming a bond between the person performing the ritual and the deity or spirit. This becomes important since communication with deities and other spirits is an important part of rituals. Similarly, animal sacrifice based on myths is usually an integral part of most rituals. Some religions use human sacrifice as part of their rituals too. However, in ritualistic sacrifices, only the best livestock is sacrificed and no inferior animals are used.

Many societies today due to factors of change and modernity no longer perform their agricultural rituals since many of these were connected to religion. This is the situation in present North-east India where a large number of tribal groups have now abandoned their traditional way of life. One of the strongest agents of change has been the introduction and adoption of Christianity to these parts. However, a few groups of people continue to use these rituals for different purposes, as they try to cling on to their traditional religion. One such community is the Garos of Garo Hills, Meghalaya, a tribe that mainly comprise of Christian converts. Nevertheless, there still remain a few pockets in the West Garo Hills district where some continue to follow their traditional religion and their traditional agricultural rituals.

The Garos are a matrilineal tribe residing in the Garo Hills of the present day Meghalaya (India) and in other areas of the Indian States of Assam, Nagaland, Tripura and West Bengal and in northern districts of Bangladesh. They call themselves *A"chik mande,* or simply mande. Linguistically they belong to the Bodo group of the Tibeto-Burman family spread all over Assam and Tripura. The languages of these people show a general similarity with the Garo language. They have a strong oral tradition about their origin and migration and their ancestors are said to have inhabited a province of Tibet called Torua, from where they started on a "voyage of discovery" under the leadership of two chiefs, Jappa-Jalimpa and Sukpa-Bongipa (Playfair, 1909: 9). They have a number of cultural and dialectical groups, each of them originally settling in a specific geographic area, though there is difference of opinion. Playfair (1909:59-62) lists twelve "tribal divisions" (or sub-tribes), which includes the A·we, Chisak, Dual, Machi, Matabeng, Kochu, Atiagra, A"beng, Chibok, Gara Ganching, Atong and Megam speaking different dialects. Numerically the three largest groups are the A"beng (or Ambeng), the A·we and the Atong. The spread of education by American Baptists missionaries in the early nineteenth century has led to the disappearance of the different dialects and they mostly speak *A·we* today.

Garo matriliny is followed at four levels in Garo Hills — descent, inheritance, residence and succession. A Garo child on birth is accepted into the folds of his/her matri-clan and not into the father's clan. Inheritance of property is from mother to daughter, while residence after marriage is uxorical. Initially there were two main clans (*chatchi*), namely Sangma and Marak. Later and at present, three more clans were added, namely Momin, Areng and Shira. These clans have a number of sub-clans called *machong*, which are named after animals, birds, trees, bamboo, rivers and hills, however, these are not totemic in nature. The simplest family structure is the household or *nok* which consists of the husband, his wife and their children. In time, the nuclear family becomes extended with the daughter's husband joining them. The inheritress daughter is called *nokna* and her husband the *nokkrom*. The traditional chieftain/ headman is called *nokma*, whose office is hereditary, passed through the inheriting daughter and it is the *nokkrom* of the chieftain's house who inherits.

Garos traditionally believe in animism. They believe in the existence of a spirit in humans which after death goes to an appointed place till it is re-incarnated. A belief in reward and punishment is inherent – the lowest form of incarnation being that of insects and plants, while the greatest reward for a virtuous life is to be reborn in one's own clan. They believe in a Supreme Being and a multitude of other benevolent and malevolent spirits (also referred to as gods or goddesses), called *mite*. These *mites* are everywhere, in rivers and lakes, mountains and hills, trees and shrubs, sticks and stones and celestial bodies. Tatara-Rabuga is the creator at whose command the whole world was made by two lesser spirits, namely *Nostu-Nopantu* and *Machi*. *Saljong* is a god, represented by the sun and responsible for the germination and growth of all crops, trees and bamboo and ripening of all fruits and grains. The Supreme Being is not worshipped for he is believed to be benevolent and therefore not in need of propitiation (Sangma, 1981). It is the numerous other deities that are the objects of their dread and therefore they offer sacrifices whenever they incur their displeasure. The introduction of Christianity by missionaries from Europe and America at the beginning of the last century brought about many changes in the religious life. Many Garos are now Baptists, with a considerable number of Roman Catholics. This has brought in a new nomenclature for traditional believers, who are now referred to as *Songsarek*. Garo Christians supposedly do not drink rice beer, take part in non-Christian rituals and do not believe in the existence of mite (gods and goddesses).

Cultivating the Plot that Shifts

Shifting cultivation, known as *a"ba chaa*, is an age-old practice of the Garos. There is no historical evidence about its origin, but it can be presumed that the Garos are practising this method of cultivation since these hills were inhabited by them. According to lore, the first man to have started shifting cultivation was Bone-Nirepa-Jane-Nitepa with the help of the god *Misi Saljong*. He had such bountiful returns that every Garo followed him. However, Playfair (1909) differs when he says that the first humans to cultivate the soil were two dwarfs, Bonejasku and his wife Jane-Gando. They cleared the forest as is done at the present time and *Tatara-Rabuga* (the supreme god), to whom they made an offering of pumpkins, rewarded their industry by causing rice to grow.

A·ba cha·a is a multicrop cultivation where a variety of crops are grown – cereals like rice, millet and maize; vegetables like beans, okra, gourd, pumpkin and sorrel; fruits like melon; condiments like ginger and chillies; and useful crops like cotton. It is said that in the past, crops were assigned for cultivation to different sub-tribes. For instance, the Chisaks were to grow millet, the A"bengs to grow and pick cotton, the Machis to grow maize, Job's tears and rear parrots, the Gara Ganchings to carve out pig troughs and wooden stools, the Kotchus to smoke fish over fire to dry, the A·wes to collect edible bamboo shoots, etc. This is said to have come about when Abong Noga, a powerful king, who had control over all the sub-tribes, forced them to cultivate different crops. However, later and at the present time, such confinement in terms of crops to specific sub-tribes is not seen.

Among all crops, rice (i.e., paddy) is the chief of all. This is proved not only by the social, cultural and emotional factors connected to it (Marak, 2014), but also by the ritualistic aspects surrounding it. There are specific rituals meant only for paddy and specific gods and goddesses looking over it.

In this method of agriculture, a plot covered by jungle is cleared in the dry months just before monsoon and allowed to dry for a month. Just before the rains come, this plot is set on fire. On the ash-covered soil, seeds of various plants are sown. After using such a plot for two years, the plot is abandoned for another ten years or more, till it grows sufficient vegetation to be cut down and burnt. Contrastingly, in olden days, a plot of land was kept fallow for over fifteen years. Today, it is with great difficulty that the plot is kept un-used even for five years. The method of shifting cultivation and the crops grown varies widely from village to village.

The various stages of shifting cultivation include the following (Marak, 2014): *A·ba nia* refers to the selection of plots (*a·ba* = field, *nia* = to see), which is made sometime in the last part of December. It is the *nokma* who allots specific plots to specific families under his jurisdiction. On the day of selection and allocation of plots, each head of the household clears a token patch and marks the boundary, even though actual clearing may be postponed for some time. Generally men do the clearing work.

This is followed by *wa·a so·a*, which refers to burning of the plot (*wa·a* = bamboo, *so·a* = to burn), when scrubby undergrowth is cut down, branches of big trees felled and left to dry for a few days. They are then set on fire on a set day after information to one and all. Immediately afterwards, men get busy building field houses called *a·ba nok, borang*, or *jamadal*.

The next stage is *bitchil sata* referring to planting of seeds (*bitchil* = seed, *sata* = to plant), which is done in different ways - *ge·a*, digging a hole with the hoe (*gitchi*), where the seed/root/head of the plant is planted and covered with soil; *sika*, pressing the digging stick into the ground to make a hole in which two or three seeds are inserted and covered with soil; *baka*, a strategy where seeds are first broadcasted and then the soil is lightly hoed, so that the seeds become embedded in soil; and finally *sata*, where the seeds are strewn over the lightly hoed plot.

The next stage in shifting cultivation, after the seeds are planted, is weeding, when the plants start sprouting. The first weeding takes place when the seeds begin to sprout. For weeding, the soil is lightly loosened with the hoe, taking care not to damage the growing saplings and unwanted weeds are disposed off. The second major weeding takes place when plants are firmly rooted. Planting, sowing of seeds and weeding is normally done by women.

Harvesting is the last stage in such a method of cultivation. Crops are harvested as and when they ripen and tools used include chopper (*ate*), axe (*rua*), hoe (*gitchi*) and the sickle (*katchi*). However, no crops can be harvested and consumed without offering the first produce to the concerned gods and goddesses of the fields.

Agricultural Calendar of the Garos

Traditionally, Garos follow an annual calendar that is based on the different stages of cultivation. Bone Nirepa Jane Nitepa, the first person to have started *jhum* (shifting) cultivation, is said to have named these stages which later began to be used as calendric months. Table 12.1 depicts the different months used in Garo calendar.

Table 12.1: Garo annual calendar

Garo Month	*Approximate Gregorian month*	*Activities*
Galmakja	March	Month of burning plots
Mebakja	April	Month of planting paddy seeds
Jagro	May	Long month of weeding
Sogalja	June	Month of burning incense in celebration
Jamebok	July	Month of fullness
Jamegap	August	Month of paddy harvest in 2nd year's plot
Mejapang	September	Month when paddy stalks are left in plot
A·anija	October	Month of selecting new plots
Berokja	November	Month of preparing plot for 2nd year's cultivation
Kilokja	December	Month of picking cotton
Awitja	January	Month of burning debris in a 2nd year's plot
Wachengja	February	Month of drying jungles in a fresh plot

A brief note on the activities connected to these months is pertinent at this point (Rongmuthu, 1960). Galmakja is the month of burning down the debris in a fresh *jhum* plot. Here, initially, trees and shrubs were cut down and left to dry and eventually in this month they are burnt. This is a dry month just before the onset of monsoon. *Mebakja* is the month of digging up the soil in previous years' *jhum* fields for sowing paddy seeds. *Jagro* is the month when paddy, millet and other cereals grow in *jhum* fields. It means a "long month," because of longing expectations of the fresh fruits of labour in the *jhum* fields. The returns have not yet been reaped and thus the months look longer for cultivators than other months.

Sogalja is the month of ritual burning of incense, accompanied by chanting age-old sacrificial songs and solemn offerings of rice flour, rice bran and rice beer out of the first fruits of the *jhum* fields on the permanent altars at home before any member of the family at home ever tastes them. This is offered to *Misi Saljong* the god of firmament and fertility.

Jamebok is the month of ripening of paddy in the *jhum* fields. This is followed by *Jagapja* (or *Jamegap*), the month of paddy harvest. *Jagapja* means the month of fullness. It is the busiest month of the year for *jhum* cultivators. The crops in the *jhum* fields need careful and vigilant watching at nights against attacks of wild pigs, deer, bear and wild elephants; the granaries need renovation, or are to be freshly constructed; baskets, mats and other things necessary for storing paddy and other *jhum* produce must be ready. In addition, paddy must be harvested and stored without the least possible delay – all within this month.

Mejapang is the month in which the paddy stalks are left in the old *jhum* fields, the harvest being over. Once the harvest is over it is the month of selecting places in the jungles for the next *jhum* clearings. This is called the month of *A·anija*. *Berokja* - the month of removing weed and millet-corn stalks in the previous year's *jhum* fields so as to convert them into *abreng* (second year's plot). *Kilokja* is the month of picking of cotton in the *jhum* fields. *Awitja* is the month of removing debris in the *abrengs*, collecting them in heaps and burning them down so as to be ready for sowing of paddy seeds. *Wachenga* is the month of drying the debris in the fresh *jhum* clearings. With this the cycle continues once again.

Agricultural Rituals

A number of rituals take place in the life of a Garo connected to agriculture (Table 12.2). After distribution of new plots by the *nokma* every head of household visits the allotted site and performs *o·pata*. This is done in order to seek permission of the deities residing in the jungles and forests. After clearing a token patch, the head of household seeks permission from the deities and he returns home. If the omens are good, then he returns to the plot in a few days' time to clear it up for cultivation. Otherwise, he returns to the *nokma* seeking another plot. It is believed that if any member of his family dreams of blood, or animal sacrifice it is a bad omen. On the other hand, if they dream of rooster feathers (dome), or plucking of cane fruits, it foretells celebrations in future and bountiful paddy harvest. In some places, such as the *A·beng* areas, in the middle of the clearing a stick of about two feet long is hammered into the ground (de Maaker, 2006). This is split at the top and a bundle of leaves is inserted. If a plot is cultivated for a year or two and is left fallow that releases the claim that was extended with the performance of the "leaves in the split" rituals.

Denbilsia or *Bilsi raa* takes place before the start of the new agricultural cycle. Throughout this ritual, the village is closed to people from outside. Lead by the *nokma*, the men of the village jointly hunt for a *ranggol* (langur). If they are unable to catch such a monkey, they substitute it for a squirrel. The priest ties it to a string and takes it through the village. He hits each house with it to have the animal soak up the *marang* (pollution) that has collected there in the preceding months. Men who accompany the priest collect old pestles, brooms and rice cooking sticks from each of the houses visited. They symbolise the old year. They are discarded outside the village in the jungle. At the same spot, the dead animal is crucified. The next day no work can be done inside the village and neither should any loud sounds be made. On the evening of the last day, the head of each house offers an egg at his granary to prepare the paddy seeds that will be sown.

Agalmaka is held just after the burning of the fields in the month of March or early April. The next morning each family sacrifices an egg in the name of *Saljong* for the sake of the growing plants in its own fields, while the *nokma* sacrifices a chicken. There are two specific rituals: *Asiroka* conducted to drive away profanities from the new *jhum* field so that the paddy goddess would come and reside therein; and *Rokkime Ringgama* to call upon the paddy goddess to come into the *jhum* fields. In the evening, the priest conducts *churugala* or pouring of rice beer to the god *Misi Saljong* at the *maljuri* post of the house. This is followed by beating of the drums (both sacred and ceremonial), blowing of buffalo horns, drinking rice beer and dancing by young boys and girls – lasting for a day.

Bang cha·a is performed when the crops of the field have germinated and started to grow. The sacrifice is made with a fowl to the god *Jugi*, the god of plants and herbs. During the sacrifice, the priest asks the god not to damage and spoil the crops of the field but to help them flourish.

Miamua is performed by the *nokma* only at the time when paddy plants begin to flower; and rites consist of sacrificing one or more fowls and a pig by the *nokma* and giving villagers a modest feast. This is performed in the last week of June and first week of July when tender saplings of paddy and millets are growing at the *jhum* fields. The purpose of the ceremony is to drive away all diseases that attack the crops through prayer. At the same location where the altar for the paddy goddess is placed, two other altars are made – one for the god *Rakasi* and another for a lesser goddess *Miasi*.

Rongchugala is performed in August just before the time of paddy harvest and ideally the festival should be held in the village and not in the fields. After the ceremonial offering of flattened rice (*rongchu*) and rice beer at the *nokma*'s house, the villagers move around the village drinking rice beer in every house. However, there is no hard and fast rule that this ceremony should always be held in the village. If this ceremony is held while the villagers are still in their field houses, then after the initial ceremonies at the *nokma*'s house in the village, they go back to the *a·ba* and drink in the field houses.

Ahaia is the forerunner of the final harvest festival *Wangala*. Essential elements of this festival are ceremonial offering of certain items of food (which are tabooed from the time of *Agalmaka* to this festival), drinking and feasting in each house. The taboos on the ceremonial drum (*dama*) and dancing and shouting by young men to indicate that their happiness are ceremonially removed from this day up to the time of the next *Agalmaka* festival. Without looking back, they carry the last of the rice harvest to their house. This is referred to as "leading the mother of rice." In the house some of this rice is tied to the *maljuri* post or placed on the house frame. If the mother of rice is not led to the house, it is believed to inhibit the germination of the paddy seeds that are stored in the granary for the next agricultural year.

Wangala is held about two weeks after the previous festival (two weeks being the minimum time required for preparation of rice beer). This is held on a grand scale and people from neighbouring villages come a day or two ahead and stay as guests. More people pour in (specially grown up boys and girls) when they hear the typical drum beats indicating the *Wangala* celebrations. There is no fixed day for this festival; the *nokma* in consultation with village elders decides a day and informs the villagers well ahead so that they find sufficient time to brew rice beer. Nor is there any fixed duration for this festival. Villagers enjoy drinks in the houses in a traditionally fixed order and move several rounds until beer is exhausted in all the households. However, the last drink is always enjoyed in the *nokma*'s house when the sacred drum (*kram*) is returned to the *nokma*'s house. This function is known as *dama gogata*. Only the *nokma*'s household enjoys the privilege of burning incense (*sasat*) in his house during the *Wangala*. Incense burning form a part of the ceremonies and at the time of burning incenses all the outlets of the house are closed. The direction of the smoke indicates the harvest in the next season. If the smoke moves along the long pole supporting the roof (*bolgro*), it gives the indication of a good harvest and if the smoke moves helter-skelter it indicates a poor harvest (Majumdar, 1980:61). With the burning of the resin or incense the *nokma* fulfills the promise that he made during the last year's *Wangala*. At the same time in the chant, *Saljong* is promised that if he renews his gift of the crops in the coming year the incense will be burned once again in the next year's *Wangala*. The promise is sworn at the smoke.

Gods and Goddesses of the Fields

Among the Garos, there are numerous gods and goddesses of whom some are directly connected to the agricultural cycle and hence are propitiated through various rituals (Tables 12.2 and 12.3). Some of the common deities include the following:

Saljong is the god of fertility. He is represented by the sun and is worshipped because all crops are in his care and without his favour no harvests would be reaped. The *Wangala* is celebrated in his honour, but the actual sacrifice is offered to him in the fields before the village festival begins. Usually a rooster is killed, its blood is sprinkled on the sacrificial altar, a little liquor is poured out on the ground in front of it and the worshipper then returns to the village for the *Wangala* rejoicings (Playfair, 1909). He is also known by other names, such as *Tengsugipa-Tengtotgipa, Salgira, Salgra* and *Rengra-Balsa*. During *Agalmaka*, cooked rice, fish or chicken curry is offered to *Saljong* and *Rokkime*. Once people leave the field, crows and kites are believed to eat the food offered to the deities. These birds are regarded as representatives of *Saljong*.

Table 12.2: Rituals and gods and goddesses

Ritual	*Gods/goddesses/spirits*	*Purpose*
Aba Opata	*Abet Mite*	Permission to cultivate a fresh plot
Agalmaka	*Rokkime, Saljong*	To drive away pollution, Inviting paddy goddess to reside, Salutation to sun god
Bang cha·a	*Jugi, Bang, Nawang*	Not to damage and spoil crops
Miamua	*Rokkime, Rakasi, Miasi, Saljong*	So that paddy grows lushly
Rongchugala	*Saljong* and other spirits	Offering of first paddy
Ahaia	*Saljong, Rokkime*	Offering of first harvest of other crops, Sending off of paddy goddess.
Wangala	*Saljong, Tatara Rabuga* etc.	Thanksgiving, Renewing the relationship with Saljong

Paddy/rice is the chief crop in shifting cultivation and thus much of the rituals surround the propitiation of the paddy goddess are known as Minima *Kiri Rokkime* or *Rokkime*. She is not only the goddess who overlooks paddy and its growth and germination, but also the inherent soul in paddy. Thus, in the *Agalmaka* ritual an altar is made for her and a hen is sacrificed in order to invite her to reside in the *jhum* fields. Once the paddy seeds are sown and begins to grow, it is believed that the other malevolent gods and goddesses start wreaking havoc and the paddy goddess leaves the fields. Then the ritual of *Miamua* is held in order to entice the paddy goddess back to the fields, while at the same time appeasing the other malevolent spirits. Finally, during the ritual of *Ahaia* (also known as *Ambi Rimona*), after harvest, the paddy goddess is ceremonially sent off, only to be called again the next year during *Agalmaka*.

Jugi is a god who is propitiated during the *Bang cha·a* ritual so that the crops will not be damaged and spoiled. He is the god of herbs and plants. At the same time, a malevolent lesser god known as *Bang* along with the demon *Nawang* is sent off from the fields and the village. Both *Bang* and *Nawang* are said to create mischief and hamper in the growth of the crops. Thus, a hen or a rooster is sacrificed and offered to *Jugi*, while a pig is slaughtered for *Bang*. After the offer of the pig, *Bang* is ceremonially and through incantations chased away from the *jhum* fields. The favourite method of keeping the spirit *Bang* at a distance is to make a cylindrical cage about four feet long and two in diameters. This is filled with all kinds of old, worn-out household utensils, such as cooking pots, gourds and bamboo spoons and is hung on a pole supported by two uprights. This is placed by the side of the path leading to the village and a fowl is then sacrificed. A pestle for pounding paddy is also thought to be very efficacious in keeping the spirit away, if stuck upright in the ground by the side of the path (Playfair, 1909).

Table 12.3: Propitiation of gods and goddesses

God/goddess	*By whom*	*How*
Saljong harvest;	Usually in the field and house of *nokma* (Priest as medium)	Offer of rice beer; Offer of first Sacrifice of fowl, pig and cow; Incantation
Rokkime	Every household starting with the *nokma* (Priest as medium)	Offer of rice beer; Sacrifice of fowls and pig; Incantation
Abet Mite	Head of household	Incantation
Jugi	*Nokma* (Priest as medium)	Incantation, Sacrifice of fowl
Bang/nawang	Every household	Communal sacrifice of pig; Incantation; Effigy of Bang
Rakasi	*Nokma*	Sacrifice of pig/fowl
Miasi	*Nokma*	Sacrifice of pig/fowl

Two other lesser gods and goddesses who are also part of the cultivation process include *Rakasi* and *Miasi*. *Rakasi* is a god who eats up paddy saplings and hence leads to a poor crop. This gets manifested in the way the crops are growing and the presence of caterpillars and other insects eating the crops. *Miasi* is a lesser goddess whose main task is to help *Rokkime* in the growth of paddy, but due to the havoc created by *Rakasi*, she too goes either into hiding or becomes a mute spectator. These two spirits are also propitiated during the *Miamua* ritual along with *Rokkime*.

Abet Mite is the one who looks after all vegetation, especially in the forests and jungles. Thus, a *jhum* cultivator, once he is allotted a plot, has to seek permission of this god before he starts cultivation. This ritual is known as *Opata*. *Abet Mite* is also known as *Abet Rora, Biala Dikkima* and *Chisik Mite*.

Natural forces play an important role in agriculture. Thus, in the case of long-continued drought, the rain god/goddess is invoked in the *Wachikrita* or *Salgurua* sacrifice (Playfair, 1909: 88-89). All men of the village go to a big rock in the neighbourhood, each person holding a gourd of water in his hand. The priest recites a prayer imploring the god/goddess to have mercy on them, sacrifices a goat and smears its blood upon the rock. The assembled persons then pour the contents of their gourds over the unfortunate priest to the accompaniment of beating of drums and blowing of wind instruments.

When, on the other hand, rain has been too constant and sunshine is desired, the *Salaksoa* or "burning of the sun" ceremony is performed. This ceremony is the reverse of that for rain. Therefore, here, fires are lighted round the rocks to bring warmth and sunshine. In this, a goat or fowl is offered. In every village, a small piece of ground is set apart for the *Salaksoa* ceremony and no man may cultivate or clear it under pain of a very heavy fine.

Discussion

The main idea behind agricultural rituals is a good harvest. It is believed that if one upholds the exchange relationships with the beings, which are at its origin, then it would lead to bountiful produce. Anthropologists, following Mauss (1972) have demonstrated that such a phenomenon results from a principle inherent in the social nature of humankind. Friedberg (1989) questions about these beings that condition prosperity by acting on the soil, climate and plants. To deal with these problems, each society, therefore, develops a procedure that lead to the organisation of relations between people and the supernatural through the intermediary of officiants of different statuses.

In Songsarek areas of Garo Hills, certain bamboo structures are seen both in the *jhum* fields as well as in the village, indicating ritual significance. These vary in form according to the god or goddess for whom it is meant. A brief description of these altars is given below (after Playfair, 1909). The most common of these is the *sambasia*, which consists of an upright, oblong panel composed of a bamboo frame about four feet long and two feet broad, filled in with reeds and the leaves of certain trees. Another altar is the *chorabudi* named after the spirit, which is invoked at its base. This consists of bamboos stuck into the ground so as to form an inverted cone about three feet high, filled with earth. A third kind, is the *sekrek*, a short bamboo stuck upright in the ground, the top section of which is split into narrow strips, which, when splayed outwards and bound with cane, form a conical basket. Into this, offerings of food and sometimes money are placed. Another form of this is the *wadambeng sekrek*. This consists of two bamboos tied together in the form of a cross. The top and horizontal extremities of this cross are opened out into the conical basket described above. When an offering is made at any of these sacrificial altars, the blood of the animal or bird is smeared over it and some of the hairs or feathers are stuck on the bamboos nearby.

Inherent in every society, including the Garos, is the belief in supernatural beings whose propitiation would lead to a bountiful production (Table 12.3). The propitiation is a series of rituals which includes certain incantations, sacrifices, offerings, taboos and other socio-economic activities. The tone, manner and lyrics of the incantations are believed to have been the same since the day it has been introduced. Sacrifices include both fowl and animals, but the inherent idea behind it is to offer the best livestock available. Offerings made include rice beer and other food crops depending on the ritual concerned. For instance, in *Miamua*, the goddess *Rokkime* is offered rice beer and *chu ste* (rice from which beer was prepared); while in Rongchugala, the god *Saljong* is offered a bunch of paddy, a handful of flattened rice, *tematchu* (a citrus fruit) and rice beer. From *Agalmaka* up to *Ahaia* there exists a taboo on certain food items like paddy, melons, maize, gourd, ginger, onions and tubers including some fruits grown on trees; and on the ceremonial drum (*dama*) and dancing and shouting by young men. It is socially accepted by all that the first produce cannot be harvested without offering it to the respective gods and goddesses. The breaking of this taboo would lead to death by venomous animals such as snakes, millipedes, bird spiders and scorpions (de Maaker, 2006). Others believe that it would lead to bad harvest in coming years. Additionally, the taboo on beating of ceremonial drums and rejoicings is believed to lead to a good paddy harvest – otherwise the beating of the drums and shouting by men will frighten the paddy goddess and she will leave the *jhum* fields.

The first crops from the *jhum* fields include melons and maize which ripen at the fields in July. It is forbidden to harvest any of it before the *nokma* performs the *Ronchugala* ritual. *Rongchugala*, as mentioned earlier, involves the offering of a few stems of paddy, flattened rice, a sour fruit and rice beer. These are offered inside the house of the *nokma* at the maljuri pillar, the permanent altar inside the house. Once the *Rongchugala* offerings have been made, there are no more restrictions on the harvesting of *jhum* crops. However, some of these, such as white gourd, ginger, onions and tubers, cannot be consumed until the offerings relating to the *Wangala* festival have been made. Sour fruits, such as pomelo, lime and tamarind can only be eaten after the rituals that relate to the *Jamegapa* festival (which precedes *Wangala*) have been celebrated. These are fruits from trees that do not grow in the wild, but have been planted. Thus, all crops including fruits that have been grown or planted need to be first offered to the deities. This law, however, do not exist for crops that grow wild.

Myths form the basis of many of the prevailing practices. For instance, the Garos worship *Misi Saljong* for he is believed to be the one who taught them to cultivate as they do now. He is also the god who introduced rice to them. Therefore, they believe that he returns to the country every year, scattering the seeds which will later spring up as plants and telling the people not to forget the lessons which he taught them about keeping their fields clean. Even today in every *jhum* plot a makeshift bamboo structure is seen which is used a rubbish bin. *Misi Saljong* then sends the rain, which makes the rice grow and the other weeds. The exertions of the people in keeping down the weeds, through different phases of weeding, will lead to a corresponding harvest. The crab, *angke*, is said to have been entrusted by the spirits with the duty of watering the crops in time of drought.

Similarly, the magpies and barbets are said to have been entrusted to bring news of impending rain. These animals are commonly seen in the *jhum* fields even today.

The intermediary between the spirits and the human beings play an important role in such rituals. The priest known as *torua* or *kamal* is the one who conducts all these rituals. Without the priest no rituals can be conducted. It is the priest alone who can communicate with the gods, goddesses and demons. He is the one who has the power to call upon them, to appease them, or to propitiate them. The head priest usually has an assistant priest helping him along with a few other men who are given different tasks. For instance, there is a man in charge of sacrificing animals meant for rituals, while another man officiates as the rice beer drawer, i.e., the man who draws the rice beer for ritual purposes. Though the priest officiates at the rituals, it is the privilege of the *nokma* to provide for or sanction it.

That a belief system surrounding shifting cultivation was the crux of these rituals is undoubted. At present, due to factors of change in Garo Hills, a corresponding change is witnessed in rituals and the belief in gods and goddesses of the fields. Foremost among them is the change in the belief system due to adoption of Christianity. Now-a-days, a majority of the Garos are Christians and they do not take part in any rituals relating to the propitiation of the spirits. Christians do not believe in the existence of the supernatural *Mite* and thus do not sacrifice any animals or offer any of the first harvests to the gods and goddesses of the fields. Therefore in *jhum* fields owned by Garos, no altars can be seen. Moreover, the various taboos that exist on crops and behaviour are not seen among them. However, an alternate practice is witnessed – where they pray to the Christian god before any cultivation process begins and they offer the best harvest to the church (i.e., God).

Additionally, since many of the Garos are now changing their way of life – from subsistence to permanent wet paddy and cash crop cultivation in permanent farms – the intensity of the rituals too have gone down. The propitiation of *Misi Saljong, Rokkime* and others was intrinsically connected to shifting cultivation. Thus, with Garos adopting different lifestyles, the number of people taking part in these rituals has recently declined.

Conclusion

The question why a *Songsarek* Garo performs these rituals is one that has a culture specific answer. To others, these beliefs and practices do not make any sense for there exist no scientific basis on how cultivators can influence nature and make their crops grow aplenty by communicating with the gods and goddesses. But for the people themselves, this is much more than merely following the agricultural cycle. For them, this is a way to cope with the unknown and untameable events of the nature. They believe that the nature is governed by the diktats of supernatural beings, who demand certain observances from the people concerned.

Thus, the annual rituals are designed to preserve harmony with the supernatural beings through culture specific rituals. However, in practice, these encompass much more than mere rituals and manifests in different practices throughout the year. Thus, even though *Agalmaka* and *Ahaia* are mere rituals, it is seen that a series of observances are followed by the Garos between these two rituals. Additionally, a taboo exists on much of the crops until and unless it is first offered to the gods.

A close functional association between rituals and socio-economic activities exists in human society. Thus, with the change in a way of life from shifting cultivation to permanent cultivation, the rituals have either lost its intensity, or disappeared altogether as in the plains areas and Christian pockets. The change in subsistence and religion has thus impacted the traditional beliefs and practices.

References

de Maaker, E. (2006). *Negotiating Life: Garo Death Rituals and the Transformation of Society*. Ph.D. Thesis. Leiden Univ.

Majumdar, D. N. (1980). *A Study of Culture Change in Two Garo Villages of Meghalaya*. Guwahati: Guwahati University Press.

Marak, Q. (2014). *Food Politics: Studying Food, Identity and Difference among the Garos*. Newcastle: Cambridge Scholars Publishing.

Mauss, M. (1972). *A General Theory of Magic*. Translated by Robert Brain. London: Routledge and Kegan Paul.

Playfair, A. (1909). *The Garos* (Reprinted 1975). Guwahati: United Publishers.

Radcliffe-Brown, A. R. (1952). *Structure and Function in Primitive Society.* Glencoe, Illinois: The Free Press.

Rongmuthu, D. (1960). *Folktales of the Garos* (Reprinted 2008). Guwahati: Gauhati University Press.

Sangma, M. S. (1981). *History and Culture of the Garos*. New Delhi: Books Today.

13

Indigenous Way of Response to Gynecological and Obstetric Problems among the Dibongiya Deoris of Assam

— Juri Borah and Sarthak Sengupta

Introduction

Gynecological and obstetric problems constitute one of the major areas of reproductive health behaviour. As such for matching sound reproductive health these areas shall gain attention among the masses since reproductive health itself determines the overall health condition of an individual. Now-a-days, in India though medical science is moving towards an advance stage with the presence of improved technologies for controlling all of these problems, yet quite a substantial number of mothers are the worst sufferers of various gynecological and obstetric problems. The direct and indirect responsible factors behind such problems may be of illiteracy, poverty, premature or postponement in age at marriage, insufficient or over nutrition, exposure to heavy workload, less awareness, etc. Again, in many regions of the country transport gap, communication gap is also prevailed and as such disharmony in regards to availability of medical institution as well as higher medical facility is also observed.

It is one's general perception as well as established fact that people from tribal communities have been experiencing various reproductive problems mainly because of their illiteracy, poverty, isolation, etc. and consequently have higher maternal and child death. A large number of works have been done by different scholars, anthropologists from time to time with regards to reproductive health related problems, factors responsible behind these problems as well as mode of treatment to mitigate such problems. Among these mention may be made about few works in North-East India since it is the highly concentrated areas of tribal people.

Meitei *et al.*, (2005) had worked on the awareness and prevalence of reproductive tract infections (RTI) in North-East India (districts level). The knowledge of both males and females about RTI was observed to be relatively poor. The level of awareness of RTI among males and females have observed only in 11 and 9 districts respectively out of 34 districts in northeastern states in India.

Hazarika and Chutia (2013) worked on incidence of abortion, still birth and reproductive risk among Deori and Mishing women of North East India. The study reveals that average conception per women and abortion-conception ratio estimates confirm the worsening of reproductive health conditions and loss of reproductivity of tribal women.

Krishnakumari *et al.*, (2014) had worked about women's perception of reproductive illness among Andro community in Manipur, India. They found that women in Andro community refer to health problem relating to reproductive organ and function not as reproductive illness but as women's illness. These people have perceived that poverty is the root cause of women's illness.

Baidya *et al.*, (2014) conducted their study on reproductive health problems and also to ascertain healthcare seeking behaviour among rural adolescent girls of Mohanpur block of West Tripura district, Tripura. Their study indicates enormous reproductive problems among the population. Regarding the knowledge of HIV, STD and AIDS also, the respondents were poorly knowledgeable.

Chanu and Arunkumar (2015) worked on traditional reproductive healthcare practices and knowledge among the Thadou of Manipur. They found that Thadou women still believe in traditional method for care and treatment for reproductive illness like vaginal discharge and other diseases during pregnancy and post partum period.

Alakananda along with her associates (2015) has tried to evaluate the age at menopause and prevalence of menopausal symptoms and also to determine the awareness and attitude towards menopause and treatment seeking behaviour among women attending Guwahati Medical College and Hospital, Assam. Their findings reveal the common occurrence of menopausal symptoms mainly because of lack of awareness among the masses.

Gogoi and Prusty (2013) tried to examine the prevalence of reproductive health complications and treatment seeking behaviour among tribal women in North East India based on DLHS-3 data. Their study revealed that tribal women were reporting less awareness about RTI/STD's but non-tribal women reporting relatively more complications than tribal women. Women use to go for public source for treatment seeking, while very high proportion of women does not receive any treatment for their problems.

Objective

The present chapter attempts to examine the prevalence of certain gynecological and obstetric problems among the Dibongiya Deori women of Assam. Attempts have also been made to understand their perception and the way of response to get relief from such problems.

Materials and Methods

To have an overall idea about the gynecological and obstetric problems among the Dibongiya Deori women, 178 ever married women from two villages namely, village Borchapori and Kinapather Deori Gaon of Lakhimpur district of Assam were studied. These two villages were exclusively inhabited by the Dibongiya Deori population only. Data were collected from only those women whose husbands are alive and having at least one child. Moreover, women who volunteered were only taken into consideration. Observation, interview and case study methods are the basis for collection of the data. Their indigenous knowledge regarding preventive measures in the form of ethno-medicine against the gynecological and obstetric problems were collected from traditional ethno-medicinal practitioners as well as few knowledgeable aged persons of both sexes of the villages.

Deori, a priestly tribal community with rich cultural traditions, inhabit in few districts of upper Assam as well as in Lohit district of Arunachal Pradesh. Dibongiya Deori is a sub-tribe of Deori population and owes its name from their original habitation on the bank of the river Dibong. According to 2011 census, the total Deori population in Assam is 41,161 in numbers. This population group is trying to maintain their discrete identity by preserving their traditional Deori dialect. They are strictly endogamous. Now-a-days, the Dibongiya Deori populations show an interest to higher education as well as are getting exposure to various governmental jobs also.

Results and Discussion

Various types of gynecological and obstetric problems experienced by the Dibongiya Deori women have been shown in Table 13.1 to 13.4. Accordingly, the way of response of the population to mitigate the problems they face is also attempted.

Table 13.1 illustrates the frequency distribution of the Dibongiya Deori women according to menstrual related problems. It has been observed that out of 178 women, 45.51 per cent of them have experienced various menstrual related problems like heavy or low bleeding, irregular bleeding, very short or prolong duration of bleeding and also severe lower abdominal pain during menstruation, etc. Among these, some women are suffering from a couple of problems at a time while some are suffering from one or two of such problems. The problem most frequently encountered is in regards to lower abdominal pain during menstruation period (26.97 per cent). Women having irregular bleeding (6.74 per cent) and very insignificant bleeding (15.17 per cent) and short duration of bleeding (5.62 per cent) are also observed that suggests nutritional imbalance among the Dibongiya Deori women.

Table 13.2 shows the frequency distribution of the Dibongiya Deori women suffering from leucorrhea. The incidence of leucorrhea (32.02 per cent) is observed to be relatively common in the studied population. The most commonly occurred gynecological and obstetric problems are reported as menstrual related problems and problem of white discharge. The frequency of women having menstrual related problem is more frequently met with in comparison to white discharge sufferers.

Table 13.1: Menstrual related problems among the Dibongiya Deori women

Character	*Frequency*	*Percentage*
Regularity		
Regular	166	93.26
Irregular	12	6.74
Lower abdominal pain		
Yes	48	26.97
No	130	73.03
Menstrual flow		
Low	27	15.17
Normal	134	75.28
Over	17	9.55
Menstrual duration		
Less (< 2 days)	10	5.62
Normal (3-5 days)	138	77.53
Heavy (6 days & above)	30	16.85

Table 13.2: Incidence of leucorrhea among Dibongiya Deori Women

Problem of White discharge	***Frequency***	***Percentage***
Yes	57	32.02
No	121	67.98

Frequency distribution of the pregnancy related problems among the Dibongiya Deori women is shown in Table 13.3. From the table it is observed that a great variety of obstetric problems have been experienced by the Dibongiya Deori women. The frequency of pregnancy complicacy is encountered in 57.87 per cent of women. The incidence of severe headache during pregnancy (18.58 per cent) and women experiencing spontaneous abortion (12.02 per cent) is quite common. Other commonly occurred problems associated with pregnancy in the studied population are edema of body and feet (8.74 per cent), anemia (8.74 per cent), less appetite (7.65 per cent), too much vomiting tendency/nausea (7.10 per cent) etc.

Table 13.3: Pregnancy complications among the Dibongiya Deori women

Cesarean	16	8.74
Anemia	16	8.74
Occasional Bleeding	8	4.37
Headache	34	18.58
Edema of body and feet	16	8.74
Spontaneous Abortion	22	12.02
Pain at body and feet	5	2.73
Stomach pain	8	4.37
Fever	8	4.37
Jaundice	2	1.09
Vomiting	13	7.10
Mal position of the baby	2	1.09
Stunted growth	1	0.55
Lack of appetite	14	7.65
Excessive breast pain	1	0.55
Low pressure	3	1.64
Sitting and sleeping problem	2	1.09
High pressure	1	0.55
Weakness	6	3.28
Urinary problem	2	1.09
Constipation	1	0.55
Convulsion	2	1.09
Total	**183**	**100.00**

Table 13.4 provides an idea about the ethno-medicinal plants, parts used, the local name along with their scientific name used to cure the gynecological and obstetric problems experienced by the Dibongiya Deori women. With regards to gynecological problems

majority of the women are in the habit of using various ethno-medicines and follow various traditional ways of healing and generally ignore the modern medical treatments. The following are some of the traditional medicines that are used by the Dibongiya Deori population for curing various gynecological and obstetric problems they have experienced in their lifetime.

Table 13.4: Ethno-medicinal plants and animal parts used to cure gynecological and obstetric problems

Ethno Medicine				*Disease*
Local name	*English equivalent*	*Scientific name*	*Part used*	
Munuma Penchu	Ripe betel	*Piper betel*	Leaf	Boil in reproductive organ
Dasiya	Tobacco	*Nicotiana tabacum*	Leaf	
Satmul	Tree garden asparagus	*Asparagus recemosus*	Root	White discharge
Tonasinga	-	-	Root	
Kaliya Tulashi	Holy basil	*Ocimum tenuiflorum*	Leaf	Stomach pain during menstruation
Laijabori	Heart leaf drymary	*Drymaria cordata*	Leaf	
Mukagu Naharu	Garlic	*Allium sativum*	Seed	
Dubori Bon	Dog grass	*Cynodon dactylon*	Leaf	Over bleeding
Kakini Tamul	Kakini nut	-	Root	Unable to conceive
Hukloti	Patchouli	*Pogostemon cablin*	Leaf	Edema of body and feet
Goroichiya	Snakehead	*Channa punctatus*	Entire fish	
Gakhiroti Bon	Asthma weed	*Euphorbia hirta*	Leaf	Insufficient amount of breast milk
Tagodhiya	Sweet potato	*Ipomoea batatas*	Leaf	
Mikaci	Duggal fiber tree	*Debregeasia wallichiana*	Leaf	Excess amount of breast milk

Boil abscess in reproductive organ (local name. *tuturu higari*): When an individual irrespective of sex is suffering from boil in reproductive organ and also have itching/ irritation due to it, ripe betel leaves (local name. *munuma penchu;* Sc. Name. *piper betel;* Assamese term. *Burha pan*) and tobacco (local name. *dasiya*; Sc. Name. *Nicotiana tabacum*; Assamese term. *dhapat*) is grinded and mixed with water and wrap in a cloth for extracting the juice into a bottle. The extracted juice is applied in the affected area by a quill of fowl (local name. *du pakhi;* Assamese term. *kukura pakhi*) as applicator.

White Discharge (local name. *purusat kebasi*): When a woman is suffering from white discharge, the root of a plant, known as *tonasinga* in Deori dialect is cut into small pieces and kept in one cup of water for about two hours. Then it is mixed with one-fourth liters of milk and advised to drink in empty stomach for seven days.

The root of a tree garden asparagus (local name. *satmul*; Sc. Name. *Asparagus recemosus*; Assamese term. *satmul*) is cut into three pieces and grinded. Then it is mixed with milk and prescribed to consume in empty stomach for three days.

Stomach pain during menstruation (local name. *utusaba*): The juice extracted from the leaf of holy basil (local name. *kaliya tulashi*; Sc. Name. *Ocimum tenuiflorum*; Assamese term. *Kaliya tulashi*) and half-spoon honey (local name. *giya miji*; Assamese term. *mou*) is taken from fourth days onwards during menstruation for three days in empty stomach. During medication sour food, spicy food and any kind of mucilaginous food item is restricted.

Another medicine for this problem is grinding and boiling the leaf of heart leaf drymary (local name. *laijabori*; Sc. Name. *Drymaria cordata*; Assamese term. *laijabori*), three pieces of garlic (local name. *mukagu naharu;* Assamese term. *naharu*) with little amount of salt together taken in empty stomach for three consecutive days. The same medicine is also prescribed to a woman who is unable to conceive a baby. During the time of taking the medicine, sour and spicy food item is restricted.

Excessive bleeding during menstruation (local name. *chi luba*): When a woman is suffering from extreme bleeding during menstruation and after birth of a child, few leaves of *Cynodon dactylon* (local name. *dubori bon;* Assamese term. *dubori bon*) is grinded with any variety of rice except the *bora and lahi* variety and is given to consume in empty stomach for three days. Any sour and spicy type of food is prohibited during medication.

Sterility (local name. *moicha chahiya*): The root of a betel nut tree known as *Kakini nut* (local name. *kakini tamul),* leaves of piper betel that is creeping in that particular tree mixed together to make paste and given to a woman during her menstrual period.

Occasional bleeding during caring period: It has been reported that if a woman had experienced occasional bleeding during caring period, they took the recourse of some traditional folk medicine like using of special wrath (*mala*) prepared by the traditional healer of the village.

Edema of body and feet (local name. *ga fula*): To get relief from edema of body and feet they consume patchouli (local name. *hukloti*; Sc. Name. *Pogostemon cablin*; Assamese term. *sukloti*) and dried snake headed fish (local name. *goroichiya*; Sc. Name. *Ophiocephalus (Channa) punctatus*; Assamese term. *Goroi mash*) together either by boiling or by steaming after rapping the fish in banana leaf.

Insufficient or surplus production of breast milk: When the mother suffers from insufficient lactation, she is given some locally available herbs like asthma weed (local name. *gakhiroti bon*, Sc. Name. *Euphorbia hirta;* Assamese term. *gakhiroti bon*), sweet potato (local name. *tagodhiya*, Sc. Name. *Ipomoea batatas;* Assamese term. *gariya aalu*) etc. On the other hand, when a mother has excess secretion of breast milk, she is given duggal fiber tree (local name. *mekaci*, Sc. Name. *Debregeasia wallichiana;* Assamese term. *mecaki*) to come again to normal state of breast milk production.

Apart from the above mentioned herbs used for curing various ailments, diseases, some special food items are also prepared for the maintenance of normal health condition in combination with various wild vegetations which are available in their own backyard.

Conclusion

The present chapter records relatively poor reproductive health condition with regard to the occurrence of various gynecological and obstetric problems among the Dibongiya Deori women of Assam. No doubt few of them are taking preventive measures either from governmental institution or from traditional healers of the village yet majority of the women considered it as the normal phenomenon associated with women's life. Even they have constrained and hesitations to discuss such problems with others and consequently considered it as taboos. Establishment of medical institution with improved medical facility at affordable price will be helpful for the people to move forward in this regards. As they have strong belief in supernatural forces for getting relief from many prevailing ailments, they are seeking help from traditional healers. Therefore, scientific study on the ethno-medicinal plants used by the Dibongiya Deori of Assam, to understand their efficacy and reliability and if required step should be taken for their preservation.

Acknowledgement

The authors are thankful to all the respondent women as well as their respective husbands of the village Borchapori and Kinapather Deori Gaon for their response and co-operation during the survey. Gratitude is also to the entire traditional ethno-medicinal practitioners contacted for sharing their invaluable knowledge and experiences regarding the treatment of various gynecological and obstetric ailments with the first author.

References

Alakananda; N. Das and B. P. Das. (2015). Age of menopause and menopausal symptoms among women attending Guwahati Medical College and Hospital, Guwahati, Assam: A cross sectional study, *Scholars Journal of Medical Sciences*, 3(7C): 2621-2629.

Baidya, S.; M. Debnath and R. Das, (2014). 'A study of reproductive health problems among rural adolescent girls of Mohanpur block of West Tripura district', *Al Ameen Journal of Medical Science'*, 7(1): 78-82.

Chanu, J. T. and M. C. Arunkumar, (2015). 'Traditional reproductive health care practices and knowledge: A case study of the Thadou of Manipur', *IOSR Journal of Humanities and Social Sciences*, 20(7): 86-88.

Gogoi, M. and R. K. Prusty. (2013). Reproductive health complications among tribal women in India: A special focus on north-east India, *Etawah Journal of Social Sciences*, pp. 8-14.

Hazarika, P. and N. Chutia (2013). 'Abortion incidents, still birth and reproductive health risk of Deori and Mishing women in north east India', *International Journal of Scientific and Technology Research*, 2(8): 259-266.

Krisnakumari, P.; P. C. Joshi; M. C. Arunkumar and M. Meghachandra. (2014). Women's perception of reproductive illness in Manipur, India, *Journal of Anthropology*, 2014, Article ID 321480.

Meitei, M. H.; K. Latashori and Ksh. Gopal. (2005). 'Awareness and prevalence of reproductive tract infections in north-east districts of India', *Health and Population-Perspective and Issues*, 28 (3): 132-145.

14

Women Power Structure in Matrilineal Jaintia Society

— *R. P. Athparia*

The People

The "name Jaintia could be an Aryanised form of the name Synteng by which the people of Jaintia Hills used to be called even today (Passah and Sarma, 2002: XI). From the word Synteng we get Syntein, Syntiang, Zontain, Zontia and ultimately Jaintia". Again, the name "Synteng" could also be an Aryanised form of the name "Sutong", the original clan of the Jaintia royal dynasty from which was also derived the names "Suteng" and "Sutnga".

It is wrong to say that the ethnic name "Jaintia" has now been largely replaced by the term "Pnar" (Simon, 1996:1). In fact, the people residing in the central region of Jaintia Hills are called "Pnars" by those living in the southern and northern regions and who are in turn being called as "Wars" and "Bhois" respectively by the Pnars. But all the three are collectively known by a generic name "Jaintia" or "Synteng" (Passah and Sarma, 2002, XI).

The Jaintias are believed to have come from South-East Asia. Probably they started their migration from Mongolia via West Asia and along the foothills of the Himalayas to South-east Asia, thence to their present habitat through Burma (Pakem, 1977). Bareh (1997: 9-10) states that "Khasi is a general name given to the various tribes and sub-tribes that inhabit the Khasi and Jaintia Hills. The name includes the following sub-tribes – (1) Khynriams or Nonglums (Khasis proper) inhabiting the middle ranges of Khasi Hills, comprising the Khynriams and their allied tribes in the central plateau; (2) the Jaintias are called Syntengs but they prefer to be called Pnars; (3) the War people of the south comprising the Shella people and their allied groups of tribes; (4) The Amwi people and their allied War Synteng in the south of Jainta Hills who appear to form a parent tribe of Khasi during earliest period of settlement in the land; (5) The Bhoi people both Khasi and Pnar, inhabiting the north of Khasi and Jaintia Hills with their different sub-groups, were also in some cases, a result of diversion of the people from the central plateau forming an intermixing with the Mikirs on the outer fringes of this land".

Chattopadhayaya (1988:3-4) states that the Jaintias do not like the term "Synteng" because it is associated with "Sahteng" which means either the people who were left behind in their westward migration or simply a "backward" community. However, according to Chatterjee (1976) in his "Kirata Jana Kriti", the word Jaintia (Zantain or Zonten) was derived from the word "Synteng". According to Pakem (1972), the word Synteng was derived from the word "Sutnga" (Suteng), the ruling dynasty of the Jaintias, or from the word "Sohkynting" (Smynting or Synting), a village through which the Khasis came to the Jaintia Hills. Tradition has it that "Teng" is the ancient mother and therefore Syntengs means the children of the ancestral mother. Jaintians seem to have an organisation and the original Khasi word Synteng (Zeintein) developed into Jaintia (Chattopadhayaya, 1988:4). According to Gurdon (1975:1-2), the Khasis inhabit the Khasi Hills proper and the Syntengs or Pnars, the Jaintia Hills. The Jaintia Hills take their name from the Rajas of Jaintia, the rulers of this part of the country, who had as their capital Jaintiapur, a place situated at the foot of the Jaintia Hills on the southern side, now falls within the boundaries of the Sylhet district (now Bangladesh).

According to Paul (1956:151), the Jaintias were the original inhabitants of a State in the Chinese region called T'Sin-tiang. This is an Austric word and the people of this State were called T'Sin-Tiang or T'Sin-tien. In course of time they came to be known as

Synteng or Syntien. This term got corrupted into Chyntien and then as Zyntein and ultimately as Jaintia which is the present name.

According to Chatterjee (1976), except the Khasis and the connected Jaintias (Syntengs) of Assam, the Mongoloid peoples who are found in India are speakers of languages and dialects belonging to the Sino-Tibetan or Tibeto-Chinese speech family. But Chatterjee's opinion that the Jaintias are Mongoloid by race and Austric by speech is not correct. It could not be possible for the Khasis and Jaintias to retain the Austric language after being surrounded by the Indo-Mongoloid, by Sino-Tibetan or Tibeto-Chinese and also by Aryan speakers. The Khasi-Jaintias could retain their linguistic and racial characteristics because of their strong foundation. Again it is difficult to accept the opinion of Chatterjee that the mixture produced completely different races like Mon, Wa, Paloung etc. Then again how could the Khasi Jaintias be Mongoloid when they have close relation with Mon-Khmer Palaung, Wa of Burma and Indo-China and in South Burma and Indo-China Mon-Khmer are an Austric people? According to Bareh (1997:16), Khasi is strictly connected with the Palaung-Wa dialects spoken by the tribes that live along the central and upper reaches of the Mekong River. The close sisters of Khasi appear to have been the Mon and Palaung-Riang-Wa dialects of Burma. It is clear that from the first, Khasi is described as a sub-group of the Mon-Khmer and Palaung. But there exist also some important phonetic relations between Khasi and Vietnamese. Khasi has also shown a few relations with Wancho, a tribe in the Tirap district of Arunachal Pradesh.

From the above it is clear that there is a possibility of the mingling of these Proto-Australoids with Mongoloids in very early time in Burma and Indo-China, as Chatterjee himself said. Thus, Jaintias are neither Mongoloid by race nor *Kirata*. Their language is Austric and by race, it is quite possible that purity of the Austric race could not be maintained because they lived all along with Mongoloid. Chattopadhayaya (1988:6) quoting Bareh said that the Khasis lost a good deal of Austric racial features due to the pressure of strong and sturdy Mongoloid types. The changes in the physical features are more visible in the urban area in recent years due to admixture through matrimonial connections with plains people.

Rymbai (1979) is in the opinion that the origin of the Khasi is a vexed question. It is still shrouded in mystery and yet to be resolved (c.f. Chattopadhayaya, 1988:6). Regarding origin of the Jaintias, Gassah (1994:69) states that there are two schools of thought which represents the outer or non-local sources, the Jaintia Kingdom got its name from the southern plains tract which was originally known as Jaintiapur because of the presence of the famous shrine of Jayanti Devi, an incarnation of Goddess Durga or Gouri, as mentioned in the Puranic and Tantric literature. However, the other school of thought did not accept this viewpoint. The local scholars believe that the term 'Jaintia' is entirely local in origin. In support of their contention, they say that the sanskritised term Jaintia (Zantain) is derived from the word 'Syntang'. The word 'Syntang' in turn is derived from many sources. Another local opinion is that the term has its association with the ancient mother. However, few scholars are of the opinion that the Jaintias call themselves as 'Pnar'. It was after the occupation of the Jaintia *paraganas* that the *Syiem* of Sutnga went to settle in Jaintiapur and the British called the *Syiem* and his people by the name 'Jaintia'. Such an opinion is, however, still considered debatable.

Jaintia Village

Jaintia village is a socio-cultural and socio-economic concept rather than a political unit. The household in a village are bound by social and economic bonds. The village headman always occupies an honourable place in the social set-up of the village.

The Jaintia houses were made of hard wood and stone walls. The good quality timber, like the oak, pine, jackfruit etc. was used. They plaster the space in front of the house with red earth and cow dung, the latter indicating an influence of Hinduism. They have comparatively large houses. The house of the *Doloi* of Sutnga in Jaintia Hills was more than 80 ft. long in the 1970s (Prakash, 2007:1675).

As the hill villages go, the Jaintia villages are fairly big. Nongtalang in the War area is the biggest village over 100 houses. In the interior hills, the people live in groups of small villages. About 75 per cent of the Jaintias live in the villages. The *Lyngdoh* (priest) is highly respected. The villagers are deeply attached to the place of their birth and were reluctant to leave for new avenues which offered jobs and professions away from their houses (Prakash, 2007: 1676).

Nongtalang, the summer capital of the Kingdom, came under the influence of the Hinduism when the Jaintia Kings embraced the faith. It still has a Hindu temple with a Brahmin priest, a descended from the Brahmin family from the days of the Jaintia Raj (Prakash, 2007:1676).

The position of the ancestral mother is great among the Jaintias and as the originator of the clan and family occupies an important and responsible position. The married sons and daughters start living separately except the youngest daughter who remains in the ancestral home, to inherit the position, place and importance of her mother.

It is observed that in a patrilineal society there is always a gender bias in every field or aspects of life, for instance in many religious books like The Holy Bible, the Quran and the Gita, has portrayed only the male figure as the supreme most powerful being. Whereas, on the contrary, women are always portrayed as a weak, gentler sex, submissive to their husbands and family etc, so the questions revolve around us today is that whether it is the society or the customs that have given a particular image or character to the women? If she doesn't fulfilled the above criteria she is considered as unfit mother, wife, sister, etc. Is it the customs or traditions that control the behaviour of particular sexes in a great extend? Customs and traditions have always been a great impact to shape the society of particular communities. It has its own rules. Do's and Don'ts, either approved or disapproved by one's culture. The present study is based on the field work conducted in ten villages in Jaintia Hills, namely, Shangpung, Amlaren, Tuber, Rymbai, Umkiang, Wahiajer, Jowai, Syndia, Raliang and Nartiang. We will try to look into the various customs and practices followed by the Jaintias in inheritance of property and how it affects on the status of women? How much the women folk have benefited after the introduction of modern democratic system in post-Independence period in the societies? It is rightly said by Jawaharlal Nehru that, "You can tell the condition of a nation by looking at the status of its women".

Customary Law, Community and Women

The customs and its laws vary from region to region and so is the case for North Eastern region. The eight Sister state is diverse in the form of practicing different customs and traditions in order to retain their identity from one another and these variations make the region unique in its own way. Ethnic and cultural diversity ensure differentiation in tribal socio-cultural and economic identity. Focusing on the status of women in tribal society also undergoes great diversity. In most of the tribes of this region women share in property rights are very minimal. They enjoy very limited or at times no control over landed properties, as we are bounded by patrilineal practices and ideologies where man enjoys the overall power in the family. But the situation and the practice of patriarchy contradicts totally when it comes to matrilineal societies like the Garos, the Khasis, the Jaintias or the Lyngngams from the state of Meghalaya.

The women are often associated or considered as a homemaker. Nath (2003) in his book, 'Rural Women Workforce in India' talks about the dual role of women both in home as well as outside home. He says, "In the social context, due to the low status attached to manual labour in our society and the cultural value associated with women's confinement to home, the work of rural and urban as wage labourers, unskilled factory workers and menials are not conducive to a better status. The average woman in rural can give little attention to the upbringing up of her children. With dual roles and without any mechanical aids for house-work, she is really overworked. So also are the women engaged in unskilled or semi-skilled work in organised and unorganised sectors attitude of unconcern about the public affairs, is responsible for the limited participation of women in activities like those of Trade Unions or political parties" (Nath, 2003:13).

The customary laws are not uniform but most of the societies there is a clear separation between the family in which the woman is the in-charge and society where the man represented the family. She controls the family economy including the *jhum* which most of the hill tribes practice. The village headman or council allotted land to each family according to the number of mouths to feed in it. After it the man of the house chose the plot of land and the woman took charge of it. As a result, division of work is more gender sensitive than that in settled agriculture. That gives the women a relatively high status. Besides, women share much of the work at home with men but they are not allowed in the village council. Thus, their status is higher than that of woman in caste societies but they are not equal to men (Fernandes and Barbora, 2002: 30-31).

Besides, social and inheritance laws evolve according to the environment in which the people live and there is diversity in the tribal customary laws but common to all of them is patriarchy based on the central pivot of women as homemakers and men as providers and protectors. Their myths and beliefs legitimise its assumption that harmony and co-existence depend on women (Vitso, 2003:58). Their ownership and inheritance laws reflect it. All of them discriminate against women in their legally enforceable right to benefit from, control or alienate their assets. Thus, the gender issue not merely one of legitimacy but is principally of rules affecting the allocation of resources and life chances (Mann, 1983:307). Inheritance or right to own, use and control immovable property is basic to it. Immovable property includes land, water sources and house. Movable items are personal assets like agricultural tools, weapons, clothes, ornaments, weaving looms, food grains and livestock.

While enjoying a better status than in patrilineal societies, women in matrilineal tribes are not equal to men. Despite inheritance being through the mother, the Khasi and Jaintia vest much decision-making power and control with men. Among the Jaintias, the youngest daughter is the *khadduh* or heiress. Their tradition treats the girl as *Ka Blei Ing* (Goddess) and *Ka Likhimai* (guardian spirit) of the house. These titles suggest not only moral attributes of virtue, purity and goodness but also her role in maintaining the continuity of her family, sub-clan (*kpoh*) or clan (*kur*). The other sisters leave the house after marriage. The *khadduh* as the guardian of the family property and custodian of its religion meets the expenses of family ceremonies such as weddings, naming and religious rites. She looks after members who suffer misfortunes like disability, a spouse's death or divorce and gathers the family at the *ing-seng* (foundation house) for family rituals prepares for the religious rites and assists her maternal uncles in their performance. In practice her maternal uncle (*ki kni*) and brothers control her property. She is not the heiress in the strict sense of the word. She does not have any control or rights to sell property without the consent and counsel of her maternal uncles and other siblings. The family property is more a joint trust.

Thus, the Jaintia women look after the family, rear and train and educate children and are in control of household affairs. The notion of visiting husband among the Jaintia is now discouraged by the society. Among the Christian Jaintias this system is not generally observed. Urban people like to have independent house. Even non-Christian Jaintia husbands now come to stay with the wife and they take much care for their children and share the burden of the house. It is not rigid in these days even among those non-Christian Jaintia husbands who follow the duo-local system of residence after marriage. Men join them in decisions on crucial matters like buying and selling of movable and immovable property, cultivation, trade and business and are expected not to interface with what she decides (Passah, 1992: 47-48). Sometimes also the youngest son inherits property. Thus, the woman does not have as much power as inheritance and descent on the mother's side indicate. Heavy responsibilities are laid on the mother to ensure the welfare of the family but both Khasi and Jaintia women are only custodians of its property. They manage the wealth and look after the old parents but men control it (Gassah, 1992: 42-43).

Women in the Traditional Political Institutions

In this section we shall study the women's role in the tribal political institutions. It is said that women are weaker than men though they play a significant role in building the family, nourish the family affairs right from the dawn to the dusk. This has made them lower than men in social activities and legitimised by keeping them subordinate to men in the society. Their subordination is also expressed in the social institutions. When asked about the women's role in traditional political institutions we gathered the information that the women are not given any role in the village council. We have to examine whether the women members are there in the village council. Though the Constitution has made provision for women the rights to be the members in the local bodies yet it is not successful in most of the cases. Now, we shall examine the political role of the women in the Governance in traditional political institutions among the Jaintia in the studied villages.

Traditional Political Institutions

Governance today is seen as paramount concern for any State. Governance, therefore, engages in new areas of articulation for a State and the people living within its jurisdiction. For many, governance refers to certain conditions necessary for a State through which it can exercise power in managing the nation's social and economic assets and also become the pre-condition for realising democratic ideals. Though the notion of governance has different meanings for different people, one common understanding of it is the decision-making process as well as the process of implementation of those decisions. This process also identifies involvement of different structures from different walks of life, signifying both the formal as well as informal actors. Thus, in the background the traditional institutions of a State also have a claim for incorporation of local structures in the issues of governance. The traditional institutions of the Jaintia also entail such claim, because of its involvement in civil, social-economic and religious jurisdiction of the local interests. Therefore, the participation of people through such institutions recognises grass rooting the democratic principle of governance in its most popular form.

We find that the Jaintia people were under the administration and leadership of *U Langdoh* both at the village and groups of villages known as *raid* level. The first incumbent of the office of the priest of the *raid* was elected from among the priestly families of the villages of the *raid* (Pakem, 1984: 52) but with the increase in the number of families and clans, area and size of population, there was also an increase in the number of duties and functions to be performed single-handedly by the *Langdoh* (ibid).The Jaintia people in their wisdom felt the need that the administrative set up should be re-structured. As a result, it was necessary to bifurcate the dual functions of sacred or religious and secular affairs which were under the concentrated power and authority of the *Langdoh*. In the process, it was decided to hand over those functions which were purely sacred or religious in nature to the priest and the other functions which were purely administrative or secular to the secular chief, *U Doloi* (Provincial Governor). Thus, the office of the *Doloi* came into existence.

U Doloi is therefore the chief of the next higher political unit called *Ka Elaka* or province, which was formed by combination of group of villages or *raids*. Occasionally, an extra tier between the *elaka* and the village was instituted wherever the *elaka* was too large to be managed by one *Doloi*. Such an extra tier was usually placed under a Lieutenant-Governor or *U Pator*. A *Doloi* could either function directly or through his deputy, *U Pator* with the assistance of *Ki Tymmen Ki San* or simply *Ki Wasan* (elders) who are the representatives of their respective clans (Pakem, 1984: 1). Once a *Doloi* takes up his office, he normally holds it for the rest of his life.

It will not be out of place to mention here that in the socio-political life of the Jaintia people, the smallest social unit is the family. The families and clans naturally formed the smallest unit of the political society called *chong* or a village. Centering on families and clans was generally a society where leadership fell on the seniormost male member called *U Kni,* literally a maternal uncle of the family or clan.

Subsequent upon the increase in the number of families and clans as well as population and territory, ultimately led to the setting up of a village. This obviously gave rise to the increase in the number of functions to be performed single-handedly by the uncle of the family or clan. The family or clan uncle under these circumstances found it very difficult to look after the multifarious affairs all by him. The people therefore felt the need of centralisation of all those functions in the hands of one person or authority but at a higher level than that of the family and clan to supervise the administration. In the process, the office of the *Waheh Chnong* or village Headman came into existence.

Before the British annexation of Jaintia Hills took place, the Jaintias had a three-tier system of administration. Under such a set up, the office of the *Syiem* or King occupied the apex position in the hierarchy; in the middle, there were and still the *Doloi* or Provincial Governors in each *elaka* and the office of the *Waheh Chnong* or Village Headman stands at the lowest rung in the ladder of administration. The office of the Jaintia *Syiem* was abolished by the British and lapsed in 1835 after the annexation and possession of the land by the latter. The British authority therefore declared the whole of Jaintia Hills along with few villages in Khasi Hills as British Areas. Though the British authority completely abolished the office of the *Syiem*, on the other hand, they retained and allowed the offices of *Doloi, Pator* and *Waheh Chnong*. These offices also continue till today aiding and assisting the District Council in the administration of the district pertaining to the welfare of the tribal people (Gassah, 1998: 11-12).

Quoting Bareh, Gassah (1998:12) said that at first there were five *Dolois,* next they increased to seven and on the eve of the British annexation it increased to twelve. However, Bareh did not explain in clear terms as to why the number of *Doloiships/Elakas* had increased from what he said the original five to twelve. But he made an interesting observation in which he stated that it was only on the eve of the British annexation of Jaintia Hills that the number of *Doloiships* was found to be twelve. However, Pakem (1985) provides a different view altogether in this respect where he stated that in fact, the Jaintia *elakas* increased from three to seven and from seven to twelve before the Jaintias formed a State (*Hima*). After the formation of the State, the *elakas* further increased with further expansion or division until there were twenty five *elakas* during the British period. According to Pakem, the number of *Doloiships* reached to twelve in number before the Jaintias formed a State (*Hima*), or in other words the period is not that of the distant past but it took place only on the eve of the British annexation of Jaintia Hills, that is, around 1830s. Hadem (1974), however, mentioned that the Jaintia King divided his whole dominion into twelve administrative units called *elakas*, under an administrator called *U Doloi*. He has also given list of names of the twelve *Doloiships* which in his opinion regarded them to be the original ones. He was also of the opinion that on the basis of twelve administrative units, the Jaintia Hills was termed as *Ka Ri Khad-ar Doloi* (the land of the twelve Dolois).

Coming to the period after Independence, the information contained in the United Khasi-Jaintia Hills Autonomous District Act, 1953, mentioned that there were eighteen *Doloiships* and one

Sirdarship in the whole of Jaintia hills. The same number of *Doloiships* and *Sirdarships* was shown by the same District Council Act of 1959. Curiously, one *Patorship* that of Sumer was missing in both the lists. But in the present list available with the Jaintia Hills Autonomous District Council, there are eighteen *Doloiships*, one *Sirdarship* and one *Patorship* (Gassah, 1998:18).

In our field investigation, we have asked the informants why females are not included as members in the traditional village council. In this regard, one male politician from Jowai, Mr. K. C. Pde said that:

> "Men and some women work together in *Durbar Shnong*. There are women secretaries in *Durbar Shnong*. Only through selection method members are selected in village councils. Regarding the office of the Headmanship, it is always occupied by the male members but no female because the headman has to hear the voice of the general mass. If there is any scheme from government, headman cannot do anything but it is the choice of people. Women have their own association called *singkenthie*/ women association. If the general body accept and support the female organisation they can work. It is up to the general mass to choose women or men. Women have right to become an active member. Women are not considered as member of the *Durbar Shnong* because women are considered to be unable in the decision-making or mostly because they are busy at home. Even in our legislative assembly there is only one female. Even though ours is matrilineal society yet males have more authority where politics is concerned and women are far behind".

When asked about the number of the members of the *Durbar Shnong, elaka* and *Dolois* among the Jaintias, a male teacher Mr. R.C. Rymbai who is also *Doloi* of Jowai *elaka* said that:

> "There are seven members in the village *Durbar* and the tenure for each member is for five years only and after five years we have to renew the members and these members are only men. An *elaka* consists of many villages. It has an open *Durbar* and each and every *elaka* has elders from the villages and they elect the Doloi, the head of the *elaka* and its members are from the

village Durbars. We have a court in Jowai called as *Solangba* and four of them will be elected from the *Solangba* as traditional practice and we elect them as *Lyngdoh* (priest).

In Jaintia hill there are altogether eighteen offices of *Dolois,* one office of *Sirdarship* and once a *Doloi* is elected, he will continue the office for lifetime, but *Sirdarship* is different. It is on rotation system and after every five years it rotates through election.

The Village *Durbar* consists of all the elders as members to the *Durbar*. We have also religious *Durbar* and they only the heads from the religious field conducting all the religious responsibilities of the villages.

The election process excludes the females and only males can be nominated for membership to the *Durbar* and it has been in practice since time immemorial. Regarding the *Syiemship* and *Doloiship*, Khasi and Jaintia are different, because *Syiemship* and *Doloiship* are elected from the clans, but there is lot of differences. In Khasi hills they elect *Syiemship* only from the *Durbar* of the Kingship and not from the villages. But here in Jaintia hills the *Doloiship* is elected by all the male members who can vote for the *Doloiship* election which is not so in Khasi hills".

Women Membership in the Traditional Tribal Council

It is noted that under the traditional system, a large number of offices have been created for the smooth functioning of the Jaintia State or *Hima* which is headed by the *Dolois.* The *Doloi* cannot take any decision without the approval of his councilors. In the State, there is a large electoral *Durbar* consisting of members.

The routine administration of a village is run by the village council or *Durbar Shnong* headed by the *Waheh Chnong*. Nearly all the respondents said that they have *Durbar Shnong* or village council. All adult males of the village are the members of the village council.

The *Durbar Shnong* is assisted by seven executive members. There are President, Secretary and Treasurer to assist the *Waheh Chnong* for smooth functioning of the *Durbar Shnong.* The *Durbar*

Shnong resolves the disputes in the council. For land disputes the villagers approach the village *Durbar.* There is no restriction that the people can approach the civil court but people first choose to go to the village court. The guilty person is penalised by cash fine. The penalty depends on the nature of the crime. In case, the council fails to resolves the case it is referred to the District Council Court. However, some cases like murder are referred to the police.

It is observed that the *Waheh Chnong,* the village headman, is the in-charge of the day-to-day affairs of the village. These are both intra-village as well as inter-village activities. As such his presence is necessary in taking decisions on all matters affecting an individual's life from cradle to maturity and death. Even the aspirant leaders for contesting election in modern political field also seek advice and blessings from the village headman. The village level council, i.e., *Durbar Shnong* is found all over the Jaintia land but no where women are found as head of the village *Durbar.* But women are reported as village executive like secretary in some traditional village councils. Now, we shall examine the data collected from ten villages and see where the women stand in this traditional council. It is found that the political system of the Jaintia is democratic in nature. During the meeting of the village Council each member has a right to express his opinion freely. Only adult men can attend the *Durbar Shnong.* Their customary law confined women to the domestic sphere. This effectively forbade them from taking active part in the decision-making processes of the *Durbar Shnong.* When asked why did the customary laws did not allow women to take active role we did not get any satisfactory reply except that the women had to look after the family and agriculture activities.

Modern Political Institutions and Women

Gassah (1998:52) states that the Khasi and Jaintia society had its deep-rooted tribal institutions since time immemorial. However, these pristine institutions had to face severe stress and strains at the oncoming forces of new administrative set up and modernisation processes in the field of constitutional administration. With the advent and evolution of such agents of political modernisation and emergence of the new institutions in the area, many changes had taken place.

These changes had brought immense effects on the power and functions of the traditional institutions and the traditional chiefs. This has also certainly created a changing role and power-relationship between the two sets of political institutions. The traditional institutions have been operating in the traditional values and institutions and satisfying various traditional needs of the tradition-oriented society; the newly created constitutional institutions stand for and committed to economic, social and political change and modernisation. As such, the new political institutions which were created after Independence were in fact eroding the powers and functions of traditional councils instead of improving upon them. The immediate effect was that the powers and functions of these traditional institutions were taken away and they were put under the overall control and supervision of the District Council.

When the British authority was removed in 1947, the power of the secular authority was drastically reduced and the District Councils assumed power over them (Pakem, 1986: 44-45). The power and functions of such secular traditional institutions were therefore further curtailed and reduced by the District Council under the Sixth Scheduled to the Constitution of India. The United Khasi-Jaintia Hills Autonomous District Council which was established in 1952 passed a number of Acts, Rules and Regulations from time to time. Some of these Acts a direct bearing and tremendous effect on the power and functions of the traditional institutions and chiefs in the area. The United Khasi-Jaintia Hills Autonomous District Council passed an Act (Act No. II of 1959) known as the United Khasi-Jaintia Autonomous District (Appointment and Succession of Chiefs and Headman) Act, 1959 (hereinafter referred to as the Principal Act) on the 21st October 1959, after receiving the assent of the Governor of Assam on the 16th October 1959. This Act made provisions for the election and appointment of Chiefs and headman, confirmation of Chiefs, dispute regarding election of Chiefs etc. The United Khasi-Jaintia Hills Autonomous District Council in the aforesaid Act (Principal Act of 1959) introduced two fundamental changes from the traditional customary laws of the people as per Sections 10 and 11 of the Act which relate to the appointment of Deputy Chief (Section 10) and an Acting Chief (Section 11).

The Jaintia Hills Autonomous District Council which was established in 1964 adopted the Principal Act as it is during its initial years of existence. In the subsequent years, it made certain amendments to the Principal Act. For example, this District Council passed an Amendment Act in 1973 (the Jaintia Hills Act No. 1 of 1973) which deleted the entire Section 10 of the Principal Act of 1959 relating to the appointment of Deputy Chief. The Jaintia Hills Autonomous District Council realised the uselessness an inapplicability of such a provision of the Act in the area from the traditional customary practices of the people of Jaintia Hills. However, the Executive Committee of the Jaintia Hills District Council still retained Section 11 of the Principal Act relating to the appointment of an Acting Chief.

It may be mentioned here that the Khasi Hills Autonomous District Council in 1980, in its Fifth Amendment to the Principal Act of 1959, went even to the extent of passing an Act debarring the Chiefs, Deputy Chiefs and Acting Chiefs taking part in politics and elections either to the Parliament or the State Legislative Assembly or the District Council. To this effect, so far, the Jaintia Hills Autonomous District Council has not taken any cue from the Khasi Hills District Council in respect of debarring the Chiefs and Headman in Jaintia Hills from taking part in politics and election. Though the Chiefs and Headman in the area are treated by the District Council as its subordinate officials, no such Act was introduced. Unlike that of Khasi Hills and in the absence of any Act to debar them, the *Dolois, Pators, Waheh Chnong* in Jaintia Hills openly take part in electoral party politics.

Now we shall discuss the impact of the changes on women in order to see whether modernisation has helped them to gain any power in their society. Reservation of seats for women has inspired some women to take part in political institutions and in turn given a boost to the morale of some of them who have courage to make their voice heard but many men resist the idea of playing proactive role in public affairs.

Regarding 33.00 per cent reservation of women in modern political arena, they said that it is a democratic demand and the right of the women to be represented and manage their own affairs;

therefore it is very legitimate demand. But for smaller communities it does not work i.e., for certain women to be represented and certain women to sit at homes. The main point is that how many Jaintia men and women are actually qualified to take up such administrative responsibility. It is applicable in other parts of India but for the Jaintia people it would not be of much help.

Women Participation in Local Bodies

In order to know the participation of women in the local bodies, the respondents said that the Panchayati Raj system as well as Village Development Board does not apply to the Jaintia villages as it comes under the Sixth Scheduled. Besides, among them the traditional village council, *Durbar Shnong* continue to exist and the District Autonomous Council appointee, the *Doloi, Pator, Sirdar and Waheh Chnong* act as the liaison between the District Council Authorities and general people. In the study villages, the *Durbar Shnong* has been discharging the duties of village level grievances on behalf the *Doloi* of the respective *elaka* and the District Council without any interference. However, all of them deny political rights to women and deprive them of participation of their village structures.

Women Contesting Elections

Electoral politics came to this part of the country after Independence. Women have enrolled as voters and do cast their votes; they have contested for Assembly elections so far. Lyngdoh (1998:93-100) states that there are sporadic examples of women's participation in administration. Although it is unthinkable for women to succeed in the office of the chief, in rare circumstances, in the absence of legitimate male rulers, women were accepted as rulers. In the customary law female ruler is not allowed except when there is no legitimate male ruler. It is said that Lalitaditya, King of Kashmir invaded the Jayantia Kingdom, which they called '*Stree Rajyya*'- meaning women's Kingdom in which Lalitaditya was repulsed. In the *Hima* or State of Nongsohphoh of Nobosophoh, a female ruler, Ka Lar became the ruler in the total absence of male heir. Another tradition indicates that Hima Maram also had a female ruler - Ka Wan Rani. Another female ruler was Ka Syiem Latympang was the ruler of a small state of Manar in the Jayantia Hills. Ka Iaw Saring was another female ruler in the *raid* Iapngar of the Bhoi area.

However, for ages, the women have stood behind men on various issues although they did not take part in the *Durbar*. The role of the *Syiemsad* or high priest in the *Hima Khyrim*, as an example of women's power behind the chiefdom. The *Syiemsad* is entrusted with the rites and ceremonies of the state, in order that her moral force may serve as retraining factor behind the affairs of the state.

In the pre-independence era, the Government of India Act, 1935 gave women the right to vote. The act also provided for representation of women by reservation of a seat from the Shillong Constituency in the then Assam Legislative Assembly. This was known as a Shillong woman seat. The Act permitted the women to also contest general seats. In the 1937 election, two Khasi women contested in the Shillong reserved seat. Mavis Dunn Lyngdoh was elected and for the first time a woman became a member of the Assam Legislative Assembly. Mavis Dunn Lyngdoh was inducted in the Md. Saidulla's ministry in 1939-41 and again in 1942-45. She was the first woman in North-East to become a minister. In the 1946 Assembly election five women were contested from for the Shillong woman seat. B. K. Khongmen was elected in the Shillong woman seat.

After Independence and particularly after the attainment of statehood of Meghalaya, many changes have taken place in the Khasi-Jaintia Hills. Under the Sixth Schedule to the Constitution, the Autonomous District Councils were established in the United Khasi and Jaintia Hills in 1952. In 1967, the United Khasi and Jaintia Hills District Council for Jowai sub-division were created for administrative convenience.

In 1952, the first parliamentary election to the Lok Sabha was held. B.K. Khongmen was elected and she became the first and the only women from Assam to represent in the Lok Sabha in 1952. In 1957, she returned to stay in politics but this time she was defeated. In 1962 and in 1967 elections, no woman contested from Khasi and Jaintia Hills. In 1998 Parliamentary election Elizabeth Laitphlang contested as a BJP candidate but she was not successful.

Meghalaya came into existence as an autonomous state in 1970 and in the same year two women were nominated to the Provincial Meghalaya Legislative Assembly. After the creation of a full-fledged state in 1972, a number of women came forward to contest in the first election to the Meghalaya Legislative Assembly. No woman was elected from Khasi and Jaintia Hills. In 1978 Legislative Assembly, a number of women contested from Khasi and Jaintia Hills but only one woman, Miriam D. Shira was elected. In 1983 election, there were as many as eight women contestants but all the women defeated and only men dominated the Meghalaya Legislative Assembly. In 1993, Assembly election only Roshan Warjri was elected. She was the only woman legislator in the House of sixty. In 1998 election a number of women contested including Roshan Warjiri and two candidates came out successfully in Khasi and Jaintia Hills. They were Roshan Warjiri and Maysalin War. This brought an improvement in the otherwise poor women representation scenario in the State.

In the Autonomous District Council there were a number of women representatives who were either nominated or elected. The Khasi Jaintia Hils Autonomous District Council was bifurcated in 1967 and two separate district council for Khasi Hills and Jaintia Hills were created. In 1973, Dr K. Rymbai was nominated to the Jaintia Hills Autonomous District Council. In the Khasi Autonomous District Council women have represented since 1972 but in Jaintia Hills the picture is poor.

It is said that the Jaintia women has never been under the shadow of men as she has long been custodian of her family name (lineage) and property. However, the immense privileges guaranteed to her in other spheres are denied to her in matters of polity and public life. This has been an issue that has raised a few questions, for it represents a break with the past. The history reveals that the Jaintias were quite comfortable with the woman as ruler and an administrator. The fame of Ka Latympang and Ka Pring Saring, the queens of the Jaintia are well known. Despite many obstacles and difficulties Mavis Dunn Lyngdoh got elected as early as in 1937. Similarly, Bonniely Khongmen became Member of Parliament in 1952 and now we have Roshan Warjiri and Maysain War as Member of Legislative Assembly.

Maya Rani Kyndiah, a Jaintia woman contested the election several times but not elected, she is still an active politician (Lyndem, 2002: 102-103).

We have, therefore, tried to understand the attitude of the women across different age groups towards women contesting State and National elections. Group discussions were held with the members of different associations of men and women and younger persons. It created an atmosphere of free discussion to express their views. By and large, the younger generation was positive towards women's participation in politics. Many wanted women to be allowed to contest elections and active in politics. Most of the respondents said that women should be active in politics. All the respondents say that women understand the problems better and should be allowed to contest election. They have agreed that the customary law as the stumbling block. As practiced today it promotes patriarchal dominance though it is a matriarchal society.

Lyndem (2002; 103) has stated that the majority of political leaders in Jaintia Hills are men; they have made it clear that women do not need reservation of seats in the Assembly as they are vested with enough power under matrilineal system. It is also felt that women legislators in the state also are against reservation. In their opinion women are better off than their counterparts elsewhere because of the matrilineal system. With all these women are not sitting idle they have made their voices to be heard in several platforms. Seeking one-third reservation for women in the Municipal poll, Probity Nongpluh, a social activist, won the case in the Guwahati High Court. The matter is pending in the Supreme Court.

Conclusion

The above discussion gives us an idea that the women have not come forward in modern politics because of the hindrance of male dominance in politics. The Meghalaya Government has not initiated to implement the Panchayati Raj in the Sixth Scheduled areas in Khasi Hills District to ensure women's participation in the local bodies (Lyngdoh, 1998: 64). Unlike Nagaland there is no VDB in the Jaintia areas. Hence, there is no question of representative in the Village Development Board. Their representative is not seen in the

District Council. Again, one has to go a long journey to make 33 per cent reservations of women in the District Council. Reservations are not a panacea for equality but are only a step in undoing the historical injustice meted out to them. We have seen that there is a tendency among the people that the women can improve the political picture better if they are given a chance. It shows that there is a resistance from the people themselves that the women should not join in politics. It is due to the male domination in politics where the reservation of seats for women in politics is not fulfilling up to the mark. It is, therefore, necessary on the part of the government to implement the legal provisions to reserve seats for women in all political structures.

Awareness of political rights is another important aspect. Many respondents have said that their access to education and exposure to electoral politics women have now raising the questions about their traditions and conventions enshrined in the customary laws. When asked about their confidence in politics, they said that in many political demonstrations, rallies and meetings, the attendants are mostly women. They have played a very crucial and visible role in Jaintia politics. So, women should come up and take up more of this leadership.

From the above analysis it appears that forces of modernisation such as education, electoral politics and constitutional provisions have the capacity to transform the tribal societies in favour of gender equality. Many women who were confined at homes till now have started playing active role in social transformation. A social atmosphere should be created in favour of gender equality and the society is marching ahead of it.

During colonial rule, primacy of a rational-legal authority structure was introduced backed by institutionalised force but they just did not supersede the traditional structures. The policy-makers were also not aware of the colonial implications of the cultural policy and the changing policy parameters from protection to participation, though both did essentially address the state and global economic programmes respectively and did violence to the traditional authority structures. Under the generic policy constraints, the traditional power structures in North-East India are reeling under hopes and despair. Relocating the space for women in the public and private spheres under these circumstances is a difficult task. This has strong effect on the tribal constellation in North East India where the women play a vital role in the socio-economic lives. Empirical evidences from the North Eastern States show complex and often contradictory trends of women empowerment in the changing power structure. While the women in the North East have by and large a very significant role in the society, their space in the decision-making process both at the household and the public spheres is highly circumscribed. The studies conducted by some scholars on the subject show commonality on some broader issues like changes in the institutional aspects consequent upon the spread of education, modernisation, Christianity and urbanisation. At the same time exclusion of women from the power structure, their higher role in the domestic and social spheres exposes a contradictory scenario.

The present study draws our attention to the micro-level realities facing the women in the following crises in the increasing socio-economic and political in the region.

(a) Urbanisation-migration-lumpenisation constitutes one set of crisis;

(b) Internal shift in the institutional pattern and parallel institutional syndrome constitute another shift;

(c) Transformation of rural economy, from owner to labour and women participation in the labour force constitute the third shift;

(d) State government and administration constitute the fourth shift;

(e) Emergence of 'have' and 'have not' in the otherwise egalitarian Jaintia tribal society; and

(f) The eventual vertical division in the society constitutes the fifth shift.

References

Bareh, H. (1997). *The History and Culture of the Khasi People*. Guwahati: Spectrum Publication.

Chatterjee, S.K. (1976). *Kirata Jana Kriti*. Calcutta: Asiatic Society.

Chattopadhayaya, S.K. (1988). *The Jaintias*. New Delhi: Cosmo Publications.

Fernandez, Walter and Sanjay Borbara. (2002). *Modernisation and Women's Status in North East India: A Comparative Study of Six Tribes*. Guwahati: North Eastern Social Research Centre.

Gassah, L.S. (1992). Status of women in Jaintia culture. In: Soumen Sen (Ed): *Women in Meghalaya*. New Delhi: Daya Publishing House.

Gassah, L.S. (1998). *Traditional Institute of Meghalaya: A Study of Doloi and his Administration*. New Delhi: Regency Publication.

Lyndem, Billoris (2002). Khasi Jaintia women: Role in decision making bodies, Some Observations. In P.M. Passah and S. Sarma (Eds): *Jaintia Hills*. New Delhi: Reliance Publishing House.

Lyndoh, M.P.R. (1998), Women in Meghalaya and the Constitutional 73rd Amend-ment Act, 1992: Problems and Expectation. In M.N. Karna, L.S. Gassah and C.J.Thomas (Eds): *Power to People of Meghalaya*. New Delhi: Regency Publication.

Mann, Michael (1983). *Macmillan Student Encyclopedia of Sociology*. London and Basingstoke: Macmillan and Co.

Nath Madhuri, (2003). *Rural Women Workforce in India*. Delhi: B.R. Publishing Corporation.

Pakem, B. (1977). The changing power structures of the political institutions of Jaintia Chieftainship. *Journal of North East India Council for Social Science Research*. 1:1.

Pakem, B. (1984). State formation in Pre-Colonial Jaintia. *NEHU Journal of Social Science and Humanities*. 11(3): July-September.

Pakem, B. (1985). A Theoretical Approach to the Study of the State and Polity Formation in Meghalaya during the Pre-Colonial period with special reference to Jaintia State and Biate Chieftainship. In *Pre-History of Meghalaya and State Formation*. Govt. of Meghalaya, Education Department: 23-24 April.

Pakem, B. (1986). Political development and change in North East India. In A. P. Sinha (Ed): *Changing North East India*. Ludhiana: Gagan Publishers.

Pal, Gemini (1956). The place of Khadduh: The youngest daughter in Khasi-Synteng Society. *Vanyajati*. 4.

Passah, P.M. and S. Sarma. (2002). *Jaintia Hills*. New Delhi: Reliance Publishing House.

Passah, P.M. (1992). Status of women in Jaintia society and culture. In Soumen Sen (Ed): *Women in Meghalaya*. New Delhi: Daya Publishing House.

Prakash, Col. Ved (2007). *Encyclopaedia of North East India*. Vol. IV. Noida: Atlantic Publishers and Distributors.

Rymbai, H. (1979). The birth of Siem Raj. In U Hipshon Roy (Ed.): *The Khasi Heritage*. Shillong: Seng Khasi.

Simon, I.M. (1996). *Gazetter of India, Meghalaya, District Gazetter, Jaintia Hills*. Shillong: Government of Meghalaya, Arts and Culture Department.

Vitso, Adino (2003). *Customary Law and Women: The Chakechang Naga*. New Delhi: Regency Publication.

15

Language of the Assamese Utensils

— *Birinchi K. Medhi*

Introduction

While saying something about the utensils of Assam, it is imperative to understand the difference between the receptacles and utensils. In common parlance we consider the metallic receptacles made of brass (*pital,* an alloy of copper and zinc) or bell metal (*kanh*) as utensils. Others like the *charu* (shallow bowl), *kalah* (pitcher), etc. made of burnt clay or terracotta have their specific names and functions. These are not included into the classificatory system of utensils. They remain outside and it is a matter of cultural cognition, specific to place and time. Under transformed cultural and economic backdrops, mostly in urban contexts, the traditional utensils are in the rear seat. Here one sees the idioms, values and concept related to the traditional utensils that are neither operative nor effective as seen in the rural areas of Assam even today.

The modern culinary sets are emerged out following an evolutionary tract receptacle made initially of organic and later on of inorganic material like burnt clay, sometimes from carved-out stone and metal like copper and its alloy. This is a technological transformation that took place across time and space. Each phase of development brought about a systematic arrangement of socio-economic order. In the Western world such transformation took place by crashing the previous one; past lost its existence in time, or past cultures are put forcibly into a state of oblivion. But in Assam there is a juxtaposition of the past and present even today at the cultural and family levels. This is reflected in both material and non-material aspects of culture. Technological and socio-economic transformations have taken place over time in the form of churn-out process, which was not in isolation rather it was from within the composite socio-cultural, socio-linguistic and socio-economic situation. Today's culture of Assam carries the past elements along with the composite values, idioms, mores of different egalitarian ethnic groups and sub-groups, which contribute to the cultural development of the State. One feels their existence at each and every moment - at conscious and sub-conscious levels.

Expressions of such elements in material term can be observed in material cultural items, such as utensils and receptacles. These, when personalised, assume an animate dimension. These exist in a traditional context of this part of the country as an indivisible entity. There are products of cultural imagination and cradled by cultures in a manner the people rear up their offspring.

No culture is complete or accomplished by itself; it grows and develops by drawing cultural nutrients from the others. When any material element enters in any culture, it is internalised and becomes a part of the system. It is adopted and adapted. Culture of Assam is not exception to that. It is super organic in the sense that it does not end with a person. It passes from generation to generation through the transmission of material and non-material cultural elements in the form of visual and non-visual cultural symbols; which exist as long as the socio-cultural values, moral order and technical order remain unchanged. In Assam, because of geographical and linguistic distinctiveness and isolation or less variable socio-economic state, culture still retains the traditional values and symbols. That is why the continuation of traditional craft and its related socio-economic value are conspicuous.

Introduction of Brass or Bell Metal in Assam

The point to draw here is that prior to the introduction of brass or bell metal in this remote part of India, the mostly used culinary appliances are pottery of hand or wheel made. It is important to note that material like the rind of gourd and bamboo products are also in use. This might have entered into the flood-plains cultures from simple or egalitarian cultures, which are surrounding the flood plains. Taking into consideration the geographical, socio-cultural, socio-economic and distinct linguistic affiliation of the Assam's culture, we may divide these into two. The cultures that flourished on the flood plains, with a plough-based-agrarian economy, linguistically belong to the Indo-Aryan family with surplus production; whereas the cultures that distributed over the highland or the hills and the hills in the flood plains are linguistically affiliated to the Tibeto-Chinese family. The same is the case for the ethnic groups distributed over the foothill areas. Barring the cultures of the foothills, the highlands practice shifting cultivation and the socio-economic conditions are simple, egalitarian and lack of economic denticulations. This is contrast to the plough based flood-plains cultures.

The cultures, distributed over the two contrast situations, are distinctively affiliated to their religious faiths. In highland and foothill regions, their supernatural faiths centre round the animistic beliefs where the spirits and magico-religious beliefs play an important role. In such beliefs, practices and rituals; no receptacles are used on permanent basis as in the temple. There are, however, exceptions among the Buddhist ethnic groups, namely, the Tai-Turungs, the Duoinyas, the Khamtis and others who migrated from Thailand and Burma and settled in the area of upper courses of the river Brahmaputra probably around the twelfth century. During this period the Ahoms migrated from Burma to Upper Assam and established a powerful imperial structure. In the case of the Turung Duoniyas, they came with Buddhist rites and rituals and its associated material culture. The *sarai* (a tray mounted on a leg) and *bata* (a tray with a foot, Figure 13.1) are the two important items (these are sometimes made of bamboo, wood and cane). On the other hand, the Bodo, Rabha, Tiwa and others use the same organic receptacles as the other animistic (as mentioned) ethnic groups. It was simple initially and of late the metallic utensils started infiltrating from the neighbouring cultural groups.

The basic difference is hardly missed, one notices that the more a culture becomes socio-economically stratified or complex, the more it expresses a hierarchical order through the possession of higher forms of material cultural items. Utensils are one of such items. It is observed visually in the process of culture formation of Assam. The Ahom imperial structure based on feudal model of North Indian imperial system could be set as an example. This example shows how a Buddhist group got converted into Hinduism and accepted the Indian 'classical code' (Hinduism) to ensure their existence in the new socio-religious and economic scenario. This is no doubt a strategic and diplomatic move, but its impact on the formation of material culture, technology and a new arrangement of the socio-economic order cannot be underrated.

Socio-economic and Technological Transformation of Assam

In fact the socio-economic and technological transformation of Assam took place prior to the arrival of the Ahoms. This is evident from the reference made by the Jurung, who said that he was received by Kumar Bhaskar Barman (around the cent AD) with *Uluka* emitting fragrance in an excellently decorated earlier container (Choudhury, 1966). So there has been an existence of high level craftsmanship and it may have been the product of specialised occupational groups, who were integrated with the socio-economic system, which grew under the influence of Indian classical system.

This also gets credence from the archaeological evidences in the Ambari site of Guwahati, Assam. The archaeological strata speak of the fact that the 'Brahminical tradition' in different stages reached here prior to the arrival of the Ahoms. The extensive pottery types found in association with the stone Brahminical figurines and settlement structures developed at different phases are diverse in types and formations. Some of these still transcendent the archaeological phases and continue even today in urban and rural areas. Association of these with temples and ritual stands unchanged. Numbers of these are not many, only a few archaeological types continue to exist while the other types like *lota* (squall-shaped vessels) and carinated big bowls ceased to exist or were displaced. At time the archaeological phase being over; the replica of the archaeological carinated bowl types was replaced with the brass types found in temples or religious institutions. Forms and functions of these remain temple or ritual centric.

The main point to be mentioned here is that the making of receptacles from clay to brass and bell metal marks the beginning of the emergence of new technology and the new occupational groups like the Kahar – the makers of bell metal utensils mainly localised in Sarthebari of Barpeta district and the brass utensils makers, the Marias, who are distributed around the Hayagriva Madhava temple at Hajo and some are scattered in different parts of Assam. Here again, one witnesses that the bell metal utensils are considered to be pure, while the brass utensils are impure. The concept of 'purity and pollution' creates hierarchy between the two communities involved in utensils made of brass and bell metal. The same is true for the two potter communities – the Kumars and the Hiras. Such a traditional occupational difference imposes socio-economic movements between the two groups. The concept of 'purity and pollution' to the crafts of the two occupational groups fix their relative socio-economic sphere. This saves the two from their economic encroachment and it ensures the economic existence of each group viable in the traditional system, i.e., it integrates them with the total system. Such a development may have taken place towards the late medieval period when the occupational regimentation took a caste-like form, which seems to have got a momentum under the patronage of the Ahom rulers and it continues as the same codes underpin the socio-economic and socio-religious structure even today.

We should not forget the restricted availability of the two metals with high exchange values, which the common people cannot afford to. It limits among economically affluent groups. The brass or bell metal as raw material reached here from outside, since there is no such evidence that local people were making the alloy. The 'lost wax' process was followed while making the bronze figurines. The antiquity of this technique is yet to be determined. It may be noted that other materials like copper seen in temples or household rituals are only a few.

The introduction of new materials is being followed by the emergence of two specialised occupational groups already mentioned. They were rural based, but their products find circulation mostly in the urban and peri-urban areas generally among the affluent aristocrats or the wealthy agrarians. The others continue to depend mostly on the pottery produced by the two potter communities – the Kumars and the Hiras. If any utensil item made of bell metal is found among them, it will be a deluxe ware or a prestigious heirloom for them. Whatever it may be, this reflects the gradual transformation in socio-economic sphere; the newly emerged occupational groups get their economy oriented with the urban socio-economic needs and way of life. Their ideas and creative or aesthetic imaginations got twined with the utilitarian and the ritualistic needs of the temples grew under the patronage of the kings or the aristocrats.

The socio-economic scenario of Assam rapidly entered into a process of transformation with the emergence of the Ahom imperialism. As already mentioned, the rural economy of the flood plains entered into qualitative changes. New orders in socio-economic arrangement took place. And new technical orders give birth to new moral orders. Collective village based economic pursuits were on the wane, it is replaced by an economy tied with urban centres that influenced the socio-economic and techno-economic state of the rural areas from distance.

The moot point to be highlighted here is that the utensils are mostly produced in the remote villages, although produced sometimes near the urban or peri-urban areas. These crafts never remain subservient to rural needs as that of the pottery made by the two communities. At the same time, the blacksmith remains an integral part of the agrarian rural economy as the agrarian technology demands it to be so.

The socio-economic structure of the rural areas serves as a hinterland for the ruling royal structure. The system makes the rural economy to come within the feudal system and this has led to the emergence of socio-economic stratification. The rudimentary centralised elements of the cities' structure diffused into self-contained villages through the ruling outposts. It has been already mentioned that the production of this metallic (brass or bell metal) items have a strong commercial basis and got integrated with the needs of certain group of peoples who formed guilds around the royal or feudal structure. They came from across different socio-economic levels and such guilds or occupational groups retained the seeds of caste formations or socio-economic compartmentalisation.

The seeds of caste formation were present in flood plains, agrarian societies (i.e., Indo-Aryan speaking population), it got new momentum with the emergence of the Ahom imperialism. They came here in Assam with the Buddhist faith, but in order to ensure their existence, they accepted Hinduism with its structure and content. In fact, this era witness the emergence of a class society in Assam, where the people from various ethnic groups were drawn in. Each group has its own ethos, idioms, norms, mores, etc. This is expressed in their material cultural possession and their utilisation in their day-to-day life. This is the visual aspect of the cultural reflection of socio-cultural identity or existence of the occupational units or hierarchical status of the users in a society.

The structural and ideological content of the newly developed or pre-existing caste-based units of the plains absorbed some new culinary items trickled down from the royal system. This is apparent from the newly developed specialisations in food habits and the specialised structure of serving the foods and the incorporation of utensil items. Under such a situation, utensils, food and the nature of distribution entered into a culturally defined inter-relation. The functional involvement of a given utensil under the traditional system got much personalised and fixed. These hardly change their relative position. The functional involvement of the types of utensils as paraphernalia to the rites and rituals of a temple follows a definite order under the dictation of the 'classical codes' (Table 15.1). It is comparable to social structures where the different units on the basis of their functions are categorised.

Now the question remains how a utensil maintains its size and shape over time? To understand the phenomenon, it is imperative to comprehend cultural ecology of the utensils. To delve into the matter, it requires understanding of utensil in terms of totality the seen and unseen factors, the values added to it, the symbols (both visual and non-visual), the concepts that underpin the symbols, etc. The point to be noted here is that the ethos of culture must be understood. We are to accept the fact that visual existence or aspects of any material cultural item has its non-material or invisible counterparts. For example, broken things are reproduced, because the visual and material representation is the reflection of its non-material counterpart that exists in one's memory or imagination. Imagination means cultural imagination, which is inherited by man from his culture. The form and size of a utensil are function based; its material contents are also determined by the dictation of culture. The utensils produced by the craftsmen in this part of the country reflect the cultural imagination of the people of this region (Table 15.1).

Types and Functions

The utensils of Assam may be divided into two types – utilitarian and ritualistic. The former is made of *pital* (brass) and latter is *kanh* (bell metal). The bell metal is considered to be ritualistically pure and the brass ritualistically impure. So is their hierarchical position among other utensils, which are used in the life and culture of the Assamese society. Their relative positions, both utilitarian and religious spheres, are under the dictations of 'classical codes' - culture adds value, name and function to each item and so is each role.

Table 15.1: Functional involvement of the Assamese utensils

Utilitarian	*Ritualistic*
The items made of brass indicate very often sharp classification based on function, role and their use relative to sex, age and status of the users. Some items are exclusively earmarked for the elders of the family or outside the family. A junior member of family, by attaining appropriate age and stage, may use the utensils earmarked for his father or the elders. Each item has its name, function, and form. Name stands for identity, form and function for role and status of a utensil among the rest.	The items are made of copper (*tam*) and bell metal. The items made of copper are closest to the pantheon or the gods or goddesses or *ghat* (pipkin) – a symbolic celestial imagination for the gods or goddesses. Next to it come the brass metal utensils. The copper items come nearest to the pantheon, because of its purity (as it is not an alloy) and its colour and ancientness. Purity has higher value and position; this is irrespective of size and form.

A tacit hierarchy existing in the utensils follows an analogy with social stratification that exists in the life and culture of this area. This is maintained in the traditional context with its full vigor, sometimes in the urban situations also, even today. What it can be observed in a traditional ceremonial recognition of a bridegroom in upper caste family is that the bridegroom sits at the right side of the file of invited guest. On that day he received the highest hierarchical position, whereas the elders and the juniors were sitting in a classificatory order in terms of their roles and status. The traditional utensils are used on high-elevated metallic tetra pods exclusively for the bridegroom. Most of the utensils are bell metal on that day; the bridegroom, although junior to age, is on that day bestowed with the highest hierarchical status. This is further visually expressed through the use of utensil personalised for that occasion. It can be seen that the 'classical codes' are tacitly placed in the texture of the life and culture of the Assamese society (i.e., Indo-Aryan speaking people).

Man, society and matters are inseparable from one another. The utensils of Assamese culture when classified with reference to their functions and roles, it follows the same hierarchical orders as seen in social structure. The mostly used paraphernalia in religious institutions and rituals related to each performance received higher values and attributions. Here the 'purity and pollution' concept comes to play a major role. For example, the copper utensils receive higher value and place because of its colour, purity and ancientness. Next to it is *kanh*. Relative distance in the arrangement of these utensils follows the hierarchical order while performing rituals. If we look at the metallic values (symbolically attributed), utensils made of copper comes nearest to the deity or *ghat*. But hardly iron utensils are found in the paraphernalia of rituals or religious performance excepting a few. Iron in most cases is considered to be ritualistically impure. What is seen that *tau* (the wide and big bowl) made of brass is used for cooking and storing sacred food in the kitchen. The iron utensils are essentially for domestic purposes and utilitarian in nature. Culture hardly attaches sacred affiliation to this metal. It is felt that its colour has an important part to play in this regard. When we look at the cultural composition we see that the *kharahi* (bamboo basket) is used for serving the offering to the devotee, but that is outside the temple. The same is the case for *mala* (earthen saucer shaped wares) for distributing the offering (*prasad*) to the devotee, if it is produced by the Kumars. The potteries made by them that are used in rituals are pure for the first-time use, impure for the second-time use. Such an attribute to the pottery of the aforesaid group has an economic counterpart. It involves the question of economic survival of this group and high hierarchical position in the traditional social structure. This is being a part of their products with the temples or religious institutions. The same is the case for the craftsman Kahar and Maria (Muslim bell metal worker); their hierarchical position in the traditional setting is not as close as the Kumar are. They rank bellow the Kumar, but their socio-economic mobility got restricted as that of other occupational groups. All work within an interlocked structure.

Each group has relative position within the system and each group has ethos, idioms, cultural imaginations and concept of craft. For a son, what his father produced, he does the same. He inherits the symbols that determine the size and shape of the products more or less unchanged. Their clients or the temples share the same symbols. All in tacit manner act as an integrated whole. The existing forms of the utensils as continues today are the continuation of the symbols of the past. It changes when the ethos of the society undergoes transformation or variations.

Ethos exists in symbols (both material and non-material). The value when remain unchanged, the symbols exist without considerable variation. That's why the same type of utensils produced once continues to exist. Sometime these may remain unexpressed, but under given situations these surface again. This is the tacit language of culture. The utensils are the alphabets of the cultural sentences.

Utilitarian

Badna: A small pot with a spout made of brass metal; used by the Muslims for drinking and washing hands and feet.

Banbati: A bowl with a foot; usually made of bell metal; used to serve food (Figure 15.1c and 15.1h).

Bankanhi/Maihang: A broad plate with a foot; made of bell metal; used to serve food to a respected person (Figure 15.1i).

Bati: A bowl made of bell metal, occasionally made of brass, used for traditional present in marriage and *annaprasana*, i.e., first solid food giving ceremony to a child (Figure 15.1b).

Charia: A wash bowl made of brass

Ghati: A small metallic water pot made of brass.

Gilach: Drinking pot; made of brass; new addition to the traditional utensils; coming after British rule (Figure 15.1g).

Hatikhujia bati: A big bowl; resembles the footprints of an elephant in mud; made of bell metal.

Hatikhujia banbati: A big bowl with a stand; made of bell metal.

Heta/Karach/Karchuli: Laddle; generally made of brass.

Junjuni heta: A big ladle; tinkling objects are put inside the handle; made of brass; used in feasts.

Kalah: Pitcher for carrying water; made of brass (Figure 15.1g).

Kahi/Kanhi: Plate of different size; generally described as *adhaseri, ekseri, ek-poa*, etc. according to the weight; a popular present in marriage or *annaprasana*; made of bell metal (Figure 15.1h).

Lota: A water vessel; made of bell metal.

Pandhowa: Quarter plate; made of brass or bell metal; used to serve luncheon (Figure 15.1j).

Pitalar kharahi: A perforated thin and big washing bowl; made of brass.

Saphura bata: A bowl without stand and with a decorated lid; used to serve betel nut; made of bell metal (Figure 15.1m).

Tou: A cooking and storing vessel; made of brass (Figure 15.1p).

Ritualistic

Dagdagi lota: A water vessel with a long and narrow neck; used to fetch ritualistic water, or to wash hands and feet of a respected person; made of bell metal (Figure 15.1e).

Dunari: A disc on stand with perforated decorative lid; used to lit clay lamp inside in marriage; made of brass (Figure 15.1f).

Ou bakhalia sarai: A tray on stand with a lid decorated with many convex structures; used to offer presents to a respected person, or sacred offerings to a deity; made of bell metal.

Pushpapatra: A tray, sometime over a tripod, used to offer flowers and other offerings to a deity. It is made of a bell metal (Figure 15.1l).

Open

Bata: A tray with a foot; used to serve betel nut and sacred offerings to a deity; made of bell metal (Figure 15.1a).

Bhogjara: A water vessel with narrow neck and a spout; used to offer water to a god/goddess or to a respected person; made of bell metal (Figure 15.1b).

Sarai: A tray with or without lid mounted on a leg; used to offer present to a respected present or sacred offerings to a deity; made of brass or bell metal (Figure 15.1n and 15.1o).

Besides the above mentioned utensils sometimes article like *khundana*, i.e., a small mortar for pounding betel nut, betel vine leaf, etc. for the use of old person, *pikdani* (a vessel to spit) etc. made of brass are also found in the Assamese society, metal. Utensils made of silver also not uncommon among the Assamese people (Figure 15.1k).

(15.1a) Bata

(15.1b) Bati

(15.1c) *Banbati*

(15.1d) *Bhogjara*

(15.1e) *Dagdagi lota*

(15.1f) *Durani*

(15.1g) *A gilach* and two *kalah*

(15.1h) *A kahi* and two *banbati*

(15.1i)*Maihang*

(15.1j) *Pandhowa*

(15.1k) *Pikdani*

(15.1l) *Pushpapatra*

(15.1m) *Saphura bata*

(153.1n) *Sarai* without lid

(15.1o) *Sarai* with lid

(15.1p) *Tou*

Figure 15: Some Assamese utensils.

Reference

Choudhury, P. C. (1966). *History of Civilisation of the People of Assam to the Twelfth Century A.D.* Guwahati: Department of Historical and Antiquarian Studies in Assam.

Index